GREAT SCENES FROM WOMEN PLAYWRIGHTS

Classic and Contemporary
Selections for One to Six Actors

MARSH CASSADY

MERIWETHER PUBLISHING LTD.
Colorado Springs, Colorado

Meriwether Publishing Ltd., Publisher
P.O. Box 7710
Colorado Springs, CO 80933

Editor: Theodore O. Zapel
Typesetting: Sharon E. Garlock
Cover design: Tom Myers
Cover illustrations: Albert Giesecke

Library of Congress Cataloging-in-Publication Data

Cassady, Marsh, 1936-
    Great scenes from women playwrights / classic and contemporary
scenes for one to six actors / by Marsh Cassady. -- 1st ed.
      p.   c.m.
    ISBN 1-56608-016-9
    1. Acting. 2. American drama--Women authors. 3. American
Drama--20th century.   I. Title.
PN2080.C386   1995
812'.50809282--dc20   95-35597
                                                                   CIP
                                                                    AC

    1   2   3   4   5   6   7   8   99   98   97   96   95

To Jerine Watson

CONTENTS

INTRODUCTION

Great Scenes from Women Playwrights was written to acquaint the reader with a range of drama by women playwrights. Thus the book takes a different approach than do other collections of scenes. Instead of isolated cuttings from a large number of plays, there are a number of scenes, most often between five and eight, from each play. This gives the reader a more comprehensive view of each work (particularly since the text accompanying each work explains how the scenes are tied together and how they fit into the piece overall). The reader then can have a better feeling for the message and purpose of each play.

Unfortunately, until the present century, there were few women playwrights, perhaps harking back to the idea prevalent throughout most of history that theatre was a vocation only for men. Indeed, until the past couple of hundred years, few women even appeared as actresses in plays, except in certain types of entertainment such as the *commedia dell'arte* during the Renaissance, the roles instead often taken by pre-adolescent boys.

Except for such women as the tenth-century nun Hrovsvitha of Gandersheim and Aphra Behn in the seventeenth century, women playwrights were scarce until well into this century. So all the plays included in this collection are from the twentieth century, except for those written by Mary Inchbald and Anna Cora Ogden Mowatt.

Yet plays deal with a variety of subject matter and treatments. One purpose of the book then is to act as a stepping off place in the study of women playwrights. Just as important, student actors and directors can use the scenes for practice in building characters and for learning stage movement and voice usage, as well as in planning and executing scenes.

The scenes range from less than two minutes to ten or more minutes, so students using the books for acting and directing practice can, if so desired, begin with short scenes and move on to those that are longer. Or acting students may want to begin with monologs before interacting with others in scenes.

The plays are arranged alphabetically, according to title, so the student isn't necessarily hit with a group of plays all written at essentially the same time. This can help in giving a broader view right from the beginning.

There is an introduction to each play, providing background on most playwrights and on the plays, which should help in interpreting roles and scenes. Each scene in turn has an introduction. It might be a good idea for student actors or directors to work with different fellow students for each scene so that they will be exposed to a range of personalities and approaches.

There is no right way of interpreting and presenting characters and scenes. There are as many "right" ways as there are students. Certainly, there are "better" rules of presenting scenes, so far as voice usage, movement and placement. But no one presentation of a scene will or should appear "like" any other presentation of the same scene.

The scenes will, however, give good practice in learning to act and direct.

WORKING WITH THE SCENES

Since you will be working with each scene for at least a week or two in analyzing and preparing it for presentation, be sure to take your time in choosing one you think you will continue to enjoy.

Of course, you may be assigned scenes of a specific length or with a specific number or combination of characters. Still within these requirements, you should be able to find a number of cuttings that you like.

If the scenes are to be used for a directing class, take into consideration the actors you will be able to choose from and how well you think you can fill the roles. If the scenes will be used for an acting class, get together with the person or persons who will be your partners and try to come up with a scene and characters that each of you will want to continue to work with over a period of time.

ANALYZING THE SCENE

From the Actor's Viewpoint

Many of the questions asked about each scene will help you analyze your character.

1. Figure out what the playwright wants to convey with the scene and with your character, in other words, the central idea or theme. Then think about the best way of communicating this to your audience.

2. Figure out the mood and how to convey this. Mood is not the same as the emotions your character feels. For example, a character could be angry, but the scene itself could convey a sense of helplessness.

3. Unless, of course, you are doing a monolog, you need to get together with the others in the scene and agree both on theme and mood. You also need to agree how you can work together to show these things to an audience. Remember that it is important to be true to the playwright's intentions. For instance, when given today, Mowatt's nineteenth-century play *Fashion* sometimes is exaggerated in style, with a lot of hokey business thrown in. This is not the way Mowatt intended the play to be viewed.

3

4. You need to analyze your character, as well as the scene. Consider such things as:

 a. Present situation? Where does the person live? What country or area? What is the character's financial situation? Social status? How does all this affect what the person is like?

 b. Origin? Where did the character grow up? Live most of his or her life? Is the culture different from the one you are used to? How might all this affect the way a person thinks, feels or believes?

 c. Age? If the character's age is different from your own, what can you do to make the person convincing?

 d. Major influences in the person's life? How do they affect occupation, beliefs and so on?

 e. Personality traits? Is the character jealous, greedy, stingy, loving, caring and so on? How do you know this? How does all this affect the way the person comes across in a scene?

 f. Likeable personality? How do you feel about the character? What makes you feel this way?

 g. Relationship with the other characters? How does the character interact with others, and how do they feel about each other? How do you know this? Why is the character friends with one person, enemies with another, lukewarm with a third?

 h. Goal to be reached? Every character has something he or she is working toward in each scene. For a minor character, it can be as simple as having the goal of making a pizza delivery. Sometimes this goal differs from scene to scene. For instance, a character may want to have a happy marriage. That is the overall goal. In one particular scene this may be simpler. He or she may want to buy the marriage partner the ideal gift.

  Take into consideration what your character wants and why the goal is important. Then figure out how you might portray the character's needs or wants.

5. Next you should meet with your partners and agree on everything you've discovered. Sometimes you may need to compromise.

Then take into consideration such things as hand and set props (including furniture) you will need and decide whether this will be all imaginary, all real or a mixture. Figure out where the furniture should be placed. Continue working together in planning the movement and gestures. If you are the type of person who normally uses a lot of gestures and movement in everyday life, you probably will use more in presenting your scene. But again consider whether your use of gestures matches that of your partner(s). Each person's style of acting should match that of the others.

You should be guided by several things in planning movement and gestures: 1) the type of person your character is; 2) how you interpret the emotional situation that either calls for more movement, as anger or nervousness might, or less movement as fright could, 3) and how comfortable you are with gestures.

6. Most likely, you will need to memorize the scene (unless, for some reason, you or your teacher has decided on using scripts for the final presentation). Using all the information you have gathered, approach the memorization in whatever way you like. Some people like to memorize the text before working out movement and gestures; others like to memorize everything at the same time.

    Memorization is an individual thing, so what works well for someone else might not work for you.

    a. Be certain you know the meaning of each word and phrase. Although this is important for every type of scene, you may have to do more investigating of the meanings of words and references in historical pieces.

    b. Memorize the ideas and the flow of the scene, along with your cues, so you have the outline or the ideas firmly in mind before you try to memorize exact words.

    c. Work on memorizing the scene the last thing before you go to sleep at night; this helps you retain it.

7. Go over and rehearse the scene as many times as necessary to feel confident that you and your co-actors are presenting it to the best of your ability. This often means simply going over and over it until you are sure you have it firmly fixed in your mind. If you have access to a video camera, you may want to have someone else tape the scene so you can watch and listen

in evaluating how it is coming across.

The analysis sheet that follows can help you because it often is better to write things out so you are sure you have covered everything important. But remember you do not have to do the sheet in any particular order.

It might be a good idea for you to photocopy this sheet for each scene in which you are involved.

Analysis Sheet

Title of the Play:

Playwright:

Theme or Central Idea:

Secondary Themes:

Overall Mood:

My Character:

    Where from:

    Age:

    Environment (Time and Location of Scene):

    Major Influences:

    Personality traits:

    Motives and goals:

Interests:

    Jobs:

    Hobbies:

    Friends:

Relationship With Other Characters:

Brief Description of the Other Characters:

From the Director's Viewpoint

All of the scenes can be used for both acting and directing situations.

As a director, you should analyze each character, though not necessarily as thoroughly as each performer does his or her own character. A lot of the subtleties of interpretation can be left to the actor. Generally, this includes gestures and facial expression, except, of course, if the actor is having trouble with them.

Whether the actors are directing their own scenes or there is a different director, there are several things that are important to know, besides those on the actor's analysis sheet.

Every scene in a play has to maintain the audience's interest. You need to figure out what in your scene would do so. Are the characters unique? The situation? The setting? Often the conflict or struggle maintains interest.

As a director, you need to figure out which lines are most important for the audience to know to be able to understand the struggle (these are called plot lines), and which characters are more important at any given second. This way when directors block the scenes (plan the movement), they can place the actors where they are the most prominent when they have important lines or actions so the audience is sure to focus on what is most vital.

For instance, an actor who is upstage, that is, closer to the back wall of the set, is most prominent. A single actor commands more focus than one in a group.

An actor who is either standing or at a higher level on the stage (on a platform, for example) will gain more audience attention than one who is seated or who is at a lower level. One who is the focus of attention for the other actors also will be the focus of the audience's attention.

It can be a big help to sketch the set as seen from above to be able to keep in mind, when planning the movement, where the furniture or other set props are placed.

You can fill out an analysis sheet like the one that follows.

8

Director's Analysis

Play:

Playwright:

Theme or Central Idea:

Characters' Descriptions:

      Character 1:

      Character 2:

      Character 3:

The Goals of Each Character:

Why Each Character Is Included:

How Each Character Advances the Scene:

The Basic Struggle or Conflict of the Scene:

The Needs of Each Character:

Diagram of the set, showing placement of set pieces, such as furniture, trees, rocks, and so on.

You should also prepare a prompt book, that is, the script photocopied in the center of a sheet of eight-and-a-half by eleven inch paper, so there is plenty of space in the margins to write anything important having to do with the movement or placement of the actors. This can be done with drawings of the set showing the movement or by written directions or even with a combination of drawing and writing.

Often you will want to go back and change things because they worked better on paper than in actuality, so it is better to write in pencil, rather than pen.

Editor's Note:

The numbers at page left for all of the scenes in this book are for quick and easy reference for the actor and director. They also will aid in quick and precise back reference for note-taking when analyzing scenes.

Aftermath

by Mary Burrill

The complete text of *Aftermath* is included in the following scenes. The playwright Mary Burrill lived from 1879 to 1946, and this play first appeared in a magazine called *The Liberator* in April, 1919. The fighting, of course, refers to World War I.

At the time the play was published, the N.A.A.C.P., headed by W.E.B. DuBois, declared that it provided a hope for a new Negro drama. *Aftermath* actually echoed an editorial in the organization's publication *Crisis* that called for returning black soldiers to fight "the forces of hell" back in the States. This meant, in other words, that they should try to stem the tide of lynchings of black men in the South, and the race riots in the North.

The N.A.A.C.P. had urged young blacks to volunteer to fight America's enemies in World War I. Unfortunately, neither their war service nor the efforts of people such as Burrill and organizations such as the N.A.A.C.P. did anything noticeable to gain equality for blacks.

The play, a bleak and troubling story of a young man returned from meritorious duty as an American soldier, shows that although the United States was willing to allow black men to die for their country, still that country would not afford them equality, either morally or legally.

Mary Burrill was a teacher at Dunbar High School in Washington, D.C., from 1904 until her retirement in 1944.

SCENE 1: Two Females

Mam Sue, about 80

Millie, 16

The author sets the scene in this way:

TIME: The Present.

PLACE: The Thornton cabin in South Carolina.

It is late afternoon of a cool day in early spring. A soft afterglow pours in at the little window of the Thornton cabin. The light falls on Millie, a slender brown girl of sixteen, who stands near the window ironing. She wears a black dress and a big gingham apron. A clothes-horse weighted down with freshly ironed garments is nearby. In the rear there is a door leading out to the road. To the left there is another door leading into the other room of the cabin. To the right there is a great stone hearth blackened by age. A Bible rests on the mantel over the hearth. An old armchair and a small table on which is a kerosene lamp are near the hearth. In the center of the room sits a well-scrubbed kitchen table and a substantial wooden chair. In front of the hearth, in a low rocking chair drawn close to the smouldering wood fire, sits Mam Sue busily sewing. The many colors in the old patchwork quilt that she is mending, together with the faded red of the bandanna on her head, contrast strangely with her black dress. Mam Sue is very old. Her ebony face is seamed with wrinkles; and in her bleared, watery eyes there is a world-old sorrow. A service flag containing one star hangs in the little window of the cabin.

1. As you prepare this scene and those that follow it, pay attention to the way in which the dialects differ from person to person and even within a particular speech. For instance, the word evening is uttered both as "eben" and "evenin'." Why do you suppose the playwright wrote in this manner? If you are having trouble with the dialect, it might be better just to ignore it. Emotions and character are more important, although the dialect, of course, helps make the scene more realistic.

2. As you prepare this cutting for presentation, ask yourself its significance in the total play. Why do you suppose Burrill chose to start *Aftermath* this way?

A play, like any work that tells a story, needs to have tension. That is, things should not continue to go smoothly for the characters. The tension, often creating anxiety in the characters, continues to build and sometimes involves a disagreement or clash of wills between characters. Although this scene does not have a lot of disagreement or tension, it is present. Where can you find evidence of this? Point to specific lines and speeches. There is a conflict also brought about by differences in belief among the two characters. Figure out and discuss with the class what this stems from and how you might try to point it up for an audience.

1   **MAM SUE:** *(Crooning the old melody)*

2   **O, yes, yonder comes mah Lawd,**

3   **He is comin' dis way**

4   **Wid his sword in his han'**

5   **O, yes, yonder comes —**

6   *(A burning log falls apart, and MAM SUE suddenly stops*

7   *singing and gazes intently at the fire. She speaks in deep*

8   *mysterious tones to MILLIE, who has finished her task*

9   *and has come to the hearth to put up her irons.)* **See dat**

10   **log dah, Millie? De one fallin' tuh de side dah wid de**

11   **big flame lappin' 'round hit? Dat means big doin's**

12   **'round heah tonight!**

13   **MILLIE:** *(With a start)* **Oh, Mam Sue, don' you go**

14   **proph'sying no mo'! You seen big doin's in dat fire de**

15   **night befo' them w'ite devuls come in heah an' tuk'n**

16   **po' dad out and bu'nt him!**

17   **MAM SUE:** *(Calmly)* **No, Millie, Ah didn' see no big doin's**

18   **dat night — Ah see'd evul doin's an' Ah tole yo' po'**

19   **daddy to keep erway f'om town de nex' day wid his**

20   **cotton. Ah jes knowed dat he wuz gwine to git in a**

21   **row wid dem w'ite debbils — but he wou'd'n lis'n tuh**

22   **his ole mammy — De good Lawd sen' me dese**

23   **warnin's in dis fiah, jes lak he sen' his messiges in de**

24   **fiah to Moses. Yo' chillun bettah lis'n to —**

25   **MILLIE:** *(Nervously)* **Oh, Mam Sue, you skeers me when you**

26   **talks erbout seein' all them things in de fire —**

27   **MAM SUE: Yuh gits skeered cause yuh don' put yo' trus' in**

28   **de good Lawd! He kin tek keer o' yuh no mattuh whut**

29   **com'!**

30   **MILLIE:** *(Bitterly)* **Sometimes I thinks that Gawd's done**

31   **fu'got us po' cullud people. Gawd didn' tek no keer o'**

32   **po' dad and *he* put *his* trus' in him! He uster set evah**

33   **night by dis fire at dis here table and read his Bible**

34   **an' pray — but jes look whut happen' to Dad! That**

35   **don' look like Gawd wuz tekin' keer —**

1 **MAM SUE:** *(Sharply)* **Heish yo' mouf, Millie! Ah ain't a-**
2 **gwine to 'ave dat sinner-talk 'roun' hyeah!** *(Derisively)*
3 **Gawd don't tek no keer o' yuh? Ain't yuh bin prayin'**
4 **night an' mawnin' fo' Gawd to sen' yo' brudder back**
5 **f'om de war 'live an' whole? An' ain't yuh git dat**
6 **lettah no longer'n yistiddy sayin' dat de fightin's all**
7 **done stopp't an' dat de blessid Lawd's done brung yo'**
8 **brudder thoo all dem battuls live an' whole? Don' dat**
9 **look lak de Lawd's done 'membered yuh?**
10 **MILLIE:** *(Thoughtfully)* **I reckon youse right, Mam Sue. But**
11 **ef anything had a-happen' to John I wuz'n evah goin'**
12 **to pray no mo'!** *(MILLIE goes to the clothes-horse and*
13 *folds the garments and lays them carefully into a large*
14 *basket. MAM SUE falls again to her crooning.)*
15 **MAM SUE:**
16 **O, yes, yonder comes mah Lawd,**
17 **He's comin' dis way-a.**
18 **MILLIE: Lonnie's so late gittin' home tonight; I guess I'd**
19 **bettah tek Mis' Hart's wash home tonight myse'f.**
20 **MAM SUE: Yas, Lonnie's mighty late. Ah reckons you'd**
21 **bettah slip erlon' wid hit.** *(MILLIE gets her hat from the*
22 *adjoining room and is about to leave with the basket when*
23 *MAM SUE calls significantly.)* **Millie?**
24 **MILLIE: Yas, Mam Sue.**
25 **MAM SUE:** *(Firmly)* **Don' yo' fu'git to drap dat lettah fu'**
26 **John in de Pos' Awfus ez yuh goes by. Whah's de**
27 **lettah?**
28
29
30
31
32
33
34
35

SCENE 2: Two females; Two males

Millie, 16

Mam Sue, about 80

Rev. Moseby, probably 60-65

Lonnie, 18

1. This scene appears directly after the first. Now the tension and conflict is more apparent. Point to specific lines that show this.

2. Remembering that the play was written just after World War I, do you think the characters are realistic? Do you think anyone living in the present would have the same attitudes and beliefs toward life? Discuss this with the rest of the class.

3. Rev. Moseby appears only for this one scene. Why do you think he was included? Discuss with the class what you think his function is in furthering the plot or in building conflict and tension? What sort of person is he? How do you think he feels about the other characters in this scene? Is his view of them and of life itself realistic? Explain.

4. Before the play opens, the father, presumably Mam Sue's son or son-in-law, has been lynched and his body burned. There is no mention of any mother in this family. Why do you suppose the playwright didn't mention a mother?

5. Lonnie, of course, is John's younger brother and is two years older than Millie. What role does he play in this scene? In other words, what is his purpose here? Who is he closer to in viewpoint or outlook, Mam Sue or Millie? Point to lines that show this.

6. Why has John not been told of his father's death? Do you think it should have been kept from him? Or do you think he should have been told, as Mam Sue believes. Do you agree with Mam Sue or Millie about telling John of the lynching? Why?

1   **MILLIE:** *(Reluctantly)* **But, Mam Sue, please don' lets —**
2   *(A knock is heard. MILLIE opens the door and REVEREND*
3   *LUKE MOSEBY enters. MOSEBY is a wiry little old man*
4   *with a black, kindly face, and bright, searching eyes; his*
5   *woolly hair and beard are snow-white. He is dressed in a*
6   *rusty black suit with a coat of clerical cut that comes to his*
7   *knees. In one hand he carries a large Bible, and in the*
8   *other, a stout walking stick.)*
9   **MILLIE: Good evenin', Brother Moseby, come right in.**
10 **REV. MOSEBY: Good eben', Millie. Good eben', Mam Sue.**
11   **Ah jes drap't in to see ef you-all is still trus'in' de**
12   **good Lawd an' —**
13 **MAM SUE: Lor', Brudder Moseby, ain't Ah bin trus'n' de**
14   **good Lawd nigh onter dese eighty yeah! Whut fu' yuh**
15   **think Ah's gwine to quit w'en Ah'm in sight o' de**
16   **Promis' Lan'? Millie, fetch Brudder Moseby dat cheer.**
17 **MOSEBY:** *(Drawing his chair to the fire)* **Dat's right, Mam Sue,**
18   **you jes a-keep on trus'n' an' prayin' an evah thing's**
19   **gwine to come aw-right.** *(Observing that MILLIE is about*
20   *to leave)* **Don' lemme 'tain yuh, Millie, but whut's all**
21   **dis good news wese bin heahin' 'bout yo' brudder**
22   **John? Dey say he's done won some kind o' medal**
23   **ober dah in France?**
24 **MILLIE:** *(Brightening up)* **Oh, yes, we got a lettah day befo'**
25   **yestiddy f'om John tellin' us all erbout it. He's won**
26   **de War Cross! He fought off twenty Germuns all**
27   **erlone an' saved his whole comp'ny an' the gret**
28   **French Gen'rul come an' pinned de medal on him,**
29   **hisse'f!**
30 **MOSEBY: De Lawd bles' his soul! Ah know'd dat boy wud**
31   **mek good!**
32 **MILLIE:** *(Excited by the glory of it all)* **An' he's been to Paris,**
33   **an' the fines' people stopp't him when they seen his**
34   **medal, an' shook his han' an' smiled at him — an' he**
35   **kin go evahwhere, an' dey ain't nobody all the time**

1   a-lookin' down on him, an' a-sneerin' at him cause
2   he's black; but evahwhere they's jes gran' to him! An'
3   he sez it's the firs' time evah in his life he's felt lak
4   a real, sho-nuf man!

5   MOSEBY: Well, honey, don't de Holy Book say, "De fust
6   shill be las' and de las' shill be fust"?

7   MAM SUE: *(Fervently)* Dat hit do! An' de Holy Book ain't
8   nebber tole no lie!

9   MOSEBY: Folks ober in Char'ston is sayin' dat some sojers
10   is gwine to lan' dah today or tomorrer. Ah reckons
11   day'll all be comin' 'long soon now dat de war's done
12   stopp't.

13   MILLIE: I jes hates the thought of John comin' home an'
14   hearin' 'bout Dad!

15   MOSEBY: *(In astonishment)* Whut! Yuh mean to say yuh
16   ain't 'rite him 'bout yo' daddy, yit?

17   MAM SUE: Dat she ain't! Millie mus' 'ave huh way! She
18   'lowed huh brudder ough'n be tole, an' dat huh could
19   keep on writin' to him jes lak huh dad wuz livin' —
20   Millie allus done de writin' — An' Ah lets huh 'ave
21   huh way —

22   MOSEBY: *(Shaking his head in disapproval)* Yuh mean tuh
23   say —

24   MILLIE: *(Pleadingly)* But, Brother Moseby, I couldn't write
25   John no bad news w'ilst he wuz way over there by
26   hisse'f. He had 'nuf to worry him with death a-starin'
27   him in the face evah day!

28   MAM SUE: Yas, Brudder Moseby, Millie's bin carryin' on
29   dem lies in huh lettahs fu' de las' six months; but
30   today Ah jes sez to huh — Dis war done stopp't now,
31   an' John he gwine to be comin' home soon, an' he
32   ain't agwine to come hyeah an' fin' me wid no lie on
33   mah soul! An' Ah med huh set down an' tell him de
34   whole truf. She's gwine out to pos' dat lettah dis
35   minute.

1   **MOSEBY:** *(Still disapproving)* **No good nebher come —**

2   *(The door is pushed violently open, and LONNIE, a sturdy*

3   *black boy of eighteen rushes in breathlessly.)*

4   **LONNIE: Mam Sue! Millie! Whut'da yuh think? John's**

5   **come home!**

6   **MILLIE:** *(Speechless with astonishment)* **John? Home?**

7   **Where's he at?**

8   **MAM SUE:** *(Incredulously)* **Whut yuh sayin'? John done**

9   **come home? Bles' de Lawd! Bles' de Lawd! Millie,**

10   **didn' Ah tell yuh sumpin wuz gwine tuh happen?**

11   **LONNIE:** *(Excitedly)* **I wuz sweepin' up de sto' jes befo'**

12   **leavin' an' de phone rung — it wuz John — he wuz at**

13   **Char'ston — jes landid! His comp'ny's waitin' to git**

14   **de ten o'clock train fu' Camp Reed, whah dey's goin'**

15   **to be mustered out.**

16   **MOSEBY: But how's he gwine to get erway?**

17   **LONNIE: Oh, good evenin', Brother Moseby, Ise jes so**

18   **'cited I didn' see yuh — Why his Cap'n done give him**

19   **leave to run over heah 'tell de train's ready. He ought**

20   **tuh be heah now 'cause it's mos' two hours sence he**

21   **wuz talkin' —**

22   **MAM SUE: Whuffo yuh so long comin' home an' tellin' us?**

23   **LONNIE:** *(Hesitatingly)* **I did start right out but when I git to**

24   **Sherley's corner I seen a whole lot of them w'ite**

25   **hoodlums hangin' round de feed sto' — I jes felt like**

26   **dey wuz jes waitin' dah to start sumpin, so I dodged**

27   **'em by tekin' de long way home.**

28   **MILLIE: Po' Lonnie! He's allus dodgin' po' w'ite trash!**

29   **LONNIE:** *(Sullenly)* **Well, yuh see whut Dad got by not**

30   **dodgin' 'em.**

31   **MOSEBY:** *(Rising to go)* **Ah mus' be steppin' 'long now. Ah**

32   **got to stop in to see ole man Hawkins; he's mighty**

33   **sick. Ah'll drap in on mah way back fu' a word o'**

34   **prayer wid John.**

35   **MAM SUE: Lonnie, yu'd bettah run erlon' as Brudder**

1 **Moseby go an' tote dat wash tuh Mis' Ha't. An' drap**
2 **in Mis' Hawkins' sto' an' git some soap an' starch; an'**
3 **Ah reckons yu'd bettah bring me a bottle o' linimint**
4 **— dis ole pain done come back in mah knee.** *(To*
5 *MOSEBY)* **Good eben, Brudder Moseby.**
6 MOSEBY: **Good eben, Mam Sue; Good eben, Millie, an'**
7 **Gawd bles' yuh.**
8 LONNIE: *(As he is leaving)* **Tell John I'll git back fo' he**
9 **leaves.**
10 *(LONNIE and MOSEBY leave. MILLIE closes the door*
11 *behind them and then goes to the window and looks out*
12 *anxiously.)*
13 MILLIE: *(Musingly)* **Po' John. Po' John!** *(Turning to MAM SUE)*
14 **Mam Sue?**
15 MAM SUE: **Yas, Millie.**
16 MILLIE: *(Hesitatingly)* **Who's goin' to tell John 'bout Dad?**
17 MAM SUE: *(Realizing for the first time that the task must fall to*
18 *someone)* **Dunno. Ah reckons yu'd bettah.**
19 MILLIE: *(Going to MAM SUE and kneeling softly at her side)*
20 **Mam Sue, don' let's tell him now! He's got only a li'l**
21 **hour to spen' with us — an' it's the firs' time fu' so**
22 **long! John loved daddy so! Let 'im be happy jes a li'l**
23 **longer — we kin tell 'im the truth when he comes**
24 **back fu' good. Please, Mam Sue!**
25 MAM SUE: *(Softened by MILLIE's pleading)* **Honey chile, John**
26 **gwine to be askin' for his daddy fust thing — dey**
27 **ain't no way —**
28 MILLIE: *(Gaining courage)* **Oh, yes, 'tis! We kin tell 'im Dad's**
29 **gone to town — anything, jes so's he kin spen' these**
30 **few lil'l minutes in peace! I'll fix the Bible jes like**
31 **Dad's been in an' been a-readin' in it! He won't know**
32 **no bettah!**
33 *(MILLIE takes the Bible from the mantel and opening it at*
34 *random lays it on the table; she draws the old armchair*
35 *close to the table as her father had been wont to do every*

1   *evening when he read his Bible.)*

2   **MAM SUE:** *(Shaking her head doubtfully)* **Ah ain't much on**

3   **actin' dis lie, Millie.**

4   *(The soft afterglow fades and the little cabin is filled with*

5   *shadows. MILLIE goes again to the window and peers*

6   *out. MAM SUE falls again to her crooning.)*

7   **MAM SUE:** *(Crooning)*

8   **O, yes, yonder comes mah Lawd,**

9   **He's comin' dis way**

10   **Wid his sword in his han' —**

11   *(To MILLIE)* **Millie, bettah light de lamp; it's gittin'**

12   **dark. —**

13   **He's gwine ter hew dem sinners down**

14   **Right lebbal to de groun'**

15   **O, yes, yonder comes mah Lawd-**

16   *(As MILLIE is lighting the lamp, whistling is heard in the*

17   *distance. MILLIE listens intently, then rushes to the*

18   *window. The whistling comes nearer, it rings out clear and*

19   *familiar — "Though the boys are far away, they dream of*

20   *home!")*

21

22

23

24

25

26

27

28

29

30

31

32

33

34

35

SCENE 3: Two Females and One Male

Millie, 16

Mam Sue, about 80

John, probably early 20s

1. Up until this scene, the other characters have only talked about John. From what the other characters said about him, is he the sort of person you expected him to be? Why or why not?

2. As you know, Mam Sue has been against not telling John that his father is dead. Her religious beliefs strongly prohibit lying. Yet even now she continues to go along with what Millie wants. Why do you think she does this? Is it realistic that she do so?

3. In what way does the tension increase in this scene? Point to specific lines that show this. Remember that a play involves a clash of forces, a protagonist and an antagonist. Usually, the protagonist is a person, but sometimes a group of people is opposed in some way by other people or forces. A play continues to build with the protagonist and antagonist pitted against each other. Their conflict and struggle continues to build until it reaches a point where it can go no further without something occurring that is irreversible. Sometimes the antagonist is a person, or sometimes a group of people. At other times it can be a "force" such as society or nature. Who is the protagonist here? Who is the antagonist? Why do you think so?

4. Do you like the characters you've met so far? Why or why not?

1   **MILLIE:** *(Excitedly)* **That's him! That's John, Mam Sue!**
2   *(MILLIE rushes out of doors. The voices of JOHN and*
3   *MILLIE are heard from without in greetings. Presently,*
4   *JOHN and MILLIE enter the cabin. JOHN is tall and*
5   *straight—a good soldier and a strong man. He wears the*
6   *uniform of a private in the American Army. One hand is*
7   *clasped in both of MILLIE's. In the other, he carries an old-*
8   *fashioned valise. The War Cross is pinned on his breast.*
9   *On his sleeve three chevrons tell mutely of wounds*
10 *suffered in the cause of freedom. His brown face is aglow*
11 *with life and the joy of homecoming.)*
12 **JOHN:** *(Eagerly)* **Where's Dad? Where's Mam Sue?**
13 **MAM SUE:** *(Hobbling painfully to meet him)* **Heah's ole Mam**
14   **Sue!** *(JOHN takes her tenderly in his arms.)* **Bles' yo'**
15   **heart, chile, bles' yo' heart! Tuh think dat de good**
16   **Lawd's done lemme live to see dis day!**
17 **JOHN: Dear old Mam Sue! Gee, but I'm glad to see you an'**
18   **Millie again!**
19 **MAM SUE: Didn' Ah say dat yuh wuz comin' back hyeah?**
20 **JOHN:** *(Smiling)* **Same old Mam Sue with huh faith an' huh**
21   **prayers! But where's Dad?** *(He glances toward the open*
22   *Bible.)* **He's been in from de field, ain't he?**
23 **MILLIE:** *(Without lifting her eyes)* **Yes, he's come in but he**
24   **had to go out ag'in — to Sherley's feed sto'.**
25 **JOHN:** *(Reaching for his cap that he has tossed upon the table)*
26   **That ain't far. I've jes a few minutes so I'd bettah run**
27   **down there an' hunt him up. Won't he be surprised!**
28 **MILLIE:** *(Confused)* **No — no, John — I fu'got; he ain't gone**
29   **to Sherley's, he's gont to town.**
30 **JOHN:** *(Disappointed)* **To town? I hope he'll git in befo' I'm**
31   **leavin'. There's no tellin' how long they'll keep me at**
32   **Camp Reed. Where's Lonnie?**
33 **MAM SUE: Lonnie's done gone to Mis' Ha't's wid de wash.**
34   **He'll be back to-reckly.**
35 **MILLIE:** *(Admiring the medal on his breast)* **An' this is the**

1   **medal? Tell us all erbout it, John.**

2   **JOHN: Oh, Sis, it's an awful story — wait 'til I git back fu'**

3   **good. Let's see whut I've got in dis bag fu' you.** *(He*

4   *places the worn valise on the table and opens it. He takes*

5   *out a bright-colored dress pattern.)* **That's fu' you, Millie,**

6   **and quit wearin' them black clothes.**

7   *(MILLIE takes the silk and hugs it eagerly to her breast,*

8   *suddenly there sweeps into her mind the realization that*

9   *she cannot wear it, and the silk falls to the floor.)*

10   **MILLIE:** *(Trying to be brave)* **Oh, John, it's jes lovely!** *(As she*

11   *shows it to MAM SUE)* **Look, Mam Sue!**

12   **JOHN:** *(Flourishing a bright shawl)* **An' this is fu' Mam Sue.**

13   **Mam Sue'll be so gay!**

14   **MAM SUE:** *(Admiring the gift)* **Who'd evah b'lieved dat yo' ole**

15   **Mam Sue would live to be wearin' clo'es whut huh**

16   **gran'chile done brung huh f'om Eu'ope!**

17   **JOHN: Never you mind, Mam Sue, one of these days I'm**

18   **goin' to tek you an' Millie over there, so's you kin**

19   **breathe free jes once befo' yuh die.**

20   **MAM SUE: It's got tuh be soon, 'cause dis ole body's mos'**

21   **wo'e out; an' de good Lawd's gwine to be callin' me to**

22   **pay mah debt 'fo' long.**

23   **JOHN:** *(Showing some handkerchiefs, with gay borders)* **These**

24   **are fu' Lonnie.** *(He next takes out a tiny box that might*

25   *contain a bit of jewelry.)* **An' this is fu' Dad. Sum'pin**

26   **he's been wantin' fu' years. I ain't goin' to open it 'til**

27   **he comes.**

28   *(MILLIE walks into the shadows and furtively wipes a tear*

29   *from her eyes.)*

30   **JOHN:** *(Taking two army pistols from his bag and placing them*

31   *on the table)* **An' these las' are fu' you***ahs truly.*

32   **MILLIE:** *(Looking at them, fearfully)* **Oh, John, are them**

33   **youahs?**

34   **JOHN: One of 'em's mine; the other's my lieutenant's. I've**

35   **been cleanin' it fu' him. Don' tech 'em — 'cause**

1   mine's loaded.
2   **MILLIE:** *(Still looking at them in fearful wonder)* **Did they learn**
3   **yuh how to shoot 'em?**
4   **JOHN: Yep, an' I kin evah mo' pick 'em off!**
5   **MILLIE:** *(Reproachfully)* **Oh, John!**
6   **JOHN: Nevah you worry, li'l Sis, John's nevah goin' to use**
7   **'em 'less it's right fu' him to.** *(He places the pistols on*
8   *the mantel — on the very spot where the Bible has lain.)*
9   **My! but it's good to be home! I've been erway only**
10   **two years but it seems like two cent'ries. All that life**
11   **ovah there seems like some awful dream!**
12   **MAM SUE:** *(Fervently)* **Ah know it do! Many's de day yo' ole**
13   **Mam Sue set in dis cheer an' prayed fu' yuh.**
14   **JOHN: Lots of times, too, in the trenches when I wuz dog-**
15   **tired, an' sick, an' achin' wid the cold I uster say:**
16   **well, if we're sufferin' all this for the oppressed, like**
17   **they tell us, then Mam Sue, an' Dad, an' Millie come**
18   **in on that — they'll git some good ou'n it if I don't!**
19   **An' I'd shet my eyes an' fu'git the cold, an' the pain,**
20   **an' them old guns spittin' death all 'round us; an' see**
21   **you folks settin' here by this fire — Mam Sue,**
22   **noddin, an' singin'; Dad a spellin' out his Bible —** *(He*
23   *glances toward the open book.)* **Let's see whut he's been**
24   **readin' —** *(JOHN takes up the Bible and reads the first*
25   *passage upon which his eye falls.)* **"But I say unto you,**
26   **love your enemies, bless them that curse you, an' do**
27   **good to them that hate you" —** *(He lets the Bible fall to*
28   *the table.)* **That ain't the dope they been feedin' us**
29   **soljers on! 'Love your enemies!' It's been — git a**
30   **good aim at 'em, an' let huh go!**
31   **MAM SUE:** *(Surprised)* **Honey, Ah hates to hyeah yuh talkin'**
32   **lak dat! It sound lak yuh done fu'git yuh Gawd!**
33   **JOHN: No, Mam Sue, I ain't fu'got God, but I've quit**
34   **thinkin' that prayers kin do everything. I've seen a**
35   **whole lot sence I've been erway from here. I've seen**

1   some men go into battle with a curse on their lips,
2   and I've seen them same men come back with never
3   a scratch; an' I've seen men whut read their Bibles
4   befo' battle, an' prayed to live, left dead on the field.
5   Yes, Mam Sue, I've seen a heap an' I've done a tall lot
6   o' thinkin' sence I've been erway from here. An' I
7   b'lieve it's jes like this — beyon' a certain point
8   prayers ain't no good! The Lawd does jes so much for
9   you, then it's up to you to do the res' fu' yourse'f.
10 The Lawd's done his part when he's done give me
11 strength an' courage; I got tuh do the res' fu' myse'f!
12
13
14
15
16
17
18
19
20
21
22
23
24
25
26
27
28
29
30
31
32
33
34
35

SCENE 4: Three Females and Two Males

Mam Sue, about 80

John, probably early 20s

Lonnie, 18

Millie, 16

Mrs. Hawkins, young to middle-aged

1. This scene, of course, is the climax to the play. It shows the point where the action can go no further without something irrevocable happening. What is that something? Point to specific lines that show it. Discuss with the rest of the class the conditions that led to this.

2. Do you think John's action here is realistic? Do you agree with what he's going to do? Why or why not? Given his circumstances, do you think it logical that he decides on this course of action?

3. How do you think Lonnie feels throughout the scene? Do you think John should have asked him to go along at the end? How would you feel about this if you were Lonnie? Why do you think John wants Lonnie to go with him?

4. The more minor the character, the less the audience needs to know about him or her. If the character is too fully developed, the audience will feel cheated if the person disappears, never to return. Often these minor characters are devices to further the action or to carry on the plot. One such character is Mrs. Hawkins, who really is only a device, rather than a fully developed character. Why did the playwright include her? What purpose does she serve? How would you go about playing this role?

5. Do you think *Aftermath* is a good play? Do you like it? Why? Do you think it has any relevancy to life today? Why? Would you ever want to appear in or direct a play such as this for a wider audience than your fellow students? Why?

1 MAM SUE: *(Shaking her head)* **Ah don' lak dat kin' o' talk —**
2 **it don' 'bode no good!** *(The door opens and LONNIE*
3 *enters with packages. He slips the bolt across the door.)*
4 JOHN: *(Rushing to LONNIE and seizing his hand)* **Hello,**
5 **Lonnie, ole man!**
6 LONNIE: **Hello, John. Gee, but Ah'm glad tuh see yuh!**
7 JOHN: **Boy, you should 'ave been with me! It would 'ave**
8 **taken some of the skeeriness out o' yuh, an' done**
9 **yuh a worl' o' good.**
10 LONNIE: *(Ignoring JOHN's remark)* **Here's the soap an'**
11 **starch, Millie.**
12 MAM SUE: **Has yuh brung mah linimint?**
13 LONNIE. **Yassum, it's in de packige.**
14 MILLIE: *(Unwrapping the package)* **No, it ain't, Lonnie.**
15 LONNIE: **Mis' Hawkins give it tuh me. Ah mus' a lef' it on de**
16 **counter. Ah'll git it w'en Ah goes to de train wid John.**
17 MILLIE: *(Showing him the handkerchief)* **See whut John done**
18 **brought you! An' look on de mantel!** *(Pointing to the*
19 *pistols)*
20 LONNIE: *(Drawing back in fear as he glances at the pistols)*
21 **You'd bettah hide them things! No cullud man bettah**
22 **be seen wid dem things down heah!**
23 JOHN: **That's all right, Lonnie, nevah you fear. I'm goin' to**
24 **keep 'em an' I ain't a-goin' to hide 'em either. See**
25 **them,** *(Pointing to the wound chevrons on his arm)* **well,**
26 **when I got them wounds, I let out all the rabbit-blood**
27 **'at wuz in me!** *(Defiantly)* **Ef I kin be trusted with a gun**
28 **in France, I kin be trusted with one in South Car'lina.**
29 MAM SUE: *(Sensing trouble)* **Millie, yu'd bettah fix some**
30 **suppah fu' John.**
31 JOHN: *(Looking at his watch)* **I don' want a thing. I've got to**
32 **be leavin' in a little while. I'm 'fraid I'm goin' to miss**
33 **Dad after all.**
34 *(The knob of the door is turned as though someone is*
35 *trying to enter. Then there is a loud knock on the door.)*

1   **JOHN:** *(Excitedly)* **That's Dad! Don't tell him I'm here!**
2   *(JOHN tips hurriedly into the adjoining room. LONNIE*
3   *unbolts the door and MRS. SELENA HAWKINS enters.)*
4   **MRS. HAWKINS. Lonnie fu'got de liniment so I thought I'**
5   **bettah run ovah wid hit, 'cause when Mam Sue sen'**
6   **fu' dis stuff she sho' needs hit. Brudder Moseby's**
7   **been tellin' me dat John's done come home.**
8   **JOHN:** *(Coming from his hiding place and trying to conceal his*
9   *disappointment)* **Yes, I'm here. Good evenin', Mis'**
10   **Hawkins. Glad to see you.**
11   **MRS. HAWKINS:** *(Shaking hands with JOHN)* **Well, lan' sakes**
12   **alive! Ef it ain't John sho'nuf! An' ain't he lookin'**
13   **gran'! Jes look at dat medal a-shining' on his coat!**
14   **Put on yuh cap, boy, an' lemme see how yuh look!**
15   **JOHN: Sure!** *(JOHN puts on his overseas cap and, smiling,*
16   *stands at attention a few paces off, while MAM SUE,*
17   *LONNIE, and MILLIE form an admiring circle around him.)*
18   **MRS. HAWKINS: Now don' he sholy look gran'! I knows yo'**
19   **sistah, an' gran'-mammy's proud o' yuh!** *(A note of*
20   *sadness creeps into her voice.)* **Ef only yuh po' daddy**
21   **had a-lived to see dis day!**
22   *(JOHN looks at her in amazement. MILLIE and MAM SUE*
23   *stand transfixed with terror over the sudden betrayal.)*
24   **JOHN:** *(Looking from one to the other and repeating her words as*
25   *though he can scarcely realize their meaning)* **'Ef your po'**
26   **daddy had lived —** *(To MILLIE)* **Whut does this mean?**
27   *(MILLIE sinks sobbing into the chair at the table and*
28   *buries her face in her hands.)*
29   **MRS. HAWKINS: Lor', Millie, I thought you'd tole him!**
30   *(Bewildered by the catastrophe that she has precipitated,*
31   *SELENA HAWKINS slips out of the cabin.)*
32   **JOHN:** *(Shaking MILLIE almost roughly)* **Come, Millie, have**
33   **you been lyin' to me? Is Dad gone?**
34   **MILLIE:** *(Through her sobs)* **I jes hated to tell you — you wuz**
35   **so far erway —**

1   JOHN: *(Nervously)* **Come, Millie, for God's sake don' keep**
2   **me in this su'pense! I'm a brave soldier — I kin stan'**
3   **it — did he suffer much? Wuz he sick long?**
4   MILLIE: **He wuzn't sick no time — them w'ite devuls come**
5   **in heah an' dragged him —**
6   JOHN: *(Desperately)* **My God! You mean they lynched Dad?**
7   MILLIE: *(Sobbing piteously)* **They burnt him down by the big**
8   **gum tree!**
9   JOHN: *(Desperately)* **Whut fu', Millie? What fu'?**
10   MILLIE: **He got in a row wid ole Mister Withrow 'bout the**
11   **price of cotton — an' he called Dad a liar an' struck**
12   **him — an' Dad he up an' struck him back —**
13   JOHN: *(Brokenly)* **Didn' they try him? Didn' they give him**
14   **a chance? Whut'd the sheriff do? An' the gov-nur?**
15   MILLIE: *(Through her sobs)* **They didn't do nothin'.**
16   JOHN: **Oh, God! Oh, God!** *(Then recovering from the first bitter*
17   *anguish and speaking)* **So they've come into ouah**
18   **home, have they!** *(He strides over to LONNIE and seizes*
19   *him by the collar.)* **An' whut wuz you doin' when them**
20   **hounds come in here after Dad?**
21   LONNIE: *(Hopelessly)* **They wuz so many of 'em come an'**
22   **git 'im — whut could Ah do?**
23   JOHN: **Do? You could 'ave fought 'em like a man!**
24   MAM SUE: *(Pleadingly)* **Don't be too hard on 'im, John,**
25   **wese ain't got no gun 'round heah!**
26   JOHN: **Then he should 'ave burnt their damn kennels ovah**
27   **their heads! Who was it leadin' em?**
28   MILLIE: **Old man Withrow and the Sherley boys, they**
29   **started it all.**
30   *(Gradually assuming the look of a man who has deter-*
31   *mined to do some terrible work that must be done, JOHN*
32   *walks deliberately toward the mantel where the revolvers*
33   *are lying.)*
34   JOHN: *(Bitterly)* **I've been helpin' the w'ite man git his**
35   **freedom, I reckon I'd bettah try now to get my own!**

1   MAM SUE: *(Terrified)* **Whut yuh gwine ter do?**
2   JOHN: *(With bitterness growing in his voice)* **I'm sick o' these**
3   **w'ite folks doin's — we're fine, trustworthy feller**
4   **citizuns' when they're handin' us out guns, an' Liberty**
5   **Bonds, an' chuckin' us off to die; but we ain't a damn**
6   **thing when it comes to handin' us the rights we done**
7   **fought an' bled fu'! I'm sick o' this sort o' life — an'**
8   **I'm goin' to put an' end to it!**
9   MILLIE: *(Rushing to the mantel, and covering the revolvers with*
10   *her hands)* **Oh, no, no, John! Mam Sue, John's gwine**
11   **to kill hisse'f!**
12   MAM SUE: *(Piteously)* **Oh, mah honey, don' yuh go do**
13   **nothin' to bring sin on yo' soul! Pray to de good Lawd**
14   **to tek all dis fiery feelin' out'n yo' heart! Wait 'tel**
15   **Brudder Moseby come back — he's gwine to pray —**
16   JOHN: *(His speech growing more impassioned and bitter)* **This**
17   **ain't no time fu' preachers or prayers! You mean to**
18   **tell me I mus' let them w'ite devuls send me miles**
19   **erway to suffer an' be shot up fu' the freedom of**
20   **people I ain't nevah seen, while they 're burnin' an'**
21   **killin' my folks here at home! To hell with 'em!** *(He*
22   *pushes MILLIE aside, and seizing the revolvers, thrusts*
23   *the loaded one into his pocket and begins deliberately to*
24   *load the other.)*
25   MILLIE: *(Throwing her arms about his neck)* **Oh, John, they'll**
26   **kill yuh!**
27   JOHN: *(Defiantly)* **Whut ef they do! I ain't skeered o' none**
28   **of 'em! I've faced worse guns than any sneakin'**
29   **hounds kin show me! To hell with 'em!** *(He thrusts the*
30   *revolver that he has just loaded into LONNIE's hand.)* **Take**
31   **this, an' come on here, boy, an' we'll see what Withrow**
32   **an' his gang have got to say!**
33   *(Followed by LONNIE, who is bewildered and speechless,*
34   *JOHN rushes out of the cabin and disappears in the gath-*
35   *ering darkness.)*

Family Scenes

by Ivette M. Ramirez

Winner of the 1989 Drama League Award, *Family Scenes* explores the relationships among members of a family, consisting of a mother and her two grown daughters. The major theme is families or members of families are not always what they appear to be.

Each of the three women has secrets or presumed secrets, which are revealed as the play unravels. Margarita, the mother, assumes the role of a woman whose husband has deserted her, forcing her to raise their two children alone. Yet this is not true, any more than are the roles the daughters assume.

The play seems to say that the family will never be united in the way they all seem to wish possible. Yet they will go on, and so will their relationships with each other.

This is a one-act play, consisting of seven scenes.

SCENE 1: Three Females

Sophia, 20

Paula, 23

Margarita, 40

This scene opens the play and introduces the three central characters. It consists of about three-fourths of the play's "Scene One."

1. Taking only the first five speeches in this scene, what can you presume about the family as a whole, about each of the members, and about the relationships among them? Use the specific lines to support what you say.

2. Almost immediately there is conflict of various sorts. Can you discover it? Can you think of possible reasons for this type of family clash? Are there ever similar clashes in your own family or in families you know? How can you take the personal knowledge that comes from this and use it in portraying one of the three women here?

3. Are these characters likeable? Why do you think so?

1   *The set is a small three-room apartment located in a poor,*
2   *but well-kept neighborhood in the Bronx. The three rooms*
3   *are set on a low platform. The center of the apartment is*
4   *the kitchen with a bedroom on stage left with a doorway*
5   *leading to the bathroom and the living room barely visible*
6   *behind the kitchen. Stage right is the door to the apart-*
7   *ment and the stoop of the brownstone building. The front*
8   *of the stage represents the street, with a fire hydrant and*
9   *lamppost. The apartment is furnished with mostly old*
10   *furniture which is kept in good condition.*
11   *PAULA, dressed casually but fashionably, is in the*
12   *bedroom admiring a wedding dress which hangs on a*
13   *closet door. A light flickers from the living room television as*
14   *MARGARITA watches it. SOPHIA comes up the steps of the*
15   *brownstone to the door, fumbles for the house keys in her*
16   *bag, drops it, tries the door and, finding it open, goes in.*
17   **SOPHIA: Mami, I'm home.**
18   **MARGARITA:** *(From the living room)* **It's time you got home.**
19   **Your food's on the counter. Eat it before it gets cold.**
20   **I wish you would call when you're going to be late.**
21   **SOPHIA:** *(Looking at the plate of food)* **I had to work late.** *(To*
22   *herself)* **Nag, nag, nag.** *(SOPHIA places her handbag on*
23   *the kitchen counter, picks up the plate and places it on the*
24   *table. She goes to the refrigerator and pours herself a*
25   *glass of milk; she then sits down at the kitchen table*
26   *to eat.)*
27   **PAULA:** *(From the bedroom)* **Was that the door?** *(PAULA comes*
28   *out of the bedroom with a bride's magazine in her hand.)*
29   **Oh, it's you.**
30   **SOPHIA:** *(Seeing the magazine)* **How come you're still**
31   **looking at those? Didn't you tell Mami you were**
32   **wearing her dress?**
33   **PAULA: I know, but it doesn't hurt to look. Besides, there's**
34   **other things in here.**
35   **SOPHIA: You shouldn't have told her you were wearing her**

1   **dress. You're going to hurt her feelings if you don't**
2   **wear it.**
3   PAULA: *(Reluctantly)* **I wouldn't do that. There's stuff in**
4   **here about how to wear your hair...**
5   SOPHIA: **Anything in there about when not to get**
6   **married?**
7   PAULA: **Shut up, okay. I know you don't like Benny, but**
8   **I'm the one who's marrying him, not you.**
9   SOPHIA: *(Mocking her)* **Oh, well, ain't that precious.** *(Pause)*
10   **Sorry, I didn't mean it.**
11   PAULA: **He's not such a bad person, if you just give him a**
12   **chance.**
13   SOPHIA: **I'm not saying nothing. I'm minding my own**
14   **business.**
15   PAULA: **I really wish you would. He's coming over in a**
16   **little while, so you better behave yourself.**
17   SOPHIA: **I'll be a good little girl, just like I always am.**
18   PAULA: **Please don't mess this up for me.**
19   SOPHIA: **What?**
20   PAULA: *(Begins to go back into the bedroom.)* **I want my**
21   **wedding to be special.**
22   SOPHIA: *(To herself)* **Well, maybe you should change the**
23   **bridegroom.**
24   PAULA: **What did you say?**
25   SOPHIA: **Nothing.**
26   PAULA: **Can't you see how important this is to me?**
27   SOPHIA: **Yeah, sure.**
28   PAULA: **He's really a nice person. He has problems, but he**
29   **loves me.**
30   SOPHIA: **You know, I'm sick of hearing about this. I'm sick**
31   **of him hanging around here.**
32   PAULA: **He's my boyfriend and he can come whenever he**
33   **wants.**
34   SOPHIA: **Big deal. I personally wouldn't go telling that to**
35   **people I knew.** *(MARGARITA enters carrying a plate and*

1   *glass to the sink. She's in a housedress with a flower*
2   *print, her hair is pinned up. She has the tired look about*
3   *her but becomes animated when speaking to her daugh-*
4   *ters.)* **Mami, tell her she can't have Benny over here**
5   **every night.**

6   **PAULA: What do you care, you're never around, anyway.**

7   **MARGARITA: Will you stop fighting?**

8   **SOPHIA: Sure, go ahead take her side.**

9   **MARGARITA:** *(Being patient)* **I'm not taking sides.**

10   **SOPHIA: Then tell her Benny can't come over every night.**

11   **MARGARITA: Do your dishes...and mine.**

12   **SOPHIA: Mom, I just got home.**

13   **PAULA: You're so damn lazy.**

14   **SOPHIA:** *(To PAULA)* **You know you're really stupid.** *(PAULA*
15   *reaches over to hit SOPHIA and MARGARITA steps*
16   *between them.)*

17   **PAULA: Sure, defend her, that's why she's such a**
18   **spoiled...** *(MARGARITA grabs PAULA by the face.)*

19   **MARGARITA: I thought you said you had a date with**
20   **Benny?**

21   **PAULA: Yeah, yeah.** *(PAULA reluctantly exits to the bedroom.*
22   *MARGARITA turns to her youngest daughter; she slaps*
23   *her gently on the head.)*

24   **SOPHIA: Hey, what's that for?**

25   **MARGARITA: Haven't I told you a million times to leave**
26   **your sister alone about Benny?**

27   **SOPHIA: But, Mom, he's just so...**

28   **MARGARITA: He loves your sister and wants to marry her,**
29   **so leave it alone.**

30   **SOPHIA: If you knew how people talk about him...**
31   *(MARGARITA slaps her on the head again, this time a little*
32   *harder.)* **Ma, you're giving me a headache.**

33   **MARGARITA: I don't want to hear gossip, is that clear?**

34   **SOPHIA: Mom, why do you want her to marry Benny?**

35   **MARGARITA: I don't want anything. She's a good girl, she**

1   **works hard and she should marry and settle down**
2   **and have a family.**
3   **SOPHIA: Ugh, gross.** *(PAULA comes out of the bedroom,*
4   *looking at her watch.)*
5   **MARGARITA: What time is Benny picking you up?**
6   **PAULA: Twenty minutes ago.**
7   **MARGARITA: Maybe he had to work late.**
8   **PAULA: I talked to him at home.**
9   **SOPHIA:** *(Smiling)* **Maybe he's not coming.**
10   **PAULA: Why do you say that?**
11   **SOPHIA:** *(Wide grin)* **Maybe he found something better**
12   **along the way, maybe Dolores across the street got to**
13   **him before he made it here.**
14   **MARGARITA: I warned you.** *(MARGARITA reaches over and*
15   *slaps SOPHIA on the head.)*
16   **SOPHIA: Jesus, it's a miracle I'm not retarded.**
17   **MARGARITA: Sophia, don't you have something to do so**
18   **you won't be in the same room as your sister?**
19   **SOPHIA: I'm eating, where would you like me to go, the**
20   **toilet?**
21   **PAULA: That's a good place for you.** *(BENNY comes strutting*
22   *up the steps. When he gets to the door he stops a moment*
23   *to smooth his hair before ringing the doorbell. MARGARITA*
24   *raises her head up as if praying for peace.)* **I'll get it.**
25   **Hopefully it's Benny so I can get the hell out of here.**
26   **SOPHIA: You owe me one, I won't forget it.** *(PAULA opens*
27   *the door and BENNY enters.)*
28
29
30
31
32
33
34
35

SCENE 2: Three Females and Male

Paula, 23

Margarita, 40

Benny, 27

Sophia, 20

This scene immediately follows the other one, and actually is a continuation of the play's "Scene One."

1. Why do you think Sophia doesn't like Benny?

2. From these few speeches, what sort of person do you think Benny is? Point out specific lines that support what you say.

3. What do you think Sophia means when she says, "The condemned man speaks?"

4. Who do you think is the protagonist in this play? Who or what do you think is the antagonist? Explain.

1   **PAULA:** *(Kisses him lightly and clutches his arm.)* **I told Mom**
2   **we're going out for a while.**
3   **MARGARITA: Don't be too late, we all have to work**
4   **tomorrow.**
5   **BENNY: Hello, Doña Margarita, how are you doing?**
6   **MARGARITA:** *(Forcing a smile)* **Just fine, Benny; how are**
7   **you?**
8   **BENNY:** *(Rubs SOPHIA's head as if she's a kid.)* **Hi, Sophie.**
9   **SOPHIA:** *(Pushes his hand away.)* **Don't do that.**
10   **BENNY: What's with you?**
11   **SOPHIA: Nothing, just keep your hands off me.** *(SOPHIA*
12   *picks up her dish and takes it to the sink.)* **Mami, do I**
13   **have to do the dishes?**
14   **MARGARITA: Yes, and you better do them now, 'cause one**
15   **of your friends will call you and you'll be out the door**
16   **and forget to do them.**
17   **PAULA: Mom, did I get a letter from Dad today?**
18   **MARGARITA: No, we didn't get any mail today.**
19   **PAULA: I need to know if he's going to be here for the**
20   **wedding to give me away.**
21   **BENNY: What's the hurry, we still have six months.**
22   **SOPHIA:** *(Without looking up from the sink)* **The condemned**
23   **man speaks.**
24   **BENNY:** *(To SOPHIA)* **Have I done something to you?**
25   **SOPHIA: You're breathing, ain't you?**
26   **PAULA:** *(To SOPHIA)* **If you don't stop it ...**
27   **SOPHIA: What did I do?**
28   **MARGARITA:** *(Exits to the living room.)* **Paula, Benny, why**
29   **don't you go, so I can get some peace around here?**
30   **PAULA:** *(Going into the bedroom)* **I have to get my purse.**
31   **BENNY:** *(To SOPHIA)* **Really, sweetie, couldn't you even try**
32   **to like me a little?**
33   **SOPHIA: What for?** *(PAULA comes out of the bedroom.)*
34   **PAULA: I'm ready.** *(BENNY and PAULA exit the apartment and*
35   *stop by the stoop.)*

1   **SOPHIA:** *(Wipes her hands and takes a letter out of her bag.*
2   *The letter is still sealed, she looks it over and then tears it*
3   *into pieces. The phone rings and she goes into the*
4   *bedroom to answer it. While in there she picks up a picture*
5   *of her father on the dresser, looks at it for a moment, then*
6   *opens a drawer and throws it in.)*
7
8
9
10
11
12
13
14
15
16
17
18
19
20
21
22
23
24
25
26
27
28
29
30
31
32
33
34
35

SCENE 3: Two Females

Margarita, 40

Sophia, 20

"Scene Two" is between Benny and Paula. He is miffed at the way Sophia has treated him. He asks Paula to borrow money, which he says he'll give back the following week.

The following scene is most of "Scene Three" from the play. The scene opens with Sophia's talking on the phone to her boyfriend, Jimmy. She tells him she wants to go out with just him, not a group of people. Margarita yells for her to get off the phone. Before Sophia hangs up, she tells Jimmy she'll meet him later.

1. Whose view of Benny do you feel is more correct? Why? It appears that Margarita really wants Paula and Benny to marry. Can you think of reasons why this might be so?

2. What can you find in this scene that further defines the relationship Sophia has with her mother? Do you think their relationship is realistic given that Margarita and Sophia are mother and daughter?

3. Why do you think Paula insists that Margarita is going out with Samuel, instead of to bingo? Can you think of any logical reason Margarita would deny going out with a man?

1   MARGARITA: Hello...yes, I'm leaving now...okay. *(She*
2   *hangs up the phone.)*
3   SOPHIA: Where are you going?
4   MARGARITA: Bingo.
5   SOPHIA: Like I needed to ask. Don't you get tired of that?
6   MARGARITA: Do you get tired of dancing?
7   SOPHIA: That's different.
8   MARGARITA: Kids always think that.
9   SOPHIA: Ma, I'm not a kid. Is Samuel going to be there?
10   MARGARITA: *(Ignoring the question)* Where are you going?
11   SOPHIA: Just out, no place special.
12   MARGARITA: With who?
13   SOPHIA: With Jimmy.
14   MARGARITA: Why doesn't he pick you up here? You
15   ashamed of something?
16   SOPHIA: No, Ma, of course not. It's just easier to meet at
17   the...uhh, bowling alley.
18   MARGARITA: What kind of boy is this Jimmy?
19   SOPHIA: Ma, he's just a friend, I ain't marrying the guy.
20   MARGARITA: Why can't you be more like your sister, huh?
21   Find yourself a nice steady boy?
22   SOPHIA: Well, I think she should be more like me and
23   maybe she wouldn't even think of marrying someone
24   like Benny. Me, I'm never getting married.
25   MARGARITA: Don't say that. What's wrong with Benny?
26   He works, is with her all the time, and is going to
27   marry her.
28   SOPHIA: What about all the women he was involved with,
29   huh? They still come around I hear. And that job,
30   God, he only has it because his uncle owns the store.
31   MARGARITA: I don't want you talking that way about
32   Benny to people.
33   SOPHIA: Why, Mom? Why is it so important that she get
34   married to Benny? Or is it that you don't care who
35   she marries as long as she gets married?

40

1   MARGARITA: Don't you talk to me like that. I've only
2   wanted what's best for you and Paula, always,
3   nothing else have I thought of. Maybe I just know a
4   little more than you since I've been through so much.
5   SOPHIA: All right, Mom, truce, I don't want to get into
6   your troubles with Dad, okay.
7   MARGARITA: I used to be real smart, just like you.
8   SOPHIA: *(Kissing her mother)* **Mom, you go out with Samuel**
9   and have a good time, okay.
10   MARGARITA: I'm going to bingo.
11   SOPHIA: Yeah, I know, and so is Samuel, I know he goes
12   same as you. So have a good time, okay.
13   MARGARITA: You watch that new boy.
14   SOPHIA: Mami, don't start. Jimmy's a nice guy.
15   MARGARITA: No such thing as a nice guy.
16   SOPHIA: Mom, stop living in the dark ages, don't be
17   paranoid.
18   MARGARITA: You listen to me, no boy respects a girl who
19   is easy. Paula is very smart that way.
20   SOPHIA: Yeah, sure, Mom, I thought we called a truce.
21   MARGARITA: *(MARGARITA smiles, pinches her daughter's*
22   *cheek.)* **Yeah, be careful, okay. You're the one I worry**
23   about.
24   SOPHIA: Don't worry about me.
25
26
27
28
29
30
31
32
33
34
35

SCENE 4: One Male and One Female

Margarita, 40

Samuel, 55

Paula comes home late, and Sophia says Margarita has gone to bed angry. She then asks why Paula has written to "Dad to come to the wedding." She feels that Margarita will not want to see him and that it will hurt her.

Paula tells her to mind her own business; she doesn't want to hurt Margarita but does want her father to give her away. Sophia says he deserted them and hasn't sought them out in all the years since.

Paula asks why Sophia hates him so much. She admits she wrote in the letter to him that Sophia also was looking forward to seeing him.

In "Scene Five" Sophia and Paula are getting ready for work. As they're leaving, Samuel enters. This picks up just a few lines later.

1. Do you think Margarita has a right to be worried about Eduardo's showing up for the wedding? Why?

2. Do you think Samuel is telling the truth about divorcing his wife, or is this just a line he's giving Margarita? What makes you think so?

3. What sort of relationship do you think Samuel and Margarita have? Do they love one another? How do you know?

1   SAMUEL: What's wrong, you're the one who asked me to
2   take a day off to go look at bedroom sets for Paula's
3   wedding gift.
4   MARGARITA: Something's happening between Paula and
5   Sophia, and I can't quite figure it out. They're
6   fighting all the time.
7   SAMUEL: Sisters always fight.
8   MARGARITA: No, they weren't like that. Since Paula said
9   she's marrying Benny and told us that she's asking
10   Eduardo to walk her down the aisle, Sophia has been
11   impossible.
12 SAMUEL: Maybe she's jealous. Besides, it's only one day.
13   Once Paula is married, everything will settle down.
14 MARGARITA: Yeah, well, I heard Sophia and Paula fighting
15   last night. Sophia doesn't want anything to do with
16   her father. She's really upset that Paula wrote to him.
17 SAMUEL: It's all going to work out, you'll see.
18 MARGARITA: I'm so worried that he'll come. I really hope
19   he doesn't.
20 SAMUEL: Why?
21 MARGARITA: What if he tells them that we were never
22   married and that Paula's not his daughter?
23 SAMUEL: You should have told them a long time ago.
24 MARGARITA: Oh, sure, let me tell them that I hardly knew
25   Paula's father and that Eduardo never married me
26   because he never thought me good enough.
27 SAMUEL: What happened to you could have happened to
28   anyone.
29 MARGARITA: Yeah, I trusted him. I'll never trust another
30   man.
31 SAMUEL: You can trust me.
32 MARGARITA: Yeah, the man who's been getting a divorce
33   for the last three years.
34 SAMUEL: That's not fair, you know my wife's got me by
35   the short hairs because of the business. I can't afford

1   **to lose everything I've worked for all my life. You're**
2   **being unfair. I'm trying to get that divorce and I've**
3   **wanted to bring our relationship into the open since**
4   **the beginning.**
5 **MARGARITA: I know you have. I'm sorry, but I can't let**
6   **you meet my daughters until you're divorced and**
7   **that's final.**
8 **SAMUEL: Your mantle of respectability, uh...**
9 **MARGARITA: Oh, please, Sam, I'm really worried about**
10   **this. You don't know Eduardo. He's kept his mouth**
11   **shut all these years because it's been convenient. As**
12   **long as I didn't hassle him for child support. What if**
13   **he gets drunk and decides to confess all, where does**
14   **that leave me?**
15 **SAMUEL: Maybe you should tell them before the wedding,**
16   **then.**
17 **MARGARITA: I can't, I have to find a way to keep him**
18   **away from here. Maybe I can get Paula to change her**
19   **mind.** *(SAMUEL pours himself some coffee.)*
20 **SAMUEL: I think you should tell them the truth.** *(Pause)*
21   **You know that Sophia is a smart girl. I think she**
22   **knows about *us*.**
23 **MARGARITA: Yeah, she goes around hinting about us, but**
24   **I don't think she really knows anything.**
25 **SAMUEL: I saw her outside and she said hello and she had**
26   **this smart-ass smile.**
27 **MARGARITA: That's all I need.**
28 **SAMUEL: She's a smart girl, I don't think she disapproves.**
29 **MARGARITA: Of course she doesn't disapprove because it**
30   **stamps the seal of approval on her running around**
31   **with all different kinds of boys.**
32 **SAMUEL: I think you underestimate your daughter.**
33 **MARGARITA: I better go get dressed, if we're going to get**
34   **out of here.** *(MARGARITA goes into the living room and*
35   *SAMUEL follows her. Their shadowed figures can be seen*

1   *from the kitchen. SAMUEL puts his arms around her.)*
2   **What are you doing?**
3   **SAMUEL: Shh, I'm concentrating.**
4   **MARGARITA: Sam, we have to get to the store.**
5   **SAMUEL: I love you.**
6
7
8
9
10
11
12
13
14
15
16
17
18
19
20
21
22
23
24
25
26
27
28
29
30
31
32
33
34
35

Fashion

by Anna Cora Ogden Mowatt (Ritchie)

Anna Cora Mowatt was the first important female playwright in America. Her first published work, when she was a teenager, was poetry. Because she spent a great deal of her life in Europe, she was highly qualified to write a social satire such as *Fashion*, the first long-running play written by an American up to that time, 1845.

The title refers to wanting to be fashionable so far as one's lifestyle. The central character does this by trying to imitate everything European, especially French, as exciting and desirable and everything American as commonplace. One of the characters, Adam Trueman, describes Mrs. Tiffany's obsession with fashion this way: "Fashion! And pray what is fashion, madam? An agreement between certain persons to live without using their souls! to substitute etiquette for virtue — decorum for purity — manners for morals! to affect a shame for the words of their Creator! and expend all their rapture upon the works of their tailors and dressmakers!"

The theme is that native honesty and scruples triumph.

Briefly, the plot deals with Mrs. Tiffany who — as a result of her husband's success as a merchant — assumes all the airs of high society, and fills her home with pretentious guests and supposed nobility.

Trueman, an honest farmer, comes to visit his old friend Mr. Tiffany and takes it upon himself to see that changes occur in the Tiffany household. With the help of Gertrude, the governess, he helps rid the house of all the hangers-on and to return to a simpler life.

Trueman is an important character because he became the prototype for a series of characters who followed, all possessing native wit and Yankee ingenuity.

To Mrs. Tiffany's way of thinking, her most important guest is Count Jolimaitre, who, it turns out, is not a count at all but a cook whose former girlfriend now is a maid in the Tiffany household. Much of the plot focuses on exposing the Count. There also is a love story involving Gertrude and Howard, another honest and forthright American.

The opening scenes of the play deal with Mrs. Tiffany's efforts to embrace the European way of life, even to changing her servant Zeke's name so it will be more acceptably continental. Of course, Mrs. Tiffany, newly rich, had the humble beginnings of a milliner, a hat maker. The entire first act (out of five) consists of her attempts to appear knowledgeable of European customs and to play up to the Count. She is an insufferable snob in a scene with Trueman, where she calls him "an impertinent, audacious, ignorant old man!"

SCENE 1: Two Males

Adam Trueman, 72

Tiffany, probably in his 50s

This scene occurs near the beginning of Act II. Trueman has just been snubbed by Mrs. Tiffany. Mr. Tiffany is being blackmailed by his clerk Mr. Snobson, who wants more money and the chance to marry Seraphina, Tiffany's daughter.

1. Why do you suppose Tiffany laughs so much when Trueman mentions going to prison? Is this a natural thing to do?

2. Trueman speaks bluntly in telling Tiffany what he has observed about both him and his household. Why do you think he takes such liberties? Is this logical? Would you tell a friend things you thought were wrong about his life? Why?

3. Why do you think Tiffany responds to Trueman's remarks by saying, "I take greatest pleasure in remarking your superiority, Sir." What tone would you take if you were playing this role? Why?

4. Do you like Trueman as a person? Why? What about Tiffany? How would you describe the personalities of each man?

1 TRUEMAN: Here I am, Antony, man! I told you I'd pay you
2 a visit in your moneymaking quarters. *(Looks around.)*
3 But it looks as dismal here as a cell in the States'
4 prison!
5 TIFFANY: *(Forcing a laugh)* Ha, ha, ha! States' prison! You
6 are so facetious! Ha, ha, ha!
7 TRUEMAN: Well, for the life of me I can't see anything so
8 amusing in that! I should think the States' prison
9 plaguey uncomfortable lodgings. And you laugh, man,
10 as though you fancied yourself there already.
11 TIFFANY: Ha, ha, ha!
12 TRUEMAN: Ha, ha, ha! *(Imitating him)* What on earth do you
13 mean by that ill-sounding laugh, that has nothing of
14 a laugh about it! This *fashion*-worship has made
15 heathens and hypocrites of you all! *Deception* is your
16 household God! A man laughs as if he were crying,
17 and cries as if he were laughing in his sleeve.
18 Everything is something else from what it seems to
19 be. I have lived in your house only three days, and
20 I've heard more lies than were ever invented during
21 a presidential election! First your fine lady of a wife
22 sends me word that she's not at home — I walk
23 upstairs, and she takes good care that *I* shall not be
24 at *home* — wants to turn me out of doors. Then *you*
25 come in — take your old friend by the hand — whisper,
26 the deuce knows what, in your wife's ear, and the
27 tables are turned in a tangent! Madam curtsies —
28 says she's enchanted to see me —
29 TIFFANY: We were exceedingly happy to welcome you as
30 our guest!
31 TRUEMAN: Happy? You happy? Ah, Antony! Antony! That
32 hatchet face of yours, and those crisscross furrows
33 tell quite another story! It is many a long day since
34 you were *happy* at anything! You look as if you'd
35 melted down your flesh into dollars, and mortgaged

1   your soul in the bargain! Your warm heart has grown
2   cold over your ledger — your light spirits heavy with
3   calculation! You have traded away your youth — your
4   hopes — your tastes, for wealth! and now you *have*
5   the wealth you coveted, what does it profit you?
6   Pleasure it cannot buy; for you have lost your
7   *capacity* for enjoyment — Ease it will not bring; for
8   the love of gain is never satisfied! It has made your
9   counting-house a penitentiary, and your home a fash-
10   ionable museum where there is no niche for you! You
11   have spent so much time *ciphering* in the one, that
12   you find yourself at last a very *cipher* in the other!
13   See me, man! Seventy-two last August! — Strong as a
14   hickory and every whit as sound!
15 TIFFANY: I take the greatest pleasure in remarking your
16   superiority, sir.
17 TRUEMAN: Bah! No man takes pleasure in remarking the
18   superiority of another! Why the deuce can't you
19   speak the truth, man? But it's not the *fashion* I
20   suppose! I have not seen one frank, open face since
21   — no, no, I can't say that either, though lying is
22   catching! There's that girl, Gertrude, who is trying to
23   teach your daughter music — but Gertrude was bred
24   in the country!
25 TIFFANY: A good girl; my wife and daughter find her very
26   useful.
27 TRUEMAN: Useful? Well, I must say you have queer
28   notions of *use!* — But come, cheer up, man! I'd
29   rather see one of your old smiles, than know you'd
30   realized another thousand! I hear you are making
31   money on the true, American, high pressure system
32   — better go slow and sure — the more steam, the
33   greater danger of the boiler's bursting! All sound, I
34   hope? Nothing rotten at the core?
35 TIFFANY: Oh, sound — quite sound!

1   TRUEMAN: Well, that's pleasant — though I must say you
2   don't look very pleasant about it!
3   TIFFANY: My good friend, although I am solvent, I may
4   say, perfectly solvent — yet you — the fact is, you
5   can be of some assistance to me!
6   TRUEMAN: That's the *fact* is it? I'm glad we've hit upon
7   one *fact* at last!
8
9
10
11
12
13
14
15
16
17
18
19
20
21
22
23
24
25
26
27
28
29
30
31
32
33
34
35

SCENE 2: One Male and One Female

Colonel Howard, probably early 30s

Gertrude, probably 20s

The following scene occurs shortly after the meeting between Trueman and Tiffany, and opens Scene 2, Act II, of the play. The action takes place in "a beautiful conservatory," with a "walk through the centre; stands of flower pots in bloom; a couple of rustic seats." Gertrude is watering the flowers when Howard first addresses her.

1. Do you think Howard's opening remark is believable? Would a man address a woman this way, especially if he didn't know her well? Why?

2. What do you think Gertrude's first line means, the part where she says she learns "prudence from the reed," and how to bend in a storm?

3. What do you learn here about Gertrude's character? Point to lines that show this. Is she likeable? Why?

4. Do you think Gertrude really doesn't know why Howard is there? Why? Why does she call him a strange man?

5. Although you learn most about Gertrude in this scene, you also learn a little bit about Howard. What do you learn? Explain.

1   HOWARD: I am afraid you lead a sad life here, Miss
2   Gertrude.
3   GERTRUDE: *(Turning round gaily)* **What! Amongst the**
4   **flowers!** *(Continues her occupation.)*
5   HOWARD: No, amongst the thistles, with which Mrs.
6   Tiffany surrounds you; the tempests, which her
7   temper raises!
8   GERTRUDE: They never harm me. Flowers and herbs are
9   excellent tutors. I learn prudence from the reed, and
10   bend until the storm has swept over me.
11 HOWARD: Admirable philosophy! But still this frigid
12   atmosphere of fashion must be uncongenial to you?
13   Accustomed to the pleasant companionship of your
14   kind friends in Geneva, surely you must regret this
15   cold exchange?
16 GERTRUDE: Do you think so? Can you suppose that I
17   could possibly prefer a ramble in the woods to a
18   promenade in Broadway! A wreath of scented wild
19   flowers to a bouquet of these sickly exotics? The
20   odour of new-mown hay to the heated air of this
21   crowded conservatory? Or can you imagine that I
22   could enjoy the quiet conversation of my Geneva
23   friends more than the edifying chit-chat of a fash-
24   ionable drawing room? But I see you think me totally
25   destitute of taste?
26 HOWARD: You have a merry spirit to jest thus at your
27   grievances!
28 GERTRUDE: I have my *mania* — as some wise person
29   declares that all mankind have, — and mine is a love
30   of independence! In Geneva, my wants were supplied
31   by two kind old maiden ladies, upon whom I know
32   not that I have any claim. I had abilities, and desired
33   to use them. I came here at my own request; for here
34   I am no longer *dependent! Voila tout* as Mrs. Tiffany
35   would say.

1   **HOWARD: Believe me, I appreciate the confidence you**
2   **repose in me!**
3   **GERTRUDE: Confidence! Truly, Colonel Howard, the**
4   *confidence* **is entirely on your part, in supposing that**
5   **I confide that which I have no reason to conceal! I**
6   **think I informed you that Mrs. Tiffany only received**
7   **visitors on her reception day — she is therefore not**
8   **prepared to see you. Zeke — Oh! I beg his pardon —**
9   **Adolph, made some mistake in admitting you.**
10   **HOWARD: Nay, Gertrude, it was not Mrs. Tiffany, nor Miss**
11   **Tiffany, whom I came see; it — it was —**
12   **GERTRUDE: The conservatory perhaps? I will leave you to**
13   **examine the flowers at leisure!** *(Crosses.)*
14   **HOWARD: Gertrude — listen to me. If I only dared to give**
15   **utterance to what is hovering upon my lips!** *(Aside)*
16   **Gertrude!**
17   **GERTRUDE: Colonel Howard!**
18   **HOWARD: Gertrude, I must — must —**
19   **GERTRUDE: Yes, indeed you must, must leave me! I think**
20   **I hear somebody coming — Mrs. Tiffany would not be**
21   **well pleased to find you here — pray, pray leave me —**
22   **that door will lead you into the street.** *(Hurries him out*
23   *through door; takes up her watering pot, and commences*
24   *watering flowers, tying up branches, etc.)* **What a strange**
25   **being is man! Why should he hesitate to say — nay,**
26   **why should I prevent his saying, what I would most**
27   **delight to hear? Truly man is strange — but woman**
28   **is quite as incomprehensible!** *(Walks about gathering*
29   *flowers.)*
30
31
32
33
34
35

SCENE 3: Two Males and Two Females

Gertrude, probably 20s.

Count, late 20s to early 30s

Trueman, 72

Mrs. Tiffany, 40s

As soon as Howard leaves, the Count comes into the conservatory. He tells Gertrude he loves her and, in effect, wants her to be his mistress after he marries Seraphina Tiffany. Of course, she doesn't want to have anything to do with him. This scene follows directly after that.

1. List three or four of the Count's character traits you can discover in this scene. Back up what you say with lines of dialog. Now how would you go about portraying these things?

2. There is a lot of exaggeration of both character and action here. List as many instances of this as you can find.

3. Why do you suppose Mrs. Tiffany is so inclined to believe that whatever the Count does is acceptable? Why do you think she has the idea that anything European is an improvement over anything American?

4. Do you think Trueman is realistic in his actions? Why? Point to specific lines to support what you say.

1   *(Enter TRUEMAN unperceived.)*

2   **GERTRUDE: And therefore more entitled to respect and**

3   **protection of every *true* gentleman! Had you been**

4   **one, you would not have insulted me!**

5   **COUNT: My charming little orator, patriotism and decla-**

6   **mation become you particularly!** *(Approaches her.)* **I**

7   **feel quite tempted to taste —**

8   **TRUEMAN:** *(Thrusting him aside)* **An American hickory-**

9   **switch!** *(Strikes him.)* **Well, how do you like it?**

10   **COUNT: Old matter-of-fact!** *(Aside)* **Sir, how dare you?**

11   **TRUEMAN: My stick has answered that question!**

12   **GERTRUDE: Oh! Now I am quite safe!**

13   **TRUEMAN: Safe! Not a bit safer than before! All women**

14   **would be safe, if they knew how virtue became them!**

15   **As for you, Mr. Count, what have you to say for your-**

16   **self? Come, speak out!**

17   **COUNT: Sir — aw — aw — you don't understand these**

18   **matters!**

19   **TRUEMAN: That's a fact! Not having had *your* experience.**

20   **I don't believe I *do* understand them!**

21   **COUNT: A piece of pleasantry — a mere joke —**

22   **TRUEMAN: A joke was it? I'll show you a joke worth two of**

23   **that! I'll teach you the way we natives joke with a puppy**

24   **who don't respect an honest woman!** *(Seizing him)*

25   **COUNT: Oh! Oh! Demme — you old ruffian! Let me go.**

26   **What do you mean?**

27   **TRUEMAN: Oh! A piece of pleasantry — a mere joke —**

28   **very pleasant isn't it?** *(Attempts to strike him again;*

29   *COUNT struggles with him. Enter MRS. TIFFANY hastily,*

30   *in her bonnet and shawl.)*

31   **MRS. TIFFANY: What is the matter? I am perfectly *abimé***

32   **with terror. Mr. Trueman, what has happened?**

33   **TRUEMAN: Oh! We have been joking!**

34   **MRS. TIFFANY:** *(To COUNT, who is rearranging his dress)* **My**

35   **dear Count, I did not expect to find you here — how**

1   kind of you!

2   TRUEMAN: Your *dear* Count has been showing his *kindness*

3   in a very *foreign* manner. Too *foreign* I think, he

4   found it to be relished by an *unfashionable native!*

5   What do you think of a puppy, who insults an inno-

6   cent girl all in the way of *kindness*? This Count of

7   yours — this importation of —

8   COUNT: My dear Madam, demme, permit me to explain. It

9   would be unbecoming — demme — particularly unbe-

10   coming of you — aw — aw — to pay any attention to

11   this ignorant person. *(Crosses to TRUEMAN.)* **Anything**

12   that he says concerning a man of my standing — aw

13   — the truth is, Madam —

14   TRUEMAN: Let us have the truth by all means — if it is

15   only for the novelty's sake!

16   COUNT: *(Turning his back to TRUEMAN)* You see, Madam,

17   hoping to obtain a few moments' private conversa-

18   tion with Miss Seraphina — with *Miss Seraphina* I

19   say and — aw — and knowing her passion for flowers,

20   I found my way to your very tasteful and *recherché*

21   conservatory. *(Looks about him approvingly.)* Very beau-

22   tifully arranged — does you great credit, Madam!

23   Here I encountered this young person. She was

24   inclined to be talkative; and I indulged her with —

25   with a — aw — demme — a few *common places!* What

26   passed between us was mere *harmless bandinage* —

27   on my part. You, Madam, you — so conversant with

28   our European manners — you are aware that when a

29   man of fashion — that is, when a woman — a man —

30   is bound — amongst noblemen, you know —

31   MRS. TIFFANY: I comprehend you perfectly — *parfitte-*

32   *ment*, my dear Count!

33   COUNT: 'Pon my honor, that's very obliging of her. *(Aside)*

34   MRS. TIFFANY: I am shocked at the plebeian forwardness

35   of this conceited girl!

1   **TRUEMAN:** *(Walking up to COUNT)* **Did you ever keep a reck-**
2   **oning of the lies you tell in an hour?**
3   **MRS. TIFFANY: Mr. Trueman, I blush for you!** *(Crosses to*
4   *TRUEMAN.)*
5   **TRUEMAN: Don't do that — you have no blushes to spare!**
6   **MRS. TIFFANY: It is a man of rank whom you are addressing,**
7   **sir!**
8   **TRUEMAN: A rank villain, Mrs. Antony Tiffany! A** *rich one*
9   **he would be, had he as much** *gold* **as** *brass!*
10   **MRS. TIFFANY: Pray pardon him, Count; he knows nothing**
11   **of** *how ton!*
12   **COUNT: Demme, he's beneath my notice. I tell you what,**
13   **old fellow —** *(TRUEMAN raises his stick as COUNT*
14   *approaches, the latter starts back)* **the sight of him**
15   **discomposes me — aw — I feel quite uncomfortable**
16   **— aw—let us join your charming daughter? I can't do**
17   **you the honor to shoot you, sir —** *(To TRUEMAN)* **you**
18   **are beneath me — a nobleman can't fight a**
19   **commoner! Good-bye, old Truepenny! I — aw — I'm**
20   **insensible to your insolence!**
21   *(Exeunt COUNT and MRS. TIFFANY.)*
22   **TRUEMAN: You won't be insensible to a cowhide in spite**
23   **of your nobility! The next time he practices any of**
24   **his foreign fashions on you, Gertrude, you'll see how**
25   **I'll wake up his sensibilities!**
26
27
28
29
30
31
32
33
34
35

SCENE 4: One Male and One Female

Tiffany, 50s

Mrs. Tiffany, 40s

This next scene actually is Scene 1 of Act III and takes place in "Mrs. Tiffany's Parlor." In the interim between the last scene and this, Trueman has asked Prudence, a friend of Mrs. Tiffany's from the old days when they worked together, if she knows whom Gertrude loves. She tells him it is Mr. Twinkle, a poet. She goes on to say that Seraphina loves Count Jolimaitre, and that Howard loves Seraphina.

Trueman is disappointed about Gertrude, feeling it would be better if she loved Howard, "the only, frank, straightforward fellow that I've met..." Prudence then makes a play for Trueman, who isn't interested.

1. One type of humor is exaggeration. What can you find that is exaggerated in this scene? Why is it funny? There is a lot of other humor in the scene. Can you point out specific lines where it occurs? Discuss this with the class.

2. Is Mrs. Tiffany at all a believable character? Does she have traits that you like? Traits that you dislike? Explain. Why do you suppose she wants to forget her past?

3. Why do you suppose Mr. Tiffany has allowed his wife's love of fashion to progress to the point where she can easily ruin him financially? Why wouldn't he have put a stop to this earlier?

4. List as many points of conflict as you can find in this scene. How would you portray them, in playing either of the characters?

5. Why do you suppose Mr. Tiffany says he will never allow Seraphina to marry the Count? Can you find hints of this in any of his dialog so far?

1   TIFFANY: Your extravagance will ruin me, Mrs. Tiffany!
2   MRS. TIFFANY: And your stinginess will ruin me, Mr.
3   Tiffany! It is totally and *toot a fate* impossible to
4   convince you of the necessity of *keeping up appear-*
5   *ances.* There is a certain display which every woman
6   of fashion is forced to make!
7   TIFFANY: And pray who made *you* a woman of fashon?
8   MRS. TIFFANY: What a vulgar question! All women of
9   fashion, Mr. Tiffany —
10   TIFFANY: In this land are *self-constituted*, like you, Madam
11   — and *fashion* is the cloak for more sins than charity
12   ever covered! It was for *fashion's* sake that you
13   insisted upon my purchasing this expensive house —
14   it was for *fashion's* sake that you ran me in debt at
15   every exorbitant upholsterer's and extravagant furni-
16   ture warehouse in the city — it was for *fashion's* sake
17   that you built that ruinous conservatory — hired
18   more servants than they have persons to wait upon —
19   and dressed your footman like a harlequin!
20   MRS. TIFFANY: Mr. Tiffany, you are thoroughly plebeian,
21   and insufferably *American*, in your grovelling ideas!
22   And, pray, what was the occasion of these very
23   *mal-ap-pro-pos* remarks? Merely because I requested
24   a paltry fifty dollars to purchase a new style of head-
25   dress — a *bijou* of an article just introduced in France.
26   TIFFANY: Time was, Mrs. Tiffany, when you manufactured
27   your own French headdresses — took off their first
28   gloss at the public balls, and then sold them to your
29   shortest sighted customers. And all you knew about
30   France, or French either, was what you spelt out at
31   the bottom of your fashion plates — but now you
32   have grown so fashionable, forsooth, that you have
33   forgotten how to speak your mother tongue!
34   MRS. TIFFANY: Mr. Tiffany, Mr. Tiffany! Nothing is more
35   positively vulgarian — more unaristocratic than any

1   allusions to the past!

2 TIFFANY: Why I thought, my dear, that *aristocrats* lived

3   principally upon the past — and traded in the market

4   of fashion with the bones of their ancestors for

5   capital.

6 MRS. TIFFANY: Mr. Tiffany, such vulgar remarks are only

7   suitable to the counting house, in my drawing room

8   you should —

9 TIFFANY: Vary my sentiments with my locality, as you

10   change your *manners* with your *dress!*

11 MRS. TIFFANY: Mr. Tiffany, I desire that you will purchase

12   Count d'Orsay's "Science of Etiquette," and learn

13   how to conduct yourself — especially before you

14   appear at the grand ball, which I shall give on Friday!

15 TIFFANY: Confound your balls, Madam; they make *foot-*

16   *balls* of my money, while you dance away all that I

17   am worth! A pretty time to give a ball when you know

18   that I am on the very brink of bankruptcy!

19 MRS. TIFFANY: So much the greater reason that nobody

20   should suspect your circumstances, or you would lose

21   your credit at once. Just at this crisis it is absolutely

22   *necessary* to save your reputation. There is Mrs.

23   Adolphus Dashaway — she gave the most splendid fête

24   of the season — and I hear on very good authority that

25   her husband has not paid his baker's bill in three

26   months. Then there was Mrs. Honeywood —

27 TIFFANY: Gave a ball the night before her husband shot

28   himself — perhaps, you wish to drive me to follow his

29   example? *(Crosses.)*

30 MRS. TIFFANY: Good gracious! Mr. Tiffany, how you talk!

31   I beg you won't mention anything of the kind.

32   I consider black the most unbecoming color. I'm

33   sure I've done all that I could to gratify you. There

34   is that vulgar old torment, Trueman, who gives one

35   the lie fifty times a day — haven't I been very civil

1   to him?

2   TIFFANY: Civil to his *wealth*, Mrs. Tiffany! I told you that

3   he was a rich, old farmer — the early friend of my

4   father — my own benefactor — and that I had reason

5   to think he might assist me in my present embar-

6   rassments. Your civility was *bought* — and like most

7   of your own purchases has yet to be *paid* for. *(Crosses.)*

8   MRS. TIFFANY: And will be, no doubt! The condescension

9   of a woman of fashion should command any price.

10   Mr. Trueman is insupportably indecorous—he has

11   insulted Count Jolimaitre in the most outrageous

12   manner. If the Count was not so deeply interested —

13   so *abimé* with Seraphina, I am sure be would never

14   honor us by his visits again!

15   TIFFANY: So much the better — he shall never marry my

16   daughter! — I am resolved on that. Why, Madam, I

17   am told there is in Paris a regular matrimonial stock

18   company, who fit out indigent dandies for this

19   market. How do I know but this fellow is one of its

20   creatures, and that he has come here to increase its

21   dividends by marrying a fortune?

22   MRS. TIFFANY: Nonsense, Mr. Tiffany. The Count, the most

23   fashionable young man in all New York — the intimate

24   friend of all the dukes and lords in Europe — not

25   marry my daughter? Not permit Seraphina to become

26   a Countess? Mr. Tiffany, you are out of your senses!

27   TIFFANY: That would not be very wonderful, considering

28   how many years I have been united to you, my dear.

29   Modern physicians pronounce lunacy infectious!

30   MRS. TIFFANY: Mr. Tiffany, he is a man of fashion —

31   TIFFANY: Fashion makes fools, but cannot *feed* them.

32

33

34

35

SCENE 5: One Male and Two Females

Mrs. Tiffany, 40s

Count, 20s to 30s

Seraphina, 18-20

Snobson, late 20s, early 30s

The preceding scene ends with Tiffany's telling Mrs. Tiffany that Snobson will be coming to the ball and that he expects both her and Seraphina to be civil to him. Snobson arrives and doesn't understand Mrs. Tiffany's speech, a combination of English and imperfect French. She tells Snobson that it is the French custom not to allow a daughter to be alone with a young man. Shortly afterward, the Count arrives.

1. How would you characterize Snobson? Point to lines that illustrate the type of person he is.

2. What type of person is Seraphina? Explain. Why do you believe she is taken in by the Count and the whole idea of "fashion"?

3. This scene also contains exaggeration. Point out and discuss whether you think it is humorous or not.

4. Are any of these characters likeable? Why? Which is the least likeable? Why?

1 MRS. TIFFANY: My dear Count, I am overjoyed at the very
2   sight of you.
3 COUNT: Flattered myself you'd be glad to see me, Madam
4   — knew it was not your *jour de reception.*
5 MRS. TIFFANY: But for you, Count, all days —
6 COUNT: I thought so. Ah, Miss Tiffany, on my honor,
7   you're looking beautiful. *(Crosses.)*
8 SERAPHINA: Count, flattery from you —
9 SNOBSON: What? Eh? What's that you say?
10 SERAPHINA: Nothing but what etiquette requires. *(Aside*
11   *to him)*
12 COUNT: *(Regarding MR. TIFFANY through his eye glass)* **Your**
13   **worthy Papa, I believe? Sir, your most obedient.**
14   *(MR. TIFFANY bows coldly; COUNT regards SNOBSON*
15   *through his glass, shrugs his shoulders and turns away.)*
16 SNOBSON: *(To MRS. TIFFANY)* **Introduce me, will you? I**
17   **never knew a Count in all my life — what a strange-**
18   **looking animal!**
19 MRS. TIFFANY: Mr. Snobson, it is not the fashion to intro-
20   duce in France!
21 SNOBSON: But, Marm, we're in America. *(MRS. TIFFANY*
22   *crosses to COUNT.)* **The woman thinks she's some-**
23   **where else than where she is — she wants to make an**
24   **alibi?** *(Aside)*
25 MRS. TIFFANY: I hope that we shall have the pleasure of
26   seeing you on Friday evening, Count?
27 COUNT: Really, Madam, my invitations — my engage-
28   ments — so numerous — I can hardly answer for
29   myself: and you Americans take offence so easily —
30 MRS. TIFFANY: But, Count, everybody expects you at our
31   ball — you are the principal attraction —
32 SERAPHINA: Count, you *must* come!
33 COUNT: Since you insist — aw — aw — there's no resisting
34   you, Miss Tiffany.
35 MRS. TIFFANY: I am so thankful. How can I repay your

1   **condescension!** *(COUNT and SERAPHINA converse.)* **Mr.**
2   **Snobson, will you walk this way? — I have such a**
3   **cactus in full bloom — remarkable flower! Mr.**
4   **Tiffany, pray come here — I have something partic-**
5   **ular to say.**
6   TIFFANY: Then speak out, my dear — I thought it was
7   highly improper just now to leave a girl with a young
8   man? *(Aside to her)*
9   MRS. TIFFANY: Oh, but the Count — that is different!
10   TIFFANY: I suppose you mean to say there's nothing of *the*
11   man about him?
12
13
14
15
16
17
18
19
20
21
22
23
24
25
26
27
28
29
30
31
32
33
34
35

SCENE 6: One Male and Two Females

Count, 20s to 30s

Gertrude, 20s

Millinette, probably 19-20

After the close of the last scene, we meet Millinette, a French maid. When the Count sees her, he takes Seraphina aside and tells her he wants to elope with her instead of having a big wedding ceremony. The following scene explains why.

1. Do you think it's believable that Millinette is working for the same people who have the Count as a guest? Why?

2. This scene in ways is very melodramatic; that is, it has a lot of sentiment thrown in and involves a character the audience does not know. Why do you suppose the author did this? Pick out instances of this in the scene. Why do you think they are important to the play?

3. In a comedy the audience does not usually become as involved with the characters as they do with the characters in a serious play. In this play, of course, you know that most of the characters are not true to life. What would have happened had Mowatt made them realistic? How would this make the play different?

4. What do you think are Gertrude's feelings in discovering the Count and Millinette together?

5. In playing the role of the maid, what traits or mannerisms do you think an actress should emphasize? Explain.

6. Gertrude, of course, is a very moral person; she doesn't want to do any wrong. How do you react to this trait of hers? Explain.

1   *(Enter COUNT)*

2   COUNT: Ah! Millinette, my dear, you see what a good-
3   natured dog I am to fly at your bidding —

4   MILLINETTE: Fly? Ah! *Trompeur!* Vat for you fly from
5   Paris? Vat for you leave me — and I love you so
6   much. Ven you sick — you almost die — did I not
7   stay by you — take care of you — and you have no
8   else friend? Vat for you leave Paris?

9   COUNT: Never allude to disagreeable subjects, *mon enfant!*
10   I was forced by uncontrollable circumstances to fly to
11   the land of liberty —

12   MILLINETTE: Vat you do vid all de money I give you? The
13   last sou I had — did I not give you?

14   COUNT: I dare say you did, ma petite — wish you'd been
15   better supplied! *(Aside)* Don't ask any questions here
16   — can't explain now — the next time we meet —

17   MILLINETTE: But ah! Ven shall ve meet — ven? You not
18   deceive me, not any more.

19   COUNT: Deceive you! I'd rather deceive myself — I wish I
20   could! I'd persuade myself you were once more
21   washing linen in the Seine! *(Aside)*

22   MILLINETTE: I vil tell you ven ve shall meet — on Friday
23   night Madame give one grand ball — you come *sans*
24   *doute* — den ven de supper is served — de Americans
25   tink of noting else ven de supper come — den you
26   steal out of de room, and you find me here — and you
27   give me one grand explanation!

28   *(Enter GERTRUDE, unperceived.)*

29   COUNT: Friday night — while supper is serving — *parole*
30   *d'honneur* I will be here — I will explain everything
31   — my sudden departure from Paris — my — demme,
32   my countship — everything! Now let me go — if any
33   of the family should discover us —

34   GERTRUDE: *(Who during the last speech has gradually*
35   *advanced)* They might discover more than you think

1   it advisable for them to know!

2   COUNT: The devil!

3   MILLINETTE: *Mon Dieu!* Mademoiselle Gertrude!

4   COUNT: *(Recovering himself)* **My dear Miss Gertrude, let me**

5   **explain — aw — aw — nothing is more natural than**

6   **the situation in which you find me —**

7   GERTRUDE: I am inclined to believe that, sir.

8   COUNT: Now — 'pon my honor, that's not fair. Here is

9   Millinette who will bear witness to what I am about

10   to say —

11   GERTRUDE: Oh, I have not the slightest doubt of that, sir.

12   COUNT: You see, Millinette happened to be lady's-maid in

13   the family of — of — the Duchess Chateau D'Espagne

14   — and I chanced to be a particular friend of the

15   Duchess — *very* particular I assure you! Of course I

16   saw Millinette, and she, demme, she saw me! Didn't

17   you, Millinette?

18   MILLINETTE: Oh! *Oui* — mademoiselle, I knew him very vell.

19   COUNT: Well, it is a remarkable fact that — being in corre-

20   spondence with this very Duchess — at this very time —

21   GERTRUDE: That is sufficient, sir — I am already so well

22   acquainted with your extraordinary talents for improvi-

23   sation, that I will not further tax your invention —

24   MILLINETTE: Ah! Mademoiselle Gertrude do not betray us

25   — have pity!

26   COUNT: *(Assuming an air of dignity)* **Silence, Millinette! My**

27   **word has been doubted — the word of a nobleman! I**

28   **will inform my friend, Mrs. Tiffany, of this young**

29   **person's audacity.** *(Going)*

30   GERTRUDE: His own weapons alone can foil this villain!

31   *(Aside)* **Sir — SIR — Count!** *(At the last word the COUNT*

32   *turns.)* **Perhaps, Sir, the least said about this matter**

33   **the better!**

34   COUNT: *(Delightedly)* **The least said? We won't say anything**

35   **at all. She's coming round — couldn't resist me.**

1   *(Aside)* **Charming Gertrude —**
2   **MILLINETTE: Quoi? Vat that you say?**
3   **COUNT: My sweet, adorable Millinette, hold your tongue,**
4   **will you?** *(Aside to her)*
5   **MILLINETTE:** *(Aloud)* **No, I vill not! If you do look so from**
6   **out your eyes at her again, I vill tell all!**
7   **COUNT: Oh, I never could manage two women at once —**
8   **jealousy makes the dear creatures so spiteful. The**
9   **only valor is in flight!** *(Aside)* **Miss Gertrude, I wish**
10   **you good morning. Millinette,** *mon enfant,* **adieu.** *(Exit)*
11   **MILLINETTE: But I have one word more to say. Stop, Stop!**
12   *(Exit after him)*
13   **GERTRUDE:** *(Musingly)* **Friday night, while supper is serving,**
14   **he is to meet Millinette here and explain — what?**
15   **This man is an impostor! His insulting me — his**
16   **familiarity with Millinette — his whole conduct —**
17   **prove it. If I tell Mrs. Tiffany this she will disbelieve**
18   **me, and one word may place this so-called Count on**
19   **his guard. To convince Seraphina would be equally**
20   **difficult, and her rashness and infatuation may**
21   **render her miserable for life. No — she shall be saved!**
22   **I must devise some plan for opening their eyes.**
23   **Truly, if I** *cannot* **invent one, I shall be the first**
24   **woman who was ever at a loss for a stratagem —**
25   **especially to punish a villain or to shield a friend.**
26
27
28
29
30
31
32
33
34
35

SCENE 7: Two Males

Trueman, 72

Howard, probably early 3Os

Gertrude is trying her best to thwart any plans the Count may have that involve Millinette. She has Millinette handing out flowers to the supper guests while she goes to the kitchen to wait for Jolimaitre. In the meantime, Prudence thinks the Count and Gertrude have planned a way of being together. She alerts Mrs. Tiffany and the others, including Trueman and Howard, who discover the couple together in the "housekeeper's room."

Trueman is very much disappointed in Gertrude and goes after the Count who shields himself behind Mrs. Tiffany. At this instant Millinette arrives, and the Count tells her to hold her tongue.

Later Gertrude is writing a letter on the drawing room table, and Trueman enters. In an aside, he calls her a "bold minx." She asks him to read the letter she was sending to people in Geneva. "The Wilsons?" he asks. She wonders how he knows that.

He takes the letter and discovers that she was trying to expose the Count as an imposter. This scene follows. Just before the dialog begins, Col. Howard enters.

1. Do you think it reasonable that Trueman wants to whip everyone whom he finds disagreeable? Why?

2. Point out and discuss the conflict in this scene. Anything that contributes to the suspense? How would you try to point these things up to an audience — either as a performer or as a director?

3. What do you think are Howard's feelings when he suspects Gertrude of becoming involved with the Count? How would you show them in this scene?

1   TRUEMAN: I'm out again! What is the Colonel to her?
2   *(Retires up.)*
3   HOWARD: *(Crosses to her.)* I have come, Gertrude, to bid
4   you farewell. Tomorrow I resign my commission and
5   leave this city, perhaps for ever. You, Gertrude, it is
6   you who have exiled me! After last evening —
7   TRUEMAN: *(Coming forward to HOWARD)* What the plague
8   have you got to say about last evening?
9   HOWARD: Mr. Trueman!
10   TRUEMAN: What have you got to say about last evening?
11   And what have you to say to that little girl at all? It's
12   Tiffany's precious daughter you're in love with.
13   HOWARD: Miss Tiffany? Never! I never had the slightest
14   pretension —
15   TRUEMAN: That lying old woman! But I'm glad of it! Oh!
16   Ah! Um! *(Looking significantly at GERTRUDE and then at*
17   *HOWARD)* I see how it is. So you don't choose to
18   marry Seraphina, eh? Well now, whom do you choose
19   to marry? *(Glancing at GERTRUDE)*
20   HOWARD: I shall not marry at all!
21   TRUEMAN: You won't! *(Looking at them both again)* Why you
22   don't mean to say that you don't like — *(Points with*
23   *his thumb to GERTRUDE.)*
24   GERTRUDE: Mr. Trueman, I may have been wrong to boast of
25   my good nature, but do not presume too far upon it.
26   HOWARD: You like frankness, Mr. Trueman, therefore I
27   will speak plainly. I have long cherished a dream
28   from which I was last night rudely awakened.
29   TRUEMAN: And that's what you call speaking plainly?
30   Well, I differ with you! But I can guess what you
31   mean. Last night you suspected Gertrude there of —
32   *(Angrily)* of what no man shall ever suspect her again
33   while I'm above ground! You did her injustice — it
34   was a mistake! There, now that matter's settled. Go,
35   and ask her to forgive you — she's woman enough to

1   do it! Go, go!
2   HOWARD: Mr. Trueman, you have forgotten to whom you
3   dictate.
4   TRUEMAN: Then you won't do it? You won't ask her
5   pardon?
6   HOWARD: Most undoubtedly I will not — not at any man's
7   bidding. I must first know —
8   TRUEMAN: You won't do it? Then if I don't give you a
9   lesson in politeness —
10   HOWARD: It will be because you find me your tutor in the
11   same science. I am not a man to brook an insult, Mr.
12   Trueman! But we'll not quarrel in presence of the lady.
13   TRUEMAN: Won't we? I don't know that.
14   GERTRUDE: Pray, Mr. Trueman — Colonel Howard, pray
15   desist, Mr. Trueman, for my sake! *(Taking hold of his*
16   *arm to hold him back)* Colonel Howard, if you will read
17   this letter it will explain everything. *(Hands letter to*
18   *HOWARD, who reads.)*
19   TRUEMAN: He don't deserve an explanation! Didn't I tell
20   him that it was a mistake? Refuse to beg your
21   pardon! I'll teach him, I'll teach him!
22   HOWARD: *(After reading)* Gertrude, how have I wronged you!
23   TRUEMAN: Oh, you'll beg her pardon now? *(Between them)*
24   HOWARD: Hers, sir, and yours! Gertrude, I fear —
25   TRUEMAN: You needn't — she'll forgive you. You don't
26   know these women as well as I do — they're always
27   ready to pardon; it's their nature, and they can't help
28   it. Come along, I left Antony and his wife in the
29   dining room; we'll go and find them. I've a story of
30   my own to tell! As for you, Colonel, you may follow.
31
32
33
34
35

SCENE 8: Male Monolog

Trueman, 72

In a short and silly scene, Mrs. Tiffany says it is uncouth to discuss one's bills. Tiffany then says he supposes it is "ungenteel to pay one's bills." "Certainly!" she answers. "I hear the ee-light never condescend to do anything of the kind. The honor of their invaluable patronage is sufficient for the persons they employ!"

Prudence comes in and tells them that Seraphina has eloped with the Count. Trueman enters and says he has to talk with Tiffany. This monolog is what he says. In presenting this scene, you can either have someone give the two other lines or skip them altogether.

1. In light of everything that's happening, do you think it logical Trueman says these things here? Why?

2. Do you think it realistic that he sent his granddaughter off to be raised by someone else?

3. If you were the grandchild of a man who did this, how would you feel about him?

4. Afterward Gertrude rushes into his arms. Is this realistic or melodramatic? Why?

5. The entire monolog is melodramatic, and presenting it the wrong way could make it funny. How could you try to prevent that from happening?

1 TRUEMAN: None ever saw her to forget her! Give me your
2   hand, man. There — that will do! Now let me go on. I
3   never coveted wealth — yet twenty years ago I found
4   myself the richest farmer in Catteraugus. This cursed
5   money made my girl an object of speculation. Every
6   idle fellow that wanted to feather his nest was sure to
7   come courting Ruth. There was one — my heart
8   misgave me the instant I laid eyes upon him — for he
9   was a city chap, and not over fond of the truth. But
10   Ruth — ah! She was too pure herself to look for guile!
11   His fine words and his fair looks — the old story —
12   she was taken with him — I said, "no" — but the girl
13   liked her own way better than her old father's — girls
14   always do! — And one morning — the rascal robbed
15   me — not of my money, he would have been welcome
16   to that — but of the only treasure I cherished — my
17   daughter!
18 TIFFANY: But you forgave her!
19 TRUEMAN: I did! I knew she would never forgive herself —
20   that was punishment enough! The scoundrel thought
21   he was marrying my gold with my daughter — he was
22   mistaken! I took care that they should never want;
23   but that was all. She loved him — what will not
24   woman love? The villain broke her heart — mine was
25   tougher, or it wouldn't have stood what it did. A year
26   after they were married, he forsook her! She came
27   back to her old home — her old father! It couldn't
28   last long — she pined — and pined — and — then —
29   she died! Don't call me an old fool — though I am one
30   — for grieving won't bring her back. *(Bursts into tears.)*
31 TIFFANY: It was a heavy loss!
32 TRUEMAN: So heavy, that I should not have cared how
33   soon I followed her, but the child she left! As I
34   pressed that child in my arms, I swore that my
35   unlucky wealth should never curse it, as it had

cursed its mother! It was all I had to love — but I sent it away — and neighbors thought it was dead. The girl was brought up tenderly but humbly by my wife's relatives in Geneva. I had her taught true indepen- dence — she had hands — capacities — and should use them! Money should never buy a husband! For I resolved not to claim her until she had made her choice, and found the man who was willing to take her for herself alone. She turned out a rare girl! And it's time her old grandfather claimed her. Here he is to do it! And there stands Ruth's child. Old Adam's heiress! Gertrude, Gertrude — my child!

The play ends with Gertrude and Howard getting together. Millinette comes in and tells everyone that the Count is an imposter. They met when he was a cook for a family where she was the maid. Snobson discovers Seraphina has eloped and threatens to expose the fact that Tiffany has been committing forgery. Trueman says that if Snobson knew this, then he was an accomplice. He flees. Seraphina returns, saying the clergyman wasn't home, and besides the Count wouldn't marry her because she'd forgotten her jewels.

Trueman says he will help Tiffany repay the money he stole on condition that he get rid of all the pretentious possessions. He agrees.

The Count returns, admits he's an imposter (but an excellent cook if anyone is interested in hiring him) and agrees to marry Millinette.

How the Vote Was Won

by Cicely Hamilton
and Christopher St. John

How the Vote Was Won was intended both as a comedy and as propaganda to secure voting rights for women in England. A popular play, it had a long run in London and was produced in the United States by a traveling company sponsored by the College Equal Suffrage League of Northern California.

Cicely Hamilton, who lived from 1872 to 1952, decided early on that she wanted to be an actress. However, she had not the good looks of a leading lady, and so it was months until she was cast in a touring show. During her early career she also wrote stories for the pulp (popular) magazines and later turned to playwriting because she felt the stage belonged more to the writer than to the performer.

A producer advised her to list herself as C. Hamilton when her first play was produced, so no one would realize she was a woman. When her play was successful, she no longer disguised the fact. She continued also for years as a character actress.

Christopher St. John was a successful dramatist and wrote novels as well. She also translated work by the German playwright, the nun Hrovsvitha. She and Hamilton wrote a number of other plays together.

It may be difficult now to believe that for centuries women were denied voting rights and at best were considered second-class citizens. Yet this was the case. It is interesting that Hamilton and St. John's attack on this condition took the form of humor, since it could not have been a position they or other women liked to be in. Still, as has been demonstrated again and again, satire or gentle comedy often is the best form of attack.

SCENE 1: Three Females

Ethel, 22, Cole's wife

Winifred, her sister

Lily, Cole's maid-of-all-work

The play takes place in "Sitting-room in Horace Cole's house." It "is cheaply furnished in genteel style. The window looks out on a row of little houses, all of the Cole pattern. The door leads into a narrow passage communicating at once with the front door. The fireplace has a fancy mantel border, and over it is an overmantel, decorated with many photographs and cheap ornaments. The sideboard, a small bookcase, a table, and a comfortable armchair, are the chief articles of furniture. The whole effect is modest, and quite unpleasing."

The playwrights established the time as "late afternoon on a spring day in any year in the future." This is because, of course, women had not yet received the right to vote.

The whole household, as you'll see, is pretentious, with Cole insisting on having servants, even though his own sister works as a governess.

1. Despite the fact that this play was first produced in 1909, it still holds up today. It still is enjoyable. What do you think accounts for this fact?

2. Why do you think Ethel is so afraid of opposing her husband? Do you think this is logical? Explain.

3. This scene lays the groundwork for what is to follow. Do you find it believable that women would attempt such a thing? Why? Do you really think this sort of action could be successful? Why?

4. Why do you suppose Ethel says the strike by women is "very unkind — very wicked"? What sort of woman is she? Is she believable? Why? Likeable?

5. Which woman would you rather have for a friend or relative, Winifred or Ethel? Why?

1　*(When the curtain rises, MRS. HORACE COLE is sitting in*
2　*the comfortable armchair putting a button onto her*
3　*husband's coat. She is a pretty, fluffy little woman who*
4　*could never be bad-tempered, but might be fretful. At this*
5　*minute she is smiling indulgently, and rather irritatingly,*
6　*at her sister WINIFRED, who is sitting by the fire when the*
7　*curtain rises, but gets up almost immediately to leave.*
8　*WINIFRED is a tall and distinguished-looking young*
9　*woman with a cheerful, capable manner and an emphatic*
10　*diction which betrays the public speaker. She wears the*
11　*colours of the N.W.S.P.U.)*
12　**WINIFRED: Well, good-bye, Ethel. It's a pity you won't**
13　　**believe me. I wanted to let you and Horace down**
14　　**gently, or I shouldn't be here.**
15　**ETHEL: But you're always prophesying these dreadful**
16　　**things, Winnie, and nothing ever happens. Do you**
17　　**remember the day when you tried to invade the**
18　　**House of Commons from submarine boats? Oh,**
19　　**Horace did laugh when he saw in the papers that you**
20　　**had all been landed on the Hovis wharf by mistake!**
21　　**"By accident, on purpose!" Horace said. He couldn't**
22　　**stop laughing all the evening. "What price your sister**
23　　**Winifred," he said. "She asked for a vote, and they**
24　　**gave her bread." He kept on — you can't think how**
25　　**funny he was about it!**
26　**WINIFRED: Oh, but I can! I know my dear brother-in-law's**
27　　**sense of humor is his strong point. Well, we must**
28　　**hope it will bear the strain that is going to be put on**
29　　**it today. Of course, when his female relations invade**
30　　**his house — all with the same story, "I've come to be**
31　　**supported" — he may think it excruciatingly funny.**
32　　**One never knows.**
33　**ETHEL: Winnie, you're only teasing me. They would never**
34　　**do such a thing. They must know we have only one**
35　　**spare bedroom, and that's to be for a paying guest**

1   when we can afford to furnish it.

2 WINIFRED: The servants' bedroom will be empty. Don't

3   forget that all the domestic servants have joined the

4   League and are going to strike, too.

5 ETHEL: Not ours, Winnie. Martha is simply devoted to me,

6   and poor little Lily *couldn't* leave. She has no home

7   to go to. She would have to go to the workhouse.

8 WINIFRED: Exactly where she will go. All those women

9   who have no male relatives, or are refused help by

10   those they have, have instructions to go to the

11   relieving officer. The number of female paupers who

12   will pour through the workhouse gates tonight all

13   over England will frighten the guardians into blue fits.

14 ETHEL: Horace says you'll never *frighten* the Government

15   into giving you the vote.

16 WINIFRED: It's your husband, your dear Horace, and a

17   million other dear Horaces who are going to do the

18   frightening this time. By tomorrow, perhaps before,

19   Horace will be marching to Westminster shouting out

20   "Votes for Women!"

21 ETHEL: Winnie, how absurd you are! You know how often

22   you've tried to convert Horace and failed. Is it likely

23   that he will become a Suffragette just because —

24 WINIFRED: Just because —? Go on, Ethel.

25 ETHEL: Well, you know — all this you've been telling me

26   about his relations coming here and asking him to

27   support them. Of course I don't believe it. Agatha, for

28   instance, would never dream of giving up her situa-

29   tion. But if they did come Horace would just tell them

30   he *couldn't* keep them. How could he on £4 a week?

31 WINIFRED: How could he! That's the point! He couldn't, of

32   course. That's why he'll want to get rid of them at

33   any cost — even the cost of letting women have the

34   vote. That's why he and the majority of men in this

35   country shouldn't for years have kept alive the

1   foolish superstition that all women are supported by
2   men. For years we have told them it was a delusion,
3   but they could not take our arguments seriously.
4   Their method of answering us was exactly that of the
5   little boy in the street who cries "Yah — Suffragette!"
6   when he sees my ribbon.

7 ETHEL: I always wish you wouldn't wear it when you come
8   here...Horace does so dislike it. He thinks its
9   unwomanly.

10 WINIFRED: Oh! Does he? Tomorrow he may want to
11   borrow it — when he and the others have had their
12   object-lesson. They wouldn't listen to argument...so
13   we had to expose their pious fraud about women's
14   place in the world in a very practical and sensible
15   way. At this very minute working women of every
16   grade in every part of England are ceasing work, and
17   going to demand support and the necessities of life
18   from their nearest male relatives, however distant
19   the nearest relative may be. I hope, for your sake,
20   Ethel, that Horace's relatives aren't an exacting lot!

21 ETHEL: There wasn't a word about it in the *Daily Mail* this
22   morning.

23 WINIFRED: Never mind. The evening papers will make up
24   for it.

25 ETHEL: What male relative are you going to, Winnie?
26   Uncle Joseph?

27 WINIFRED: Oh, I'm in the fighting line, as usual, so our
28   dear uncle will be spared. My work is with the great
29   army of women who have no male belongings of any
30   kind! I shall be busy till midnight marshalling them
31   to the workhouse...This is perhaps the most impor-
32   tant part of the strike. By this we shall hit men as
33   ratepayers even when they have escaped us as rela-
34   tives! Every man, either in a public capacity or a
35   private one, will find himself face to face with the

1   appalling problem of maintaining millions of women

2   in idleness. Will the men take up the burden, d'ye

3   think? Not they! *(Looks at her watch.)* **Good heavens!**

4   The strike began ages ago. I must be off. I've wasted

5   too much time here already.

6 ETHEL: *(Looking at the clock)* I had no idea it was so late. I

7   must see about Horace's tea. He may be home any

8   minute. *(Rings the bell L.)*

9 WINIFRED: Poor Horace!

10 ETHEL: *(Annoyed)* Why "poor Horace"? I don't think he has

11   anything to complain of. *(Rings again.)*

12 WINIFRED: I feel some pity at this minute for all the men.

13 ETHEL: What can have happened to Martha?

14 WINIFRED: She's gone, my dear, that's all.

15 ETHEL: Nonsense. She's been with me ever since I was

16   married, and I pay her very good wages.

17   *(Enter LILY, a shabby little maid-of-all-work, dressed for*

18   *walking, the chief effect of the toilette being a very cheap*

19   *and very smart hat.)*

20 ETHEL: Where's Martha, Lily?

21 LILY: She's left, m'm.

22 ETHEL: Left! She never gave me notice.

23 LILY: No, m'm, we wasn't to give no notice, but at three

24   o'clock we was to quit.

25 ETHEL: But why? Don't be a silly little girl. And you

26   mustn't come in here in your hat.

27 LILY: I was just goin' when you rang. That's what I've got

28   me 'at on for.

29 ETHEL: Going! Where? It's not your afternoon out.

30 LILY: I'm goin' back to the Union. There's dozens of others

31   goin' with me.

32 ETHEL: But why —

33 LILY: Miss Christabel — she told us. She says to us: "Now

34   look 'ere, all of yer — you who've got no men to go to

35   on Thursday — yer've got to go to the Union," she

1   says; "and the one who 'angs back" — and she looked
2   at me, she did — "may be the person 'oo the 'ole
3   strain of the movement is restin' on, the traitor 'oo's
4   sailin' under the 'ostile flag," she says; and I says,
5   "That won't be me — not much!"
6   *(During this speech WINIFRED puts on a sandwich board*
7   *which bears the inscription: "This way to the Work.")*
8 WINIFRED: Well, Ethel, are you beginning to believe?
9 ETHEL: Oh, I think it's very unkind — very wicked. How
10   am I to get Horace anything to eat with no servants?
11 WINIFRED: Cheer up, my dear. Horace and the others can
12   end the strike when they choose. But they're going
13   to have a jolly time first. Good-bye.
14   *(Exit WINNIE, singing the "Marseillaise.")*
15
16
17
18
19
20
21
22
23
24
25
26
27
28
29
30
31
32
33
34
35

SCENE 2: One Male and One Female

Ethel, 22

Horace, about 30

Before Lily goes off after Winifred, Ethel asks her to bring her the kettle, the chops and the frying pan, which she does. Ethel tells her: "You poor little simpleton. Do you suppose that, even if this absurd plan succeeds, you will get a vote?"

Lily responds by saying that maybe she will, "but that's not why I'm giving up work. It's so as I shan't stop them as ought to 'ave it."

Ethel calls her "a brute" and worries about how Horace, who is just arriving, will react to the situation. When Horace comes home, a friend Gerald Williams is with him. Williams tells Ethel he's come to borrow a book called "Where's the Wash-tub Now?" published by the Men's League for Opposing Women's Suffrage.

Ethel asks if Williams' wife is a suffragette. He admits she is, and Ethel wants to know if he's heard anything that is going to happen. He says no; they've agreed not to talk of such things at breakfast. He leaves and the following scene begins.

1. What is your first impression of Horace? What makes you react this way?

2. Why do you think Ethel doesn't at first want to tell him that the servants have left? Do you think it logical that she doesn't know how to cook? Why?

3. Horace is very pompous. You can see some of this tendency in the fact that although his salary is pretty low, still he has two servants. Can you point to other lines that show his pomposity? Why do you suppose he is like this? Further, why doesn't he want his wife to mention that it was her money that paid for Martha's services?

4. Can you think of any reasons for Horace to oppose women's voting rights? Explain.

5. Overall, how would you describe the way Horace treats his wife? Explain. How do you react to his wanting her to get out of his chair?

6. Why do you think Horace doesn't admit that the cab is outside his house?

7. Since Ethel obviously has her own money, and Horace does not make a lot of money, why do you suppose she married him?

8. Horace doesn't want Ethel to open the door because "it looks as if we didn't keep a servant." Why do you think this is important to him?

1   HORACE: You might have asked him to stop to tea. You
2   made him very welcome — I don't think.
3   ETHEL: I'm sorry; but I don't think he'd have stayed if I
4   *had* asked him.
5   HORACE: Very likely not, but one should always be
6   hospitable. Tea ready?
7   ETHEL: Not quite, dear. It will be in a minute.
8   HORACE: What on earth is all this?!
9   ETHEL: Oh, nothing. I only thought I would cook your
10   chop for you up here today — just for fun.
11   HORACE: I really think, Ethel, that so long as we can
12   afford a servant, it's rather unnecessary.
13   ETHEL: You know you're always complaining of Martha's
14   cooking. I thought you would like me to try.
15   HORACE: My dear child! It's very nice of you. But why not
16   cook in the kitchen? Raw meat in the sitting-room!
17   ETHEL: Oh, Horry, don't! *(She puts her arms round his neck*
18   *and sobs. The chop at the end of the toasting fork in her*
19   *hand dangles in his face.)*
20   HORACE: What on earth's the matter? Ethel, dear, don't
21   be hysterical. If you knew what it was to come home
22   fagged to death and be worried like this...I'll ring for
23   Martha and tell her to take away these beastly chops.
24   They're getting on my nerves.
25   ETHEL: Martha's gone.
26   HORACE: When? Why? Did you have a row? I suppose you
27   had to give her a month's wages. I can't afford that
28   sort of thing, you know.
29   ETHEL: *(Sobbing)* It's not you who affords it, anyhow. Don't
30   I pay Martha out of my own money?
31   HORACE: Do you call it ladylike to throw that in my face...
32   ETHEL: *(Incoherently)* I'm not throwing it in your face...but
33   as it happens I didn't pay her anything. She went off
34   without a word...and Lily's gone, too. *(She puts her*
35   *head down on the table and cries.)*

1 HORACE: Well, that's a good riddance. I'm sick of her dirty
2   face and slovenly ways. If she ever does clean my
3   boots, she makes 'em look worse than when I took
4   them off. We must try and get a charwoman.
5 ETHEL: We shan't be able to. Isn't it in the papers?
6 HORACE: What *are* you talking about?
7 ETHEL: Winifred said it would be in the evening papers.
8 HORACE: Winifred! She's been here, has she? That
9   accounts for everything. How that woman comes to
10   be your sister I can't imagine. Of course she's mixed
11   up with this wildcat scheme.
12 ETHEL: Then you know about it!
13 HORACE: Oh, I saw something about "Suffragettes on
14   Strike" on the posters on my way home. Who cares if
15   they do strike? They're no use to anyone. Look at
16   Winifred. What does she ever do except go round
17   making speeches, and kicking up a row outside the
18   House of Commons until she forces the police to
19   arrest her. Then she goes to prison and poses as a
20   martyr. Martyr! We all know she could go home at
21   once if she would promise the magistrate to behave
22   herself. What they ought to do is to try all these
23   hysterical women *in camera* and sentence them to
24   be ducked privately. Then they'd soon give up adver-
25   tising themselves.
26 ETHEL: Winnie has a splendid answer to that, but I forget
27   what it is. Oh, Horry, was there anything on the
28   posters about the nearest male relative?
29 HORACE: Ethel, my dear, you haven't gone dotty, have
30   you? When you have quite done with my chair, I —
31   *(He helps her out of the chair and sits down.)* Thank you.
32 ETHEL: Winnie said that not only are all the working
33   women going to strike, but they are going to make
34   their nearest male relatives support them.
35 HORACE: Rot!

1   ETHEL: I thought how dreadful it would be if Agatha came,
2   or that cousin of yours on the stage whom you won't
3   let me know, or your Aunt Lizzie! Martha and Lily
4   have gone to *their* male relatives; at least, Lily's gone
5   to the workhouse — it's all the same thing. Why
6   shouldn't it be true? Oh, look, Horace, there's a cab
7   — with luggage. Oh, what shall we do?
8   HORACE: Don't fuss! It's stopping next door, not here at
9   all.
10   ETHEL: No, no; it's here. *(She rushes out.)*
11   HORACE: *(Calling after her)* Come back! You can't open the
12   door yourself. It looks as if we didn't keep a servant.
13   *(Re-enter ETHEL, followed after a few seconds by*
14   *AGATHA. AGATHA is a weary-looking woman of about*
15   *thirty-five. She wears the National Union colours, and is*
16   *dowdily dressed.)*
17   ETHEL: It is Agatha — and such a big box. Where can we
18   put it?
19
20
21
22
23
24
25
26
27
28
29
30
31
32
33
34
35

SCENE 3: Two Females and One Male

Agatha Cole, Horace's sister

Ethel, about 22

The script describes Agatha as a "weary-looking woman," who "wears the National Union colours, and is dowdily dressed." The preceding scene goes directly into this one.

1. What sort of woman is Agatha? Point to lines in the scene that show this.

2. Ethel constantly worries how Horace will feel or react. Why do you think she does?

3. Why does Horace say it's illogical for daughters to be given the same "chances as sons"? Do you know anyone who still feels the way Horace does? Do you think the feeling is at all justified?

1   AGATHA: *(Mildly)* **How do you do, Horace?** *(Kisses him.)* **Dear**
2   **Ethel!** *(Kisses her.)* **You're not looking so well as usual.**
3   **Would you mind paying the cabman two shillings,**
4   **Horace, and helping him with my box? It's rather**
5   **heavy, but then it contains all my worldly belongings.**
6   HORACE: Agatha — you haven't lost your situation! You
7   haven't left the Lewises?
8   AGATHA: Yes, Horace; I left at three o'clock.
9   HORACE: My dear Agatha — I'm extremely sorry — but we
10   can't put you up here.
11 AGATHA: Hadn't you better pay the cab? Two shillings so
12   soon becomes two-and-six. *(Exit HORACE.)* I am afraid
13   my brother doesn't realize that I have some claim
14   on him.
15 ETHEL: We thought you were so happy with the Lewises.
16 AGATHA: So were the slaves in America when they had
17   kind masters. They didn't want to be free.
18 ETHEL: Horace said you always had late dinner with them
19   when they had no company.
20 AGATHA: Oh, I have no complaint against my late
21   employers. In fact, I was sorry to inconvenience
22   them by leaving so suddenly. But I had a higher duty
23   to perform than my duty to them.
24 ETHEL: I don't know what to do. It will worry Horace
25   dreadfully.
26   *(Re-enter HORACE.)*
27 HORACE: The cab was two-and-six, and I had to give a man
28   twopence to help me in with that Noah's ark. Now,
29   Agatha, what does this mean? Surely in your position
30   it was very unwise to leave the Lewises. You can't
31   stay here. We must make some arrangement.
32 AGATHA: Any arrangement you like, dear, provided you
33   support me.
34 HORACE: I support you!
35 AGATHA: As my nearest male relative, I think you are

1   obliged to do so. If you refuse, I must go to the work-
2   house.
3 HORACE: But why can't you support yourself? You've
4   done it for years.
5 AGATHA: Yes — ever since I was eighteen. Now I am going
6   to give up work, until my work is recognized. Either
7   my proper place is the home — the home provided
8   for me by some dear father, brother, husband, cousin
9   or uncle — or I am a self-supporting member of the
10   State who ought not to be shut out from the rights of
11   citizenship.
12 HORACE: All this sounds as if you had become a
13   Suffragette! Oh, Agatha, I always thought you were
14   a lady.
15 AGATHA: Yes, I *was* a lady — such a lady that at eighteen
16   I was thrown upon the world, penniless, with no
17   training whatever which fitted me to earn my own
18   living. When women become citizens I believe that
19   daughters will be given the same chances as sons,
20   and such a life as mine will be impossible.
21 HORACE: Women are so illogical. What on earth has all
22   this to do with your planting yourself on me in this
23   inconsiderate way? You put me in a most unpleasant
24   position. You must see, Agatha, that I haven't the
25   means to support a sister as well as a wife. Couldn't
26   you go to some friends until you find another situa-
27   tion?
28 AGATHA: No, Horace. I'm going to stay with you.
29 HORACE: *(Changing his tone and turning nasty)* Oh, indeed!
30   And for how long — if I may ask?
31 AGATHA: Until the bill for the removal of the sex disability
32   is passed.
33 HORACE: *(Impotently angry)* Nonsense. I can't keep you,
34   and I won't. I have always tried to do my duty by you.
35   I think hardly a week passes that I don't write to you.

1   But now that you have deliberately thrown up an
2   excellent situation as a governess and come here and
3   threatened me — yes, threatened me — I think it's
4   time to say that, sister or no sister, I will be master
5   in my own house!
6
7
8
9
10
11
12
13
14
15
16
17
18
19
20
21
22
23
24
25
26
27
28
29
30
31
32
33
34
35

SCENE 4: Male Monolog

Horace, about 30

Just after the preceding scene ends, Horace's niece Molly arrives. Horace says he hears she has "written a most scandalous book." Besides that she lives "in lodgings by yourself, when if you chose you could afford some really nice and refined boardinghouse." He also accuses her of having undesirable friends.

She says that "now's your chance of reforming me." She's come to live with him and have him support her.

"I've never heard such impertinence!" he says. "I have always understood from you that you earn more than I do."

"Ah, yes," she replies, "but you never liked my writing for money." She brings up the fact that he also wanted her to "marry that awful little bounder Weekes." Horace objects saying, "He was at Oxford." The gist of her appearance is that, like Agatha, she's going to allow her nearest male relative, who is Horace, to give her "the necessities of life."

Immediately after this a "motor" (an automobile) pulls up outside, and a third woman arrives. "The lady is dressed smartly and tastefully" and has "manners elegant, smile charming, speech resolute." It turns out that she's Horace's second cousin, whom he doesn't even know. Yet he is her nearest relative, and she's come to have him support her. She's a dress designer, known professionally as Madame Christine. "I know!" Molly says. "I've never been able to afford you."

Madame Christine announces that she's given her "motor" to the Women's Social and Political Union and the rest of her property "to the National Union and the Women's Freedom League."

Horace tells her it's a pity she doesn't have a husband to "stop your doing such foolish things." She says she had a husband once. "He liked me to do foolish things — for instance, to support him."

Horace says he's leaving to go to the theatre and that if the women are still at his house when he returns, he'll "send for the police." Just then Maudie Spark arrives, "a young woman with an aggressively cheerful manner, a voice raucous from much

93

bellowings of music-hall songs, a hat of huge size, and a heart of gold."

Maudie, whom Horace strongly disapproves of due to her vocation, is another cousin. She says she has no other place to go, no other men to support her, that "you, Horace, are the only first cousin of this poor orphan."

He tries to get past Maudie, saying he's going to the theatre. "Silly jay!" Maude says, "the theatres are all closed...The actresses have gone on strike. I've done my little bit towards that. They won't get any more work out of Maudie Spark, Queen of Comediennes, until the women have got the vote."

Maudie further states that "the big drapers can't open tomorrow. One man can't fill the place of fifteen young ladies at once...The duchesses are out in the streets begging people to come in and wash their kids. The City men are trying to get taxi-men to do their typewriting. Every man, like Horry here, has his house full of females. Most of 'em thought, like Horry, that they'd go to the theatre to escape. But there's not a blessed theatre to go to!"

Horace says that women all over London "are disgracing their sex —" to which Maudie replies, "If it comes to that, what are you doing — threatening your womankind with the police and the workhouse?" She says that other men are "running down to the House of Commons like lunatics and blackguarding the Government for not giving us the vote before!"

Shortly after this, Ethel cries out the name of Aunt Lizzie, and Horace dives underneath the table. Horace's Aunt Lizzie arrives with a spaniel and a parrot. She says she's sorry she's late, but animals hate a move and can't understand the strike.

Ethel says the dog always growls at her; Aunt Lizzie says that's because she doesn't sympathize with the cause. The women read through the paper and find all sorts of things happening in regard to the strike. For instance, "It is understood that the Naval Volunteers have been approached by the authorities with the object of inducing them to act as charwomen to the House of Commons" and that the line of women waiting for admittance to the workhouse is already a mile and a half long.

Even the Prime Minister, with the help of "the boot-boy and a Foreign Office messenger" was found making his own bed.

Ethel discovers Horace under the table, and Aunt Lizzie asks if he was hiding from her. "I hide from you?" he asks. "Aren't you always welcome in this house?"

"Not particularly," she says. She goes on to say she's given up her boarding house and is depending on Horace "to keep me until I am admitted to citizenship. It may take a long time."

Horace answers, "It must *not* take a long time...Well, you needn't all look so surprised. I know I've been against it...but I thought only a few howling dervishes wanted the vote." But now he finds Aunt Lizzie wants it too, a woman "of your firmness of character, one who has always been so careful with her money, being declared incapable of voting! The thing is absurd!"

This leads into the following monolog.

1. Do you find it logical that Horace would change his thinking? What in his character might account for this?

2. There are still remnants of Horace's old beliefs in this monolog. Can you point them out?

3. What do you think would be the best way of delivering this monolog, so far as vocal quality, emotion and movement? Why?

4. Do you think this would be a good monolog to present? Would you enjoy doing it? Why?

1   **HORACE:** *(Looking at her scornfully)* **If there are a few**
2   **women here and there who are incapable — I**
3   **mention no names, mind — it doesn't affect the posi-**
4   **tion. What's going to be done? Who's going to do it?**
5   **If this rotten Government thinks we're going to**
6   **maintain millions of women in idleness just because**
7   **they don't like the idea of my Aunt Lizzie making a**
8   **scratch on a bit of paper and shoving it into a ballot-**
9   **box once every five years, this Government have**
10   **reckoned without the men —** *(General cheering)* **I'll**
11   **show 'em what I've got a vote for! What do they**
12   **expect? You can't all marry. There aren't enough**
13   **men to go round, and if you're earning your own**
14   **living and paying taxes you ought to have a say; it's**
15   **only fair.** *(General cheering and a specially emphatic*
16   *"Hear, hear" from MADAME CHRISTINE)* **The Government**
17   **are narrow-minded idiots!** *(MADAME C.: Hear! hear!)*
18   **They talk as if all the women ought to stay at home**
19   **washing and ironing. Well, before a woman has a**
20   **washtub, she must have a home to put it in, mustn't**
21   **she? And who's going to give it her? I'd like them to**
22   **tell me that. Do they expect me to do it?** *(AGATHA:*
23   *Yes, dear.)* **I say if she can do it herself and keep**
24   **herself, so much the better for everyone. Anyhow,**
25   **who are the Government? They're only representing**
26   *me*, **and being paid thousands a year by me for**
27   **carrying out my wishes.** *(MOLLY: Oh, er — what ho!*
28   *HORACE turns on her angrily.)* **I like a woman to be a**
29   **woman — that's the way I was brought up; but if she**
30   **insists on having a vote — and apparently she does**
31   *(ALL: She does! She does!)* **— I don't see why she**
32   **shouldn't have it. Many a woman came in here at the**
33   **last election and tried to wheedle me into voting for**
34   **her particular candidate. If she has time to do that —**
35   **and I never heard the member say then that she**

1   **ought to be at home washing the baby — I don't see**
2   **why she hasn't time to vote. It's never taken up**
3   **much of *my* time, or interfered with *my* work. I've**
4   **only voted once in my life — but that's neither here**
5   **nor there. I know what the vote does for me. It gives**
6   **me a status; that's what you women want — a status.**
7   *(ALL: Yes, yes; a status.)* **I might even call it a locus**
8   **standi. If I go now and tell these rotten Cabinet**
9   **Ministers what I think of them, it's my *locus standi***
10   **— *(MAUDIE: That's a good word.)* — that will force**
11   **them to listen to me. Oh, I know. And, by gum! I'll**
12   **give them a bit of my mind. They shall hear a few**
13   **home truths for once. "Gentlemen," I shall say —**
14   **well, that won't be true of all of them to start with,**
15   **but one must give 'em the benefit of the doubt —"**
16   **gentlemen, the men of England are sick and tired of**
17   **your policy. Who's driven the women of England into**
18   **this? *You* —** *(He turns round on ETHEL, who jumps*
19   *violently)* **— because you were too stupid to know that**
20   **they meant business — because you couldn't read**
21   **the writing on the wall.** *(Hear, hear.)* **It may be nothing**
22   **to you, gentlemen, that every industry in this**
23   **country is paralyzed and every Englishman's home**
24   **turned into a howling wilderness —** *(MOLLY: Draw it*
25   *mild, Uncle. HORACE: A howling wilderness, I repeat.)* **—**
26   **by your refusal to see what's as plain as the nose on**
27   **your face; but I would have you know, gentlemen,**
28   **that it is something to us. We aren't slaves. We never**
29   **will be slaves —** *(AGATHA: Never, never!)* **— and we**
30   **insist on reform. Gentlemen, conditions have**
31   **changed, and women have to work. Don't men**
32   **encourage them to work, *invite* them to work?**
33   *(AGATHA: Make them work.)* **And women are placed in**
34   **the battle of life on the same terms as we are, short**
35   **of one thing, the *locus standi* of a vote.** *(MAUDIE:*

1   *Good old* locus standi!*)* **If you aren't going to give it to**
2   **them, gentlemen, and if they won't go back to their**
3   **occupations without it we ask you, how they're going**
4   **to live? Who's going to support them? Perhaps you're**
5   **thinking of giving them all old age pensions and**
6   **asking the country to pay the piper! The country will**
7   **see you damned first, if, gentlemen, you'll pardon the**
8   **expression. It's dawning upon us all that the women**
9   **would never have taken such a step as this if they**
10   **hadn't been the victims of gross injustice.** *(ALL:*
11   *Never.)* **Why shouldn't they have a voice in the laws**
12   **which regulate the price of food and clothes? Don't**
13   **they pay for their food and clothes?** *(MAUDIE: Paid for*
14   *mine all my life.)* **Why shouldn't they have a voice in**
15   **the rate of wages and the hours of labour in certain**
16   **industries? Aren't they working at those industries?**
17   **If you had a particle of common sense or decent**
18   **feeling, gentlemen —"**
19
20
21
22
23
24
25
26
27
28
29
30
31
32
33
34
35

Gerald Williams comes in insisting that women be given the vote and that everyone should march for their rights. Ethel calls Horace her hero. He replies: "You may depend on me — all of you — to see justice done. When you want a thing done, get a man to do it! Votes for Women!" He waves a flag triumphantly as the women cheer him on.

Letters to a Student Revolutionary

by Elizabeth Wong

Elizabeth Wong's first play, *Letters to a Student Revolutionary*, was given its initial performance in New York by the Pan Asian Repertory Theatre. It commemorated the second anniversary of the Tiananmen Square rebellion in which hundreds or perhaps thousands died at the hands of the Chinese government.

The play explores the cultural differences between an American girl Bibi and a Chinese girl who calls herself Karen. They meet and speak for only a few minutes when Bibi is vacationing in China; yet their correspondence continues for years.

The two girls put their personalities, their dreams, their accomplishments and their disappointments into the letters. Often, months separate one letter from the next. Yet there is an intimacy in the way they talk to one another.

There is also a chorus which sometimes speaks in unity. At other times members step out of place to become characters. One of them is Debbie, Karen's best friend, whom we later learn is a cat.

There are great cultural and political differences, and so often the two young women have difficulty in making themselves clear to one another.

The play takes us through job after job and boyfriend after boyfriend for Bibi, and from a regimented life to marriage to a quest for freedom for Karen. Near the end of the play, Karen writes, "I cannot begin to describe — there is this change in the air — to be here, surrounded by comrades — student activists and ordinary citizens — men and women, all patriots for a new China. I think this is what 'pursuit of happiness' must be. Bibi, for the first time in my life, I believe I can be somebody, I believe my contribution will make a difference. I believe freedom will not grow out of theory but out of ourselves."

Bibi writes back asking Karen to be careful, to seek freedom at China's own pace. Yet Karen, who has wanted freedom all her life, cannot hold back. She goes to Tiananmen Square — the Avenue of Eternal Peace — along with thousands of others, who, unafraid, advance row by row to be mowed down by tanks and gunfire.

The Chorus talks then about the world's focus turning to other things, and to China's and America's "selective historical amnesia."

The play ends in 1990 with Bibi writing once more to Karen, asking about her and her husband and asking her to write when it's safe. "Let me know you are all right," she writes. "Love, your good friend, Bibi."

The play begins in 1979 when both women are in their early twenties. The chorus is made up of three men and one woman. The production is to be "stylistic and presentational." "The set is divided into two separate areas representing China and the United States. However, the center space must be a neutral territory wherein the rules of time and geography are broken. Minimal props suggest occupation and/or location.

"The Chorus must remain on stage throughout."

SCENE 1: Multiple Characters, Male and Female

Chorus

Bibi, early 20s

Karen, early 20s

This is the scene that opens the play. "At curtain rise, the Chorus stands impassively together upstage. Bibi is downstage."

1. What mood is Bibi in during the first speech here? Why do you suppose she alludes to movie stars?

2. Do you think Bibi minded the tour as much as she says? Why?

3. Why do you suppose Karen is so much interested in the American way of life? Why does she call herself Karen, do you think?

4. Why does the chorus keep Bibi and Karen apart? Why does Karen want so badly to meet Bibi?

5. Of course the play is not at all realistic in setting and staging. Why do you think the author wanted it to be this way? Why do you suppose she used a chorus, rather than individual actors? Do you think this is effective?

6. How does Bibi's view of what she sees differ from Karen's view? What does this say about their way of life?

7. The Chorus acts a lot like the chorus of Greek plays, both interacting with the characters and commenting on the scene. What purpose does this serve? This, of course, provides a different sort of acting opportunity, choral speaking. If you are a part of the Chorus, you will have to agree with the other members on how to present the dialog. When the Chorus speaks as a unit, what are the most important qualities you would want to convey to the audience? Why?

1   BIBI: **Day thirty-five. No peanut butter. No cheese. No**
2   **toast. And I'm sick of jook. Jook is no joke. Jook for**
3   **breakfast — yesterday, today, and tomorrow. What is**
4   **jook, you ask.**
5   CHORUS ONE: *(Offers a bowl.)* **Rice porridge.**
6   CHORUS: **It's good for you.**
7   BIBI: **Boring. That's it. I've had it.** *(To audience)* **I rebelled**
8   **against breakfast. I pushed myself away from the**
9   **table. The chair went flying like a hockey puck on**
10   **ice. I struck a defiant Bette Davis pose.** *(To CHORUS*
11   *ONE)* **Get that slop away from me...you pig!** *(To audi-*
12   *ence)* **My parents were appalled at my behavior. I was**
13   **impossible. But I couldn't help it. The ghost of James**
14   **Dean.** *(Heavy sigh)* **So, for thirty-five days, wherein I**
15   **wished I was sunning in the Bahamas instead, I was**
16   **Kunta Kinte of the New Roots Generation — touring**
17   **China with Mom and Dad.**
18   *(Chinese opera music clangs. BIBI smiles a bit too broadly.)*
19   **Loved the music. Also, loved the toasting of the**
20   **honored guests...**
21   CHORUS: **Gom bei!**
22   BIBI: *(To CHORUS)* **Gom bei!** *(To audience)* **Oh sure, I loved**
23   **the endless tours — the jade factory, brocade factory,**
24   **carpet factory. But how could I appreciate it without**
25   **some proper grub. John Wayne wouldn't stand for**
26   **it, he'd shoot the cook, who was probably a Chinese**
27   **anyway.**
28   *(CHORUS ONE offers the bowl again.)*
29   **Cheerios?**
30   CHORUS ONE: **Jook.**
31   BIBI: **What a nightmare!**
32   *(BIBI abruptly runs upstage. She, not the CHORUS, sets*
33   *the scene. [Note: the CHORUS should not be individuated,*
34   *nor should they be illustrative of any particular attitude or*
35   *action.])*

1 *(To audience)* **I took to the streets of Beijing.**
2 **Wandered into Tiananmen Square — a hungry look in**
3 **my eyes, a vain hope in my heart.** *(To CHORUS FOUR)*
4 **You there, sweeper. Could you please tell me where I**
5 **might locate a golden oasis of fast food?** *(To CHORUS*
6 *TWO)* **Hey there, Mr. Chicken man, spare an egg for a**
7 **simple sunnyside up?** *(Goes downstage to audience.)*
8 **Someday, right next to that rosy-faced mug of**
9 **Chairman Mao, there'll be a golden arch and a neon**
10 **sign flashing billions and billions served. No place is**
11 **truly civilized without Mickey D and a drive-up**
12 **window.** *(Runs back upstage to CHORUS THREE.)* **'Scuse**
13 **me, Mr. Soldier, can you possibly direct me to the**
14 **nearest greasy spoon?**
15 *(CHORUS THREE slowly turns to look at BIBI.)*
16 **CHORUS ONE:** *(To audience)* **Summer, 1979. Tourism was**
17 **still so new in China.**
18 *(KAREN enters, pushing an old coaster bicycle.)*
19 **KAREN:** *(To audience)* **I am on my way home from the**
20 **factory. End of the graveyard shift. Is this the correct**
21 **phrase? Yes, I think so. Graveyard shift. This**
22 **morning, there is much mist. But it is already hot**
23 **like hell. Do I say that right? Yes, I think so.**
24 **CHORUS FOUR:** *(To audience)* **I sweep. I sweep. Everything**
25 **must be clean.**
26 **KAREN: The square is very crowded, very many people**
27 **everywhere. But I see a girl. She looks like me. But**
28 **her hair is curly like the tail of a pig. She wears pink,**
29 **lavender, indigo. She is a human rainbow.**
30 *(KAREN steps towards BIBI, but the CHORUS intimidates*
31 *her.)*
32 **CHORUS FOUR:** *(To KAREN)* **I sweep *you* if you become**
33 **unclean. Watch out for contamination!** *(Whispered, to*
34 *CHORUS ONE)* **You, you there, waiter!**
35 **CHORUS ONE:** *(Overlapped whisper to CHORUS TWO)* **Watch**

1   out! You, you there, butcher!

2   CHORUS TWO: *(Overlapped whisper to KAREN)* **Watch out!**

3   **You, you there.**

4   *(KAREN backs away from BIBI.)*

5   CHORUS FOUR: *(To audience)* **My duty to sweep all day. My**

6   **duty to sweep all night. My back hurts. But I have a**

7   **duty to perform.**

8   KAREN: **What harm is there to practice a little English?**

9   CHORUS THREE: *(To KAREN)* **I am watching her, and...** *(To*

10   *audience)* **I am watching you.**

11   BIBI: *(To audience)* **Oh look. Grandmothers with ancient**

12   **faces, pushing bamboo strollers like shopping carts.**

13   **Let's peek.** *(She does.)* **Ahhhh, sweetest little babies**

14   **with wispy, fuzzy, spiky hair.**

15   KAREN: *(To audience)* **Look, there is a butcher I know. He**

16   **carries chickens upside down, hurrying to market.**

17   **He does not see me.**

18   BIBI: *(To audience)* **Talk about ego. Check these pictures,**

19   **bigger than billboards on Sunset Boulevard. And**

20   **what's playing? That's the Mao matinee. That's**

21   **Lenin. Stalin. Is that guy Marx? Yup. Give the girl a**

22   **piece of pie.**

23   KAREN: *(To audience)* **There, a big strong worker shoulders**

24   **his load of bamboo for scaffolds. He helps to build a**

25   **hospital. He is too busy to notice me.**

26   BIBI: *(To audience)* **Bricklayers push a cartful of bricks. A**

27   **man carries a pole balanced with two hanging**

28   **baskets, filled with live fish. Great smell! I think I'm**

29   **going to faint. Bicycles everywhere in the square.**

30   CHORUS ONE: **Yes, a busy morning in the square.**

31   *(The CHORUS, one by one, builds an impenetrable human*

32   *wall between KAREN and BIBI.)*

33   CHORUS FOUR: *(To audience)* **I am not you and I am not**

34   **me. I am a good citizen of the State.**

35   CHORUS TWO: *(To audience)* **With so much going on, so**

1   **many people, who pays attention to an inconsequen-**
2   **tial girl on a bicycle?**
3 **KAREN: I will go up to her and speak to her. We will make**
4   **beautiful sentences together.**
5 **CHORUS FOUR:** *(To audience)* **I am watching too. Watching**
6   **everything. It is my duty as a good citizen of the**
7   **State.**
8   *(KAREN tries to penetrate the wall.)*
9 **CHORUS THREE:** *(To audience, overlapping)* **Anarchy will**
10   **not be tolerated.**
11 **CHORUS TWO:** *(Overlapping)* **Even a spark of spirit will be**
12   **squashed.**
13 **CHORUS ONE:** *(Overlapping)* **Wild behavior will not be**
14   **permitted.**
15 **CHORUS THREE:** *(Overlapping)* **Wild thinking will not be**
16   **permitted.**
17 **CHORUS ONE:** *(Overlapping)* **Any messes will be cleaned up.**
18 **CHORUS TWO:** *(Overlapping)* **That is what a broom is for.**
19 **CHORUS FOUR:** *(Overlapping)* **This is my sword. My broom.**
20 **CHORUS:** *(To audience)* **We must have cleanliness. The**
21   **State will insist.** *(Softly)* **Hello.**
22   *(Ignoring her)* **Like in** *Vertigo.* **Jimmy Stewart climbing**
23   **the steps, looking down from the tower. Or is it Orson**
24   **Welles with the funhouse mirrors in** *Lady From*
25   *Shanghai?* **Well, anyway, like** *everything* **going round**
26   **and round in a woozy circle.** *(She examines each*
27   *member of the CHORUS.)* **I see me and I see me and I**
28   **see me. But not really, you know. I don't fit in, not**
29   **at all.**
30   *(KAREN breaks through the wall, crosses over to BIBI.)*
31 **KAREN:** *(Tentatively)* **Hello.** *(BIBI doesn't hear. KAREN steps*
32   *closer. The CHORUS steps into a line and turns their*
33   *backs to the audience.)* **Please excuse.**
34 **BIBI: Oh, hello.**
35 **KAREN: Please. Not so loud.** *(Beat)* **Are you?**

1   BIBI: *(Whispers.)* **I am. How can you tell?**

2   **KAREN: Ahh.** *(Pause)* **Your hair.**

3   **BIBI: Completely unnatural, I know. It's called a perma-**

4   **nent. Why something's called a permanent when you**

5   **have to have it redone every six months I'll never**

6   **know. More like a temporary, if you ask me. Go figure.**

7   **KAREN: Go to figure.**

8   **BIBI: Right. It's like every time I go to the salon, they**

9   **want to give me the same old tired thing — the**

10   **classic bob and bangs, *exactly* like yours. So I plead,**

11   **"Please do something different." Understand? But**

12   **every time, without fail, I end up with...you know...**

13   *(Indicates KAREN's hair)* **that — bland and boring, like**

14   **breakfast.**

15   **KAREN: Like breakfast.**

16   **BIBI: Right. They tell me, "But, oh no, you look so cute. A**

17   **little China doll, that's what you are." Make me *puke*.**

18   **So I say, "Aldo baby darling, perm it. Wave it. Frizz**

19   **it. Spike it. Color it blue." So if you look in the light.**

20   **See? Not black, but blue with red highlights, tinged**

21   **with orange. It's unusual, don't you think?**

22   **KAREN: You want haircut like me? That easy. Very simple.**

23   **I do it for you.**

24   **BIBI: Sorry. I know I talk too fast. I'm what is known as an**

25   **energetic person. I have so much energy, I some-**

26   **times think I'll leap out of my clothes.**

27   **KAREN: No, I'm sorry. My comprehending is very bad. My**

28   **English is too stupid. But I wish to practice. I would**

29   **like to have hair curly like yours. Can you do that**

30   **for me?**

31   **BIBI: *Sure*, you come to California. And I'll set you up with**

32   **Aldo. But I warn you, he'll poof and snip, and you**

33   **think you're going to be a new woman, but you get**

34   **banged and bobbed every time.** *(KAREN starts to touch*

35   *BIBI's sleeve; then withdraws shyly.)*

1   KAREN: Here we have only a few colors. Grey and blue and
2   green.
3   BIBI: Grey and blue and green are good colors.
4   KAREN: May I ask what is your name?
5   BIBI: Bibi. My name is Bibi.
6
7
8
9
10
11
12
13
14
15
16
17
18
19
20
21
22
23
24
25
26
27
28
29
30
31
32
33
34
35

SCENE 2: Multiple Characters, Male and Female

Chorus

Karen, 20s

Bibi, 20s

This scene occurs shortly after the other one and shows the beginning of the correspondence between the two young women.

1. Why do you suppose Karen is having such difficulty getting started with her letter? What feelings of hers would you want to portray for an audience? How might you go about doing this?

2. What more can you tell about Bibi's character or personality in this scene? How would you describe her? In ways both she and Charlie are one-dimensional, lacking in depth. How is this shown? Why do you think Wong did this?

3. Why do you suppose Bibi doesn't really appreciate getting this letter? How would you feel if you were in her situation?

4. Bibi said she grew up in the slums. If so, who do you think had the worse life, she or Karen? Explain.

1   **CHORUS TWO: Bibi went back home to California, U.S.A.**
2   **And that was the beginning.**
3   **CHORUS THREE:** *(To CHORUS TWO)* **The beginning of what?**
4   **CHORUS ONE:** *(To audience)* **The beginning of a most**
5   *uncomfortable* **correspondence.**
6   *(KAREN in her bedroom)*
7   **KAREN:** *(Writes.)* **Summer, 1979. My dear American**
8   **friend...** *(Scratches out, starts again.)* **My dear new**
9   **friend...Greetings from Beijing.** *(She sits back, stares*
10   *into space.)*
11   *(BIBI on the beach)*
12   **BIBI:** *(To audience)* **Summer, 1979. This is Venice Beach. I**
13   **have my chair, hunkered down in the sand, posi-**
14   **tioned for maximum good tanning rays. The pier to**
15   **my left. The muscle boys to my right. The surfers in**
16   **their tight black wet suits. Life can't get better than**
17   **someone muscular in a tight black wet suit.**
18   *(CHARLIE, a virile young man, brings on a blaring radio*
19   *playing "Good Vibrations" by The Beach Boys. He's a nice*
20   *guy.)* **Speaking of which, my friend. A cross between**
21   **Frankie Avalon and Louis Jourdan, which I guess**
22   **makes me a cross between Annette Funicello and**
23   **Leslie Caron.**
24   **CHARLIE: Limon? Ma cheri Gidget Gigi?**
25   **BIBI:** *(To audience)* **Not bad. But temporary. I mean this guy**
26   **thinks** *Casablanca* **is a fine wine. He does try though,**
27   **and he brings me lemonade. So here we are, me and**
28   **Casanova under an umbrella of blue sky, hoping for a**
29   **beach blanket bingo state of mind. But I admit, I've**
30   **been a bit preoccupied.** *(She shows a letter to the*
31   *audience.)*
32   **CHARLIE:** *(To BIBI)* **Preoccupied nothing. You've been**
33   **downright morose. Whatsa matter punky pumpkin?**
34   **You been bluesy woozy all day.**
35   **BIBI: Turn that thing off.**

1 CHARLIE: Okay dokey, cupcake.
2   *(She resumes reading the letter.)*
3   My lady Cleopatra, Queen of the Nile, command me.
4   I live to serve.
5 BIBI: Oh, put a lid on it. *(To audience)* Like I said. He does
6   try. *(To CHARLIE)* Caesar, look on this.
7   *(BIBI shows him the letter. He takes it, examines it.)*
8 CHARLIE: Nice stamp. *(Reads.)* "Summer, 1979. Dear Bibi,
9   greetings from China. Do you remember me? I am
10   the girl with whom you have shared a conversation."
11   *(To BIBI)* Looks like you've got a pen pal. I think it's
12   very sweet.
13 BIBI: Keep reading.
14 CHARLIE: Read. All right. "I met you in Tiananmen
15   Square. I write to you from my little room..."
16   *(Lights up on KAREN.)*
17 KAREN: *(Overlapping)* ...Tiananmen Square. I write to you
18   from my little room. There is no window, but I have
19   big picture of a map to show me wondrous sights of
20   America, The Grandest Canyon and OkayDokey
21   Swamp. I share my room with my brother who
22   teaches English at the high school.
23   *(Her BROTHER steps from the CHORUS.)*
24 BROTHER: Hey ugly, turn out the light!
25 KAREN: I would like to get a new brother. Is that possible
26   in America? I think anything is possible where
27   you live.
28   *(A CAT steps from the CHORUS, sits at KAREN's feet.)*
29 CAT: *(To audience)* Meeooww.
30 BROTHER: *(To KAREN)* And get that hairball out of the
31   room. Or I'll make kitty stew!
32 KAREN: *(To BROTHER)* You wouldn't!
33 BIBI: *(To CHARLIE)* In China, cats are not kept as pets.
34 KAREN: *(To BIBI)* She is not a pet. I do not own her. She is
35   a free cat.

1   BROTHER: *(To audience)* **Cats are functional. They eat rats.**
2   *(To KAREN)* **Or they are *to be eaten*. Which is it?**
3   KAREN: *(To audience)* **I put the cat outside.** *(To CAT)* **I say,**
4   **"I am sorry, kitty cat. So very sorry, little kitty. Go**
5   **on now, go to work and catch some micey mousies."**
6   *(To audience)* **And then, she say in extreme irritable-**
7   **ness...**
8   CAT: **Meeooow.**
9   KAREN: *(To audience)* **I pretend to go to sleep. And when**
10 **my brother starts to snore, I get up and write to you,**
11 **my dear friend Bibi.**
12 BIBI: **Here it comes.**
13 CHARLIE: **Bibi, you may sound like a tough cookie, but**
14 **only I know what a soft, mushy cupcake you are.**
15 BIBI: **Oh yeah? Well, read on, *cupcake*.**
16 KAREN: *(To audience)* **It is a happy feeling I have...to have**
17 **you for a secret friend, a special friend. I have much**
18 **stupidity since I realized I never told you my name.**
19 **How do you like my name? Do you think this is a**
20 **good name?**
21 BIBI: *(To KAREN)* **Karen? Yes. I think Karen is a good name.**
22 KAREN: *(To BIBI)* **Good. I am so glad for this.** *(To audience)*
23 **I chose my new name in secret. This is my choice.**
24 **Only my best friend knows about this secret. We call**
25 **each other Debbie and Karen. Where you live, you**
26 **can be open about such matters. But here we must do**
27 **everything in secret.**
28 CHARLIE: **This is a very nice letter, Bibi. Hardly appro-**
29 **priate of you to be so provoked about it, cupcake.**
30 *(Provoked by the belittling endearment, BIBI takes the*
31 *letter from CHARLIE.)*
32 **Hey!**
33 BIBI: **You aren't helping. And *don't* you cupcake me**
34 **anymore...stud muffin. Stop patronizing me, catego-**
35 **rizing me, labeling me like some damned jar of jelly.**

1   CHARLIE: Why so miffed, love bun?

2   BIBI: There you go again.

3   CHARLIE: I just...

4   BIBI: You just what? A lot you know. *This*, for one, is not

5   a nice letter. This just *sounds* like a nice letter.

6   CHARLIE: Cupcake, not everyone has ulterior motives.

7   Not everyone is suspect. Have a little faith in human

8   nature. Not everyone is out to use and abuse.

9   BIBI: You are not listening. This letter, stud muffin, is

10   crafted on two predictable emotions — guilt and

11   more guilt. I will NOT be made to feel responsible

12   before my time.

13   CHARLIE: Are we not our brother's keeper?

14   BIBI: No, we are not. Look here, silver spoon. I have lived

15   in every ghetto slum in Los Angeles. Mom and Dad

16   slaved so I could squander their hard work on college.

17   And on top of everything, they got annoying letters

18   like this.

19   KAREN: Bibi, you have such freedom.

20   BIBI: *(Overlapping)* Bibi, you have such freedom. *(To*

21   *CHARLIE)* Mom calls them "Ailment — of — the —

22   Month" letters. Dear Mr. and Mrs. Lee, my dear rich

23   American relation, could you send us some money

24   since life here is so bad, and you have it so good.

25   KAREN: I have no freedom. None whatsoever. Is it my

26   misfortune to be born in my country and you were

27   born in yours? I look at you and it is as if I look at

28   myself in a glass.

29   CHARLIE: *(To KAREN)* You mean mirror.

30   KAREN: Thank you for this correction. *(Beat)* Yes, I look in

31   mirror, yes. I think, "You are me." I was meant to be

32   born in the United States, to live in freedom like you.

33   Do you understand? *(Beat)* Two days after I met you,

34   my boss at the factory where I am in the accounting

35   department, asked to speak to me.

1 *(The CAT gets up, and with an abrupt turn becomes the*
2 *smiling BOSS, who approaches KAREN.)*
3 **My boss has a kind voice, but a frown is in his heart.**
4 **I am taken to a small room in the basement. This is**
5 *not* **a good sign.**
6 **BOSS: Please sit down.**
7 **CHARLIE:** *(To KAREN)* **Then what happened?**
8 **KAREN: I sat down.**
9 **BOSS:** *(Kindly, as if to an errant child)* **You were seen talking**
10 **to an American. An American student. Now, you**
11 **mustn't be worried. Don't be afraid. You may talk to**
12 **Westerners now.**
13 **CHARLIE:** *(To BIBI)* **I read about this. China is relaxing**
14 **some of its policies.**
15 **BOSS: We are more relaxed under the new policies. But**
16 **you must not listen to what they say. You must not**
17 **get any ideas.** *(Pauses, recites by rote.)* **Good citizens**
18 **have only ideas that also belong to the State. The**
19 **State is your mother. The State is your father. The**
20 **State is more than your mother or your father. Do**
21 **you understand?**
22
23
24
25
26
27
28
29
30
31
32
33
34
35

SCENE 3: Two Females

Bibi, 20s

Karen 20s

This scene occurs two years later. Karen discovers that her brother is the one who reported their mother to the authorities and so was responsible for her death. Just before this scene, Bibi's mother has been complaining about being too old to have a good job. She said that before she had children, she had more choice. She says that now she lives only for Bibi. You can eliminate the first two lines of this scene, if you wish.

1. How does each of the two, Karen and Bibi, feel about their mothers?

2. How would you try to recreate the horror Karen felt at seeing her mother dead?

1   BIBI: *(Pause, thoughtfully)* **Before you had your children?**
2   **Are we your regrets, Mommy? Would it have been**
3   **better if...if I wasn't around? Would you have worked**
4   **less? Lived more?**
5   MOTHER: *(Disgustedly)* **Aiii!**
6   BIBI: Of course, my mother cares about me. She doesn't
7   mean it. All that about her life being ruined...but
8   when I think about all she's given up just because of
9   me...I sometimes ...sometimes, Karen, I wish...then
10   maybe she'd be free. Got anything in the way of a
11   razor blade?
12   KAREN: Bibi, you make abundant jokes, but I know you
13   are feeling upset and sad. *(Beat)* Bibi, we do not
14   choose to be born. In China, as in America, this is not
15   a choice we have.
16   BIBI: Sleeping pills in large quantities, however, is an
17   equal opportunity. This is America.
18   KAREN: In China, we have only few freedoms. There is a
19   saying. Do you know it? **Zu yo sung ye tai sheng. Yo**
20   **ching yu hung mao.** (Death can be as heavy as the
21   biggest mountain, or light as a feather.) **We may choose**
22   **when to die, how to die, and for what we will die. Yes,**
23   **I think there are times for such a choice. But this is**
24   **not a good choice for you, especially if you are going**
25   **to help me.**
26   BIBI: *(Choral tone)* **Spring, 1981.**
27   KAREN: You asked about my mother. My mother is dead.
28   BIBI: When did she die?
29   KAREN: When I was very young. Near my house, next to
30   the pigpens, there is a rice field. Yes, a warm day in
31   the rice field. Many mosquitoes. I am raw from the
32   bites. *(Pause)* **My mother is in the field. She has long**
33   **black hair, just like mine. I see her. I run to her. I**
34   **wave to her. I'm running and so happy. The water**
35   **from the field splashes up. The ground grabs, holds**

117

1   my feet as I run.
2   **BIBI:** *(To KAREN, softly)* **Watch out. The sheaves of rice are**
3   **sharp.**
4   **KAREN: Yes. The rice cut my legs as I run. Blood trickling**
5   **down my legs. But I don't care. I brought my mother**
6   **her lunchbox.** *(Waves.)* **MaMa! Bao bao gay ni dai fan**
7   **lai!** (Your baby brings you your lunch.) *(Beat)* **Wait! Who**
8   **is that? It is the commissar! He is the man who**
9   **reports everything.**
10   **BIBI: I see him. He's very tall.**
11   **KAREN: He is shaking my mother. He's shaking her. Why**
12   **is he doing that? Where is he taking her? MaMa!**
13   **MaMa! Where are you going? MaMa! MaMa!** *(Pause)* **I**
14   **fell in the rice, and I was wet from the water. I just**
15   **watched my mother as they took her away.**
16
17
18
19
20
21
22
23
24
25
26
27
28
29
30
31
32
33
34
35

SCENE 4: Female Monolog

Karen, about 30

This monolog occurs only a few pages from the end of the script. In all probability, Karen and her husband were later killed in the Tiananmen Square Massacre.

1. What feelings, besides optimism, do you think Karen feels here?

2. To understand the situation better, you might want to investigate what really happened in China at this time. Can you think of any similar incidents in the United States?

1   *(KAREN at Tiananmen Square)*
2   **KAREN:** *(To audience)* **May, 1989. Dear Bibi, here I am —**
3   **sitting in a tent on ChangAn Avenue in Tiananmen**
4   **Square — do you know what this means — it means**
5   **the Avenue of Eternal Peace. I cannot begin to**
6   **describe — there is this change in the air — to be**
7   **here, surrounded by my comrades — student**
8   **activists and ordinary citizens — men and women, all**
9   **patriots for a new China. I think this is what "pursuit**
10   **of happiness" must be. Bibi, for the first time in my**
11   **life, I believe I can be a somebody, I believe my**
12   **contribution will make a difference. I believe freedom**
13   **will not grow out of theory but out of ourselves. We**
14   **are fighting for a system that will respect the indi-**
15   **vidual. The individual is not dead. The government**
16   **must listen to us. The government will listen to us.**
17   **All we want is a dialog. A conversation. We want an**
18   **end to censorship. We want an end to corruption. We**
19   **are the voices of tomorrow. And our voices will be**
20   **heard. There is so much power to be here together —**
21   **singing songs, holding hands, listening to the**
22   **speeches of our student leaders.**
23
24
25
26
27
28
29
30
31
32
33
34
35

SCENE 5: Female Monolog

Bibi, about 30

This is the next to the last letter Bibi writes to Karen. The last is the one quoted in the introduction to the play, where she asks that Karen write again when it is safe.

1. What feelings do you think Bibi has as she writes this letter? Explain. How might you try to portray them?

2. Do you think it logical that Bibi would write this letter? Why? If you were writing to Karen, what else might you want to say?

1   BIBI: May, 1989. Dear Karen, I've been watching the tele-
2   vision reports. Everybody always asks me how I feel
3   about what is happening in China. I'm so envious of
4   your power — of how you have caused your govern-
5   ment, caused the world to take notice. But I am also
6   concerned about your naivete in striving towards a
7   foreign ideal. I do believe change will come, but it
8   must be at your own pace. I am not sure America is
9   the proper model for the new China that you want.
10   Perhaps you should look to make a Chinese democ-
11   racy. Please understand that I feel a deep connection
12   to you, but right now, I think that to be a somebody
13   in China is suicide. I don't mean to dampen your
14   spirits, but I am worried. Please, please be careful.
15
16
17
18
19
20
21
22
23
24
25
26
27
28
29
30
31
32
33
34
35

Machinal

by Sophie Treadwell

Machinal is an unusual play, especially for its time period. It was copyrighted in 1928 and produced for the first time the following year.

It tells the story of an ordinary woman who lives in a mechanized world. In part, the play is stating that life is impersonal like the machines we use. Although the Young Woman tries to be an individual, she ends up feeling that nothing really is hers.

The Young Woman is an individual, yet is representative of many lives. *Machinal* shows how mechanical life can appear, even in the face of heartbreak and frustration.

The style of the play is expressionistic. That means that the playwright uses a very subjective manner of writing in which she says, in effect, that this is how the central character views life. She is nearly drowned out by the machinery, the mechanics of everyday living. Her self becomes lost in everyday happenings.

In this play, the noise is almost a character in itself.

In all probability, Treadwell used a sensational murder trial of the time as a starting point for her writing.

SCENE 1: Three Males and Three Females

The characters are listed below; no ages are given for any of them.

This is how Treadwell sets the opening of the play:

THE PLOT is the story of a woman who murders her husband — an ordinary young woman, any woman.

THE PLAN is to tell this story by showing the different phases of life that the woman comes in contact with, and in none of which she finds any place, any peace. The woman is essentially soft, tender, and the life around her is essentially hard, mechanized. Business, home, marriage, having a child, seeking pleasure — all are difficult for her — mechanical nerve nagging. Only in an illicit love does she find anything with life in it for her, and when she

123

loses this, the desperate effort to win free to it again is
her undoing.

She tried to "catch the rhythm of our common city speech,
its brassy sound, its trick of repetition, etc." Treadwell also uses
a lot of sound effects, such as riveting, a priest chanting and a
jazz band both as "background" and for "their inherent
emotional effect" and to intrude on the depersonalization of
character. The stage directions also call for strong contrasts in
lighting.

The final speech in this scene can also be delivered sepa-
rately as a monolog.

1. Do you believe this type of presentation would be effective in
   pointing out that the world forces people to be depersonal-
   ized? How does this make you feel about the central
   character?

2. Do you think it would be easier or more difficult to portray
   one of the characters in a scene like the one that follows than
   would be the case with a more realistic scene?

3. Would you enjoy seeing a play done is this manner? Why?

4. What do you think is the point of the rapid-fire, seemingly
   disconnected dialog?

5. Are you able to identify with any of the characters in this
   "episode"? Explain.

6. What themes or central ideas is the playwright trying to
   convey to the audience in this scene?

7. What is the significance of repeating "hot dog"?

8. In what manner do you think the dialog should be delivered
   in this scene to keep up the idea of mechanization or depersonalization?

9. What is the Young Woman's mental attitude during the final
   speech? What are her concerns?

1   **TO BUSINESS**
2
3   **SCENE:** An office: a switchboard, filing cabinet, adding
4   machine, typewriter, manifold machine.
5   **SOUNDS:**   Office machines: typewriters, adding machine,
6   manifold, telephone bells, buzzers.
7   **CHARACTERS AND THEIR MACHINES:** A YOUNG WOMAN
8   (typewriter), A STENOGRAPHER (typewriter), A FILING
9   CLERK, AN ADDING CLERK (adding machine), A TELE-
10   PHONE OPERATOR (switchboard), JONES.
11   **BEFORE THE CURTAIN:** Sounds of machines going. They
12   continue throughout the scene, and accompany the
13   YOUNG WOMAN's thoughts after the scene is blacked out.
14   **AT THE RISE OF THE CURTAIN:**   All the Machines are
15   disclosed, and all the characters with the exception of
16   the YOUNG WOMAN.
17   Of these characters, the YOUNG WOMAN, going any
18   day to any business. Ordinary. The confusion of her own
19   inner thoughts, emotions, desires, dreams cuts her off
20   from any actual adjustment to the routine of work. She
21   gets through this routine with a very small surface of her
22   consciousness. She is not homely and she is not pretty.
23   She is preoccupied with herself — with her person. She
24   has well-kept hands and a trick of constantly arranging
25   her hair over her ears.
26   The STENOGRAPHER is the faded, efficient woman
27   office worker. Drying, dried.
28   The ADDING CLERK is her male counterpart.
29   The FILING CLERK is a boy not grown. Callow adoles-
30   cence.
31   The TELEPHONE GIRL, young, cheap and amorous.
32
33   *(Lights come up on office scene. Two desks right and left.*
34   *Telephone booth back right center. Filing cabinet back of*
35   *center. Adding machine back left center.)*

1   **ADDING CLERK:** *(In the monotonous voice of his monotonous*
2   *thoughts; at his adding machine)* **2490, 28, 76, 123,**
3   **36842, 1¼, 37, 804, 23½, 982.**
4   **FILING CLERK:** *(In the same way — at his filing desk)*
5   **Accounts — A. Bonds — B. Contracts — C. Data — D.**
6   **Earnings — E.**
7   **STENOGRAPHER:** *(In the same way — left)* **Dear Sir — in re**
8   **— your letter — recent date — will state —**
9   **TELEPHONE GIRL:** Hello — Hello — George H. Jones
10   Company good morning — hello hello — George H.
11   Jones Company good morning — hello.
12   **FILING CLERK:** Market — M. Notes — N. Output — O.
13   Profits — P. —! *(Suddenly)* **What's the matter with Q?**
14   **TELEPHONE GIRL:** Matter with it — Mr. J., — Mr. K. wants
15   you — What you mean matter? Matter with what?
16   **FILING CLERK:** Matter with Q.
17   **TELEPHONE GIRL:** Well — what is? Spring 1726?
18   **FILING CLERK:** I'm asking yuh —
19   **TELEPHONE GIRL:** WELL?
20   **FILING CLERK:** Nothing filed with it —
21   **TELEPHONE GIRL:** Well?
22   **FILING CLERK:** Look at A. Look at B. What's the matter
23   with Q?
24   **TELEPHONE GIRL:** Ain't popular. Hello — Hello — George
25   H. Jones Company.
26   **FILING CLERK:** Hot dog! Why ain't it?
27   **ADDING CLERK:** Has it personality?
28   **STENOGRAPHER:** Has it halitosis?
29   **TELEPHONE GIRL:** Has it got it?
30   **FILING CLERK:** Hot dog!
31   **TELEPHONE GIRL:** What number do you want? *(Recognizing*
32   *but not pleased)* **Oh — hello — sure I know who it is —**
33   **tonight? Uh, uh —** *(Negative, but each with a different*
34   *inflection)* **— you heard me — No!**
35   **FILING CLERK:** Don't you like him?

1   STENOGRAPHER: She likes 'em all.

2   TELEPHONE GIRL: I do not!

3   STENOGRAPHER: Well — pretty near all.

4   TELEPHONE GIRL: What number do you want? Wrong

5   number. Hello — hello — George H. Jones Company.

6   Hello, hello —

7   STENOGRAPHER: Memorandum — attention Mr. Smith —

8   at a conference of —

9   ADDING CLERK: 125 — 83 — 22 — 908 — 34 — ¼ —

10   28593 —

11   FILING CLERK: Report — R. Sales — S. Trade — T.

12   TELEPHONE GIRL: Shh —! Yes, Mr. J. —? No — Miss A.

13   ain't in yet — I'll tell her, Mr. J. — just the minute

14   she gets in.

15   STENOGRAPHER: She's late again, huh?

16   TELEPHONE GIRL: Out with her sweetie last night, huh?

17   FILING CLERK: Hot dog.

18   ADDING CLERK: She ain't got a sweetie.

19   STENOGRAPHER: How do you know?

20   ADDING CLERK: I know.

21   FILING CLERK: Hot dog.

22   ADDING CLERK: She lives alone with her mother.

23   TELEPHONE GIRL: Spring 1876? Hello — Spring 1876.

24   Spring! Hello, Spring 1876? 1876! Wrong number!

25   Hello! Hello!

26   STENOGRAPHER: Director's meeting semiannual report

27   card.

28   FILING CLERK: Shipments — Sales — Schedules — S.

29   ADDING CLERK: She doesn't belong in an office.

30   TELEPHONE GIRL: Who does?

31   STENOGRAPHER: I do!

32   ADDING CLERK: You said it!

33   FILING CLERK: Hot dog!

34   TELEPHONE GIRL: Hello — hello — George H. Jones Com-

35   pany — hello — hello —

1   STENOGRAPHER: I'm efficient. She's inefficient.

2   FILING CLERK: She's inefficient.

3   TELEPHONE GIRL: She's got J. going.

4   STENOGRAPHER: Going?

5   TELEPHONE GIRL: Going and coming.

6   FILING CLERK: Hot dog.

7   *(Enter JONES.)*

8   JONES: Good morning, everybody.

9   TELEPHONE GIRL: Good morning.

10   FILING CLERK: Good morning.

11   ADDING CLERK: Good morning.

12   STENOGRAPHER: Good morning, Mr. J.

13   JONES: Miss A. isn't in yet?

14   TELEPHONE GIRL: Not yet, Mr. J.

15   FILING CLERK: Not yet.

16   ADDING CLERK: Not yet.

17   STENOGRAPHER: She's late.

18   JONES: I just wanted her to take a letter.

19   STENOGRAPHER: I'll take the letter.

20   JONES: One thing at a time and that done well.

21   ADDING CLERK: *(Yessing)* **Done well.**

22   STENOGRAPHER: I'll finish it later.

23   JONES: Hew to the line.

24   ADDING CLERK: Hew to the line.

25   STENOGRAPHER: Then I'll hurry.

26   JONES: Haste makes waste.

27   ADDING CLERK: Waste.

28   STENOGRAPHER: But if you're in a hurry.

29   JONES: I'm never in a hurry — That's how I get ahead!

30   *(Laughs. They all laugh.)* **First know you're right —**

31   then go ahead,

32   ADDING CLERK: Ahead.

33   JONES: *(To TELEPHONE GIRL)* **When Miss A. comes in tell**

34   her I want her to take a letter. *(Turns to go in — then)*

35   It's important.

1   TELEPHONE GIRL: *(Making a note)* **Miss A. — important.**

2   JONES: *(Starts up — then)* **And I don't want to be disturbed.**

3   TELEPHONE GIRL: **You're in conference?**

4   JONES: **I'm in conference.** *(Turns — then)* **Unless it's A.B. —**

5   **of course.**

6   TELEPHONE GIRL: **Of course — A.B.**

7   JONES: *(Starts — turns again; attempts to be facetious.)* **Tell**

8   **Miss A. the early bird catches the worm.**

9   *(Exit JONES.)*

10 TELEPHONE GIRL: **The early worm gets caught.**

11 ADDING CLERK: **He's caught.**

12 TELEPHONE GIRL: **Hooked.**

13 ADDING CLERK: **In the pan.**

14 FILING CLERK: **Hot dog.**

15 STENOGRAPHER: **We beg leave to announce —**

16   *(Enter YOUNG WOMAN. Goes behind telephone booth to*

17   *desk R.)*

18 STENOGRAPHER: **You're late!**

19 FILING CLERK: **You're late.**

20 ADDING CLERK: **You're late.**

21 STENOGRAPHER: **And yesterday!**

22 FILING CLERK: **The day before.**

23 ADDING CLERK: **And the day before.**

24 STENOGRAPHER: **You'll lose your job.**

25 YOUNG WOMAN: **No!**

26 STENOGRAPHER: **No?**

27   *(WORKERS exchange glances.)*

28 YOUNG WOMAN: **I can't!**

29 STENOGRAPHER: **Can't?**

30   *(Same business)*

31 FILING CLERK: **Rent — bills — installments — miscella-**

32   **neous.**

33 ADDING CLERK: **A dollar ten — ninety — five — 3.40 —**

34   **35 — 12, 60.**

35 STENOGRAPHER: **Then why are you late?**

1 YOUNG WOMAN: Why?

2 STENOGRAPHER: Excuse!

3 ADDING CLERK: Excuse!

4 FILING CLERK: Excuse!

5 TELEPHONE GIRL: Excuse it, please.

6 STENOGRAPHER: Why?

7 YOUNG WOMAN: The subway?

8 TELEPHONE GIRL: Long distance?

9 FILING CLERK: Old stuff!

10 ADDING CLERK: That stall!

11 STENOGRAPHER: Stalled?

12 YOUNG WOMAN: No —

13 STENOGRAPHER: What?

14 YOUNG WOMAN: I had to get out!

15 ADDING CLERK: Out!

16 FILING CLERK: Out?

17 STENOGRAPHER: Out where?

18 YOUNG WOMAN: In the air!

19 STENOGRAPHER: Air?

20 YOUNG WOMAN: All those bodies pressing.

21 FILING CLERK: Hot dog!

22 YOUNG WOMAN: I thought I would faint! I had to get out

23   in the air!

24 FILING CLERK: Give her the air.

25 ADDING CLERK: Free air —

26 STENOGRAPHER: Hot air.

27 YOUNG WOMAN: Like I'm dying.

28 STENOGRAPHER: Same thing yesterday. *(Pause)* And the

29   day before.

30 YOUNG WOMAN: Yes — what am I going to do?

31 ADDING CLERK: Take a taxi!

32   *(They laugh.)*

33 FILING CLERK: Call a cop!

34 TELEPHONE GIRL: Mr. J. wants you.

35 YOUNG WOMAN: Me?

1   TELEPHONE GIRL: You!

2   YOUNG WOMAN: *(Rises.)* **Mr. J.!**

3   STENOGRAPHER: Mr. J.

4   TELEPHONE GIRL: He's bellowing for you!

5   *(YOUNG WOMAN gives last pat to her hair — goes off into*

6   *door — back.)*

7   STENOGRAPHER: *(After her)* **Get it just right.**

8   FILING CLERK: She's always doing that to her hair.

9   TELEPHONE GIRL: It gives a line — it gives a line —

10   FILING CLERK: Hot dog.

11   ADDING CLERK: She's artistic.

12   STENOGRAPHER: She's inefficient.

13   FILING CLERK: She's inefficient.

14   STENOGRAPHER: Mr. J. knows she's inefficient.

15   ADDING CLERK: 46 — 23 — 84 — 2 — 2 — 2 — 1,492 —

16   678.

17   TELEPHONE GIRL: Hello — hello — George H. Jones Com-

18   pany — hello—Mr. Jones? He's in conference.

19   STENOGRAPHER: *(Sarcastic)* **Conference!**

20   ADDING CLERK: Conference.

21   FILING CLERK: Hot dog!

22   TELEPHONE GIRL: Do you think he'll marry her?

23   ADDING CLERK: If she'll have him.

24   STENOGRAPHER: If she'll have him!

25   FILING CLERK: Do you think she'll have him?

26   TELEPHONE GIRL: How much does he get?

27   ADDING CLERK: Plenty — 5,000 — 10,000 — 15,000 —

28   20,000 — 25,000.

29   STENOGRAPHER: And plenty put away.

30   ADDING CLERK: Gas Preferred — 4s — steel — 5s — oil —

31   6s.

32   FILING CLERK: Hot dog!

33   STENOGRAPHER: Will she have him? Will she have him?

34   This agreement entered into — party of the first part

35   — party of the second part — will he have her?

1 TELEPHONE GIRL: Well, I'd hate to get into bed with him.
2   *(Familiar melting voice)* **Hello — humhum — hum —**
3   **hum — hold the line a minute — will you — hum**
4   **hum.** *(Professional voice)* **Hell, hello — A.B., just a**
5   **minute, Mr. A.B. — Mr. J.? Mr. A.B. — go ahead, Mr.**
6   **A.B.** *(Melting voice)* **We were interrupted — huh — huh**
7   **— huh — huhuh — hum — hum.**
8   *(Enter.YOUNG WOMAN — she goes to her chair, sits with*
9   *folded hands.)*
10 FILING CLERK: That's all you ever say to a guy —
11 STENOGRAPHER: Hum — hum — or uh huh — *(Negative)*
12 TELEPHONE GIRL: That's all you have to. *(To phone)* **Hum**
13   **—hum — hum hum — hum hum —**
14 STENOGRAPHER: Mostly hum hum.
15 ADDING CLERK: You've said it!
16 FILING CLERK: Hot dog.
17 TELEPHONE GIRL: **Hum hum huh hum humhumhum —**
18   **tonight?** She's got a date — she told me last night —
19   **humhumhuh — hum — all right.** *(Disconnects.)* Too
20   bad my boy friend's got a friend — but my girl
21   friend's got a date.
22 YOUNG WOMAN: You have a good time.
23 TELEPHONE GIRL: Big time.
24 STENOGRAPHER: Small time.
25 ADDING CLERK: A big time on the small time.
26 TELEPHONE GIRL: I'd ask you, kid, but you'd be up to
27   your neck!
28 STENOGRAPHER: Neckers!
29 ADDING CLERK: Petters!
30 FILING CLERK: Sweet papas.
31 TELEPHONE GIRL: Want to come?
32 YOUNG WOMAN: Can't.
33 TELEPHONE GIRL: Date?
34 YOUNG WOMAN: My mother.
35 STENOGRAPHER: Worries?

1   TELEPHONE GIRL: Nags — hello — George H. Jones

2   Company —Oh hello —

3   *(YOUNG WOMAN sits before her machine — hands in lap,*

4   *looking at them.)*

5   STENOGRAPHER: Why don't you get to work?

6   YOUNG WOMAN: *(Dreaming)* What?

7   ADDING CLERK: Work!

8   YOUNG WOMAN: Can't.

9   STENOGRAPHER: Can't?

10   YOUNG WOMAN: My machine's out of order.

11   STENOGRAPHER: Well, fix it!

12   YOUNG WOMAN: I can't — got to get somebody.

13   STENOGRAPHER: Somebody! Somebody! Always some-

14   body! Here, sort the mail, then!

15   YOUNG WOMAN: *(Rises).* All right.

16   STENOGRAPHER: And hurry! You're late.

17   YOUNG WOMAN: *(Sorting letters)* George H. Jones &

18   Company — George H. Jones Inc. George H. Jones —

19   STENOGRAPHER: You're always late.

20   ADDING CLERK: You'll lose your job.

21   YOUNG WOMAN: *(Hurrying)* George Jones — George H.

22   Jones Personal —

23   TELEPHONE GIRL: Don't let 'em get your goat, kid — tell

24   'em where to get off.

25   YOUNG WOMAN: What?

26   TELEPHONE GIRL: Ain't it all set?

27   YOUNG WOMAN: What?

28   TELEPHONE GIRL: You and Mr. J.

29   STENOGRAPHER: You and the boss.

30   FILING CLERK: You and the big chief.

31   ADDING CLERK: You and the big cheese.

32   YOUNG WOMAN: Did he tell you?

33   TELEPHONE GIRL: I told you!

34   ADDING CLERK: I told you!

35   STENOGRAPHER: I don't believe it.

1   ADDING CLERK: 5,000 — 10,000 — 15,000.

2   FILING CLERK: Hot dog.

3   YOUNG WOMAN: No — it isn't so.

4   STENOGRAPHER: Isn't it?

5   YOUNG WOMAN: No.

6   TELEPHONE GIRL: Not yet.

7   ADDING CLERK: But soon.

8   FILING CLERK: Hot dog.

9   *(Enter JONES.)*

10   TELEPHONE GIRL: *(Busy)* **George H. Jones Company —**

11   **Hello — Hello.**

12   STENOGRAPHER: Awaiting your answer —

13   ADDING CLERK: 5,000 — 10,000 — 15,000 —

14   JONES: *(Crossing to YOUNG WOMAN — Puts hand on her*

15   *shoulder, all stop and stare)* **That letter done?**

16   YOUNG WOMAN: No. *(She pulls away.)*

17   JONES: What's the matter?

18   STENOGRAPHER: She hasn't started.

19   JONES: O.K. — want to make some changes.

20   YOUNG WOMAN: My machine's out of order.

21   JONES: O.K. — use the one in my room —

22   YOUNG WOMAN: I'm sorting the mail.

23   STENOGRAPHER: *(Sarcastic)* **One thing at a time!**

24   JONES: *(Retreating — goes back C.)* **O.K.** *(To YOUNG WOMAN)*

25   **When you're finished.** *(Starts back to his room.)*

26   STENOGRAPHER: Haste makes waste.

27   JONES: *(At door)* **O.K. — don't hurry.** *(Exits.)*

28   STENOGRAPHER: Hew to the line!

29   TELEPHONE GIRL: He's hewing.

30   FILING CLERK: Hot dog.

31   TELEPHONE GIRL: Why did you flinch, kid?

32   YOUNG WOMAN: Flinch?

33   TELEPHONE GIRL: Did he pinch?

34   YOUNG WOMAN: No!

35   TELEPHONE GIRL: Then what?

1   YOUNG WOMAN: Nothing! Just his hand.

2   TELEPHONE GIRL: Oh — just his hand — *(Shakes her head*

3   *thoughtfully.)* **Uhhuh.** *(Negative)* **Uhhuh.** *(Decisively.)* **No!**

4   **Tell him no.**

5   STENOGRAPHER: If she does she'll lose her job.

6   ADDING CLERK: Fired.

7   FILING CLERK: The sack!

8   TELEPHONE GIRL: *(On the defensive)* **And if she doesn't?**

9   ADDING CLERK: She'll come to work in a taxi!

10   TELEPHONE GIRL: Work?

11   FILING CLERK: No work.

12   STENOGRAPHER: No worry.

13   ADDING CLERK: Breakfast in bed.

14   STENOGRAPHER: *(Sarcastic)* **Did Madame ring?**

15   FILING CLERK: Lunch in bed!

16   TELEPHONE GIRL: A double bed! *(In phone)* **Yes, Mr. J.** *(To*

17   *YOUNG WOMAN)* **J. wants you.**

18   YOUNG WOMAN: *(Starts to get to her feet — but doesn't.)* **I**

19   **can't — I'm not ready — In a minute.** *(Sits staring*

20   *ahead of her.)*

21   ADDING CLERK: 5,000 — 10,000 — 15,000 —

22   FILING CLERK: Profits — plans — purchase —

23   STENOGRAPHER: Call your attention our prices are fixed.

24   TELEPHONE GIRL: Hello — hello — George. H. Jones

25   Company — hello — hello —

26   YOUNG WOMAN: *(Thinking her thoughts aloud — to the*

27   *subdued accompaniment of the office sounds and voices)*

28   **Marry me — wants to marry me — George H. Jones —**

29   **George H. Jones and Company — Mrs. George H.**

30   **Jones — Mrs. George H. Jones. Dear Madame —**

31   **marry — do you take this man to be your wedded**

32   **husband — I do — to love honor and to love — kisses**

33   **— no — I can't — George H. Jones — How would you**

34   **like to marry me — What do you say — Why Mr.**

35   **Jones I — let me look at your little hands — you have**

1 such pretty little hands — let me hold your pretty
2 little hands — George H. Jones — Fat hands — flabby
3 hands — don't touch me — please — fat hands are
4 never weary — please don't — married — all girls —
5 most girls — married — babies — a baby — curls —
6 little curls all over its head — George H. Jones —
7 straight — thin — bald — don't touch me — please —
8 no — can't — must — somebody — something — no
9 rest — must rest — no rest — must rest — no rest —
10 late today — yesterday — before — late — subway —
11 air — pressing — bodies pressing — bodies — trem-
12 bling — air — stop — air — late — job — no job —
13 fired — late — alarm clock — alarm clock — alarm
14 clock — hurry — job — ma — nag — nag — nag — ma
15 — hurry — job — no job — no money — installments
16 due — no money — money — George H. Jones —
17 money — Mrs. George H. Jones — money — no work
18 — no worry — free! — rest — sleep till nine — sleep
19 till ten — sleep till noon — now you take a good rest
20 this morning — don't get up till you want to — thank
21 you — oh thank you — oh don't! — please don't
22 touch me — I want to rest — no rest — earn — got to
23 earn — married — earn — no — yes — earn — all
24 girls — most girls — ma — pa — ma — all women —
25 most women — I can't — must — maybe — must —
26 somebody — something — ma — pa — ma — can I,
27 ma? Tell me, ma — something — somebody.

(BLACK OUT)

28
29
30
31
32
33
34
35

SCENE 2: Two Females (Plus Offstage Voices)

Young Woman, no age given

Mother, no age given

In presenting this scene, you can either include the offstage voices or not.

As you can tell, this is a continuation of the Young Woman's story. Both of the first two episodes are complete, as Treadwell wrote them. In this scene the Young Woman is at home with her Mother, but still she cannot feel a real connection to life.

1. Why do you suppose the Mother isn't really listening to the fact that the Young Woman wants to talk to her about something she considers important? Why does the Mother keep going on about the potato and then about the garbage? What does this symbolize? Explain.

2. Why do you think it is so important for the Young Woman to talk to her Mother?

3. The Young Woman says someone wants to marry her and that he fell in love with her hands. What could the Mother mean when she says, "In love! Is that beginning again?"

4. What is the point of including all the off-stage voices?

5. Why does the Mother imply that love isn't important so much as security? Do you think this is a typical attitude? Explain.

6. The dialog between the Young Woman and the Mother becomes less staccato beginning with the line, "He's a decent man, isn't he?" What reason could Treadwell have had for writing it that way?

7. Why do you suppose the Young Woman is so unsure of herself?

8. The Young Woman says there's "something all tight inside" that is stifling her and can't go on much longer. What is making her feel this way? Why do you think she says she'll kill her Mother? How does this make you feel about her?

9. Later on, the Young Woman murders her husband. She does not leave fingerprints because she's wearing rubber gloves. Probably Treadwell mentioned the gloves, the feelings of being stifled, and the feelings of wanting to murder her mother to plant the seeds for the murder. Do you think this is done effectively? Why?

1   **SCENE TWO: Two Women**

2   **AT HOME**

3

4   **SCENE:** A kitchen: table, chairs, plates and food, garbage can,

5   a pair of rubber gloves. The door at the back now opens

6   on a hall — the window, on an apartment house court.

7   **SOUNDS:** Buzzer, radio (Voice of announcer, music and

8   singer).

9   **CHARACTERS:** YOUNG WOMAN, MOTHER

10   **OUTSIDE VOICES:** *(Characters heard but not seen:)* A

11   JANITOR, a BABY, a MOTHER and a SMALL BOY, a

12   YOUNG BOY and YOUNG GIRL, a HUSBAND and a

13   WIFE, another HUSBAND and a WIFE.

14   **AT RISE:** YOUNG WOMAN and MOTHER eating — radio off

15   stage — radio stops.

16

17   **YOUNG WOMAN: Ma — I want to talk to you.**

18   **MOTHER: Aren't you eating a potato?**

19   **YOUNG WOMAN: No.**

20   **MOTHER: Why not?**

21   **YOUNG WOMAN: I don't want one.**

22   **MOTHER: That's no reason. Here! Take one.**

23   **YOUNG WOMAN: I don't want it.**

24   **MOTHER: Potatoes go with stew — here!**

25   **YOUNG WOMAN: Ma, I don't want it!**

26   **MOTHER: Want it! Take it!**

27   **YOUNG WOMAN: But I — oh, all right.** *(Takes it — then)* **Ma,**

28   **I want to ask you something.**

29   **MOTHER: Eat your potato.**

30   **YOUNG WOMAN:** *(Takes a bite — then)* **Ma, there's some-**

31   **thing I want to ask you — something important.**

32   **MOTHER: Is it mealy?**

33   **YOUNG WOMAN: S'all right. Ma — tell me.**

34   **MOTHER: Three pounds for a quarter.**

35   **YOUNG WOMAN: Ma — tell me —** *(Buzzer)*

1   **MOTHER:** *(Her dull voice brightening)* **There's the garbage.**
2   *(Goes to door — or dumbwaiter — opens it.)*
3   *(Stop radio.)*
4   **JANITOR'S VOICE:** *(Offstage)* **Garbage.**
5   **MOTHER:** *(Pleased — busy)* **All right.** *(Gets garbage can —*
6   *puts it out. YOUNG WOMAN walks up and down.)* **What's**
7   **the matter now?**
8   YOUNG WOMAN: Nothing.
9   MOTHER: That jumping up from the table every night the
10   garbage is collected! You act like you're crazy.
11   YOUNG WOMAN: Ma, do all women —
12   MOTHER: I suppose you think you're too nice for anything
13   so common! Well, let me tell you, my lady, that it's a
14   very important part of life.
15   YOUNG WOMAN: I know, but, Ma, if you —
16   MOTHER: If it weren't for garbage cans where would we
17   be? Where would we all be? Living in filth — that's
18   what! Filth! I should think you'd be glad! I should
19   think you'd be grateful!
20   YOUNG WOMAN: Oh, Ma!
21   MOTHER: Well, are you?
22   YOUNG WOMAN: Am I what?
23   MOTHER: Glad! Grateful.
24   YOUNG WOMAN: Yes!
25   MOTHER: You don't act like it!
26   YOUNG WOMAN: Oh, Ma, don't talk!
27   MOTHER: You just said you wanted to talk.
28   YOUNG WOMAN: Well now — I want to think. I got to
29   think.
30   MOTHER: Aren't you going to finish your potato?
31   YOUNG WOMAN: Oh, Ma!
32   MOTHER: Is there anything the matter with it?
33   YOUNG WOMAN: No —
34   MOTHER: Then why don't you finish it?
35   YOUNG WOMAN: Because I don't want it.

1   **MOTHER: Why don't you?**

2   **YOUNG WOMAN: Oh, Ma! Let me alone!**

3   **MOTHER: Well, you've got to eat! If you don't eat —**

4   **YOUNG WOMAN: Ma! Don't nag!**

5   **MOTHER: Nag! Just because I try to look out for you —**

6   **nag! Just because I try to care for you — nag! Why,**

7   **you haven't sense enough to eat! What would become**

8   **of you I'd like to know — if I didn't nag!**

9   *(Offstage — a sound of window opening — all these*

10   *offstage sounds come in through the court window at the*

11   *back.)*

12   **WOMAN'S VOICE: Johnny — Johnny — come in now!**

13   **A SMALL BOY'S VOICE: Oh, Ma!**

14   **WOMAN'S VOICE: It's getting cold.**

15   **A SMALL BOY'S VOICE: Oh, Ma!**

16   **WOMAN'S VOICE: You heard me!** *(Sound of window slamming)*

17   **YOUNG WOMAN: I'm grown up, Ma.**

18   **MOTHER: Grown up! What do you mean by that?**

19   **YOUNG WOMAN: Nothing much — I guess.** *(Offstage sound*

20   *of baby crying. MOTHER rises, clatters dishes.)* **Let's not**

21   **do dishes right away, Ma. Let's talk — I gotta.**

22   **MOTHER: Well, I can't talk with dirty dishes around — you**

23   **may be able to but —** *(Clattering — clattering)*

24   **YOUNG WOMAN: Ma! Listen! Listen! There's a man wants**

25   **to marry me.**

26   **MOTHER:** *(Stops clattering — sits)* **What man?**

27   **YOUNG WOMAN: He says he fell in love with my hands.**

28   **MOTHER: In love! Is that beginning again?! I thought you**

29   **were over that!** *(Offstage BOY's VOICE — whistles —*

30   *GIRL's VOICE answers.)*

31   **BOY'S VOICE: Come on out.**

32   **GIRL'S VOICE: Can't.**

33   **BOY'S VOICE: Nobody'll see you.**

34   **GIRL'S VOICE: I can't.**

35   **BOY'S VOICE: It's dark now — come on.**

1   GIRL'S VOICE: Well — just for a minute.

2   BOY'S VOICE: Meet you 'round the corner.

3   YOUNG WOMAN: I got to get married, Ma.

4   MOTHER: What do you mean?

5   YOUNG WOMAN: I gotta.

6   MOTHER: You haven't got in trouble, have you?

7   YOUNG WOMAN: Don't talk like that!

8   MOTHER: Well, you say you got to get married — what do
9   you mean?

10 YOUNG WOMAN: Nothing.

11 MOTHER: Answer me!

12 YOUNG WOMAN: All women get married, don't they?

13 MOTHER: Nonsense!

14 MAN: You got married, didn't you?

15 MOTHER: Yes, I did!

16   *(Offstage voices)*

17 WOMAN'S VOICE: Where you going?

18 MAN'S VOICE: Out.

19 WOMAN'S VOICE: You were out last night.

20 MAN'S VOICE: Was I?

21 WOMAN'S VOICE: You're always going out.

22 MAN'S VOICE: Am I?

23 WOMAN'S VOICE: Where you going?

24 MAN'S VOICE: Out.

25   *(End of offstage voices)*

26 MOTHER: Who is he? Where did you come to know him?

27 YOUNG WOMAN: In the office.

28 MOTHER: In the office!

29 YOUNG WOMAN: It's Mr. J.

30 MOTHER: Mr. J.?

31 YOUNG WOMAN: The Vice President.

32 MOTHER: Vice President! His income must be — Does he
33   know you've got a mother to support?

34 YOUNG WOMAN: Yes.

35 MOTHER: What does he say?

1   YOUNG WOMAN: All right.

2   MOTHER: How soon you going to marry him?

3   YOUNG WOMAN: I'm not going to.

4   MOTHER: Not going to!

5   YOUNG WOMAN: No! I'm not going to.

6   MOTHER: But you just said —

7   YOUNG WOMAN: I'm not going to.

8   MOTHER: Are you crazy?

9   YOUNG WOMAN: I can't, Ma! I can't!

10   MOTHER: Why can't you?

11   YOUNG WOMAN: I don't love him.

12   MOTHER: Love! — What does that amount to! Will it

13   clothe you? Will it feed you? Will it pay the bills?

14   YOUNG WOMAN: No! But it's real just the same!

15   MOTHER: Real!

16   YOUNG WOMAN: If it isn't — what can you count on in life?

17   MOTHER: I'll tell you what you can count on! You can

18   count that you've got to eat and sleep and get up and

19   put clothes on your back and take 'em off again —

20   that you got to get old — and that you got to die.

21   That's what you can count on! All the rest is in

22   your head!

23   YOUNG WOMAN: But Ma — didn't you love Pa?

24   MOTHER: I suppose I did — I don't know — I've forgotten

25   — what difference does it make — now?

26   YOUNG WOMAN: But then! — Oh Ma, tell me!

27   MOTHER: Tell you what?

28   YOUNG WOMAN: About all that — love!

29   *(Offstage voices)*

30   WIFE'S VOICE: Don't.

31   HUSBAND'S VOICE: What's the matter — don't you want

32   me to kiss you?

33   WIFE'S VOICE: Not like that.

34   HUSBAND'S VOICE: Like what?

35   WIFE'S VOICE: That silly kiss!

1 **HUSBAND'S VOICE:** Silly kiss?

2 **WIFE'S VOICE:** You look so silly — oh I know what's

3   coming when you look like that — and kiss me like

4   that — don't — go away —

5   *(End of offstage voices)*

6 **MOTHER:** He's a decent man, isn't he?

7 **YOUNG WOMAN:** I don't know. How should I know — yet.

8 **MOTHER:** He's a Vice President — of course he's decent.

9 **YOUNG WOMAN:** I don't care whether he's decent or not. I

10   won't marry him.

11 **MOTHER:** But you just said you wanted to marry —

12 **YOUNG WOMAN:** Not him.

13 **MOTHER:** Who?

14 **YOUNG WOMAN:** I don't know — I don't know — I haven't

15   found him yet!

16 **MOTHER:** You talk like you're crazy!

17 **YOUNG WOMAN:** Oh, Ma — tell me!

18 **MOTHER:** Tell you what?

19 **YOUNG WOMAN:** Tell me— *(Words suddenly pouring out)*

20   Your skin oughtn't to curl — ought it — when he just

21   comes near you — ought it? That's wrong, ain't it?

22   You don't get over that, do you — ever, do you or do

23   you? How is it, Ma — do you?

24 **MOTHER:** Do you what?

25 **YOUNG WOMAN:** Do you get used to it — so after a while

26   it doesn't matter? Or don't you? Does it always

27   matter? You ought to be in love, oughtn't you, Ma?

28   You must be in love, mustn't you, Ma? That changes

29   everything, doesn't it — or does it? Maybe if you just

30   like a person it's all right — is it? When he puts a

31   hand on me, my blood turns cold. But your blood

32   oughtn't to run cold, ought it? His hands are — his

33   hands are — fat, Ma — don't you see — his hands are

34   fat — and they sort of press — and they're fat —

35   don't you see? — Don't you see?

143

1   **MOTHER:** *(Stares at her bewildered.)* **See what?**
2   **YOUNG WOMAN:** *(Rushing on)* **I've always thought I'd find**
3   **somebody — somebody young — and — and attrac-**
4   **tive — with wavy hair — wavy hair — I always think**
5   **of children with curls — little curls all over their**
6   **head — somebody young — and attractive that I'd**
7   **like — that I'd love — But I haven't found anybody**
8   **like that yet — I haven't found anybody — I've**
9   **hardly known anybody — you'd never let me go with**
10   **anybody and —**
11 **MOTHER: Are you throwing it up to me that —**
12 **YOUNG WOMAN: No — let me finish, Ma! No — let me**
13   **finish! I just mean I've never found anybody—**
14   **anybody — nobody's ever asked me — till now — he's**
15   **the only man that's ever asked me — and I suppose I**
16   **got to marry somebody — all girls do.**
17 **MOTHER: Nonsense.**
18 **YOUNG WOMAN: But, I can't go on like this, Ma — I don't**
19   **know why — but I can't — it's like I'm all tight inside**
20   **— sometimes I feel like I'm stifling! — You don't**
21   **know — stifling.** *(Walks up and down.)* **I can't go on**
22   **like this much longer — going to work — coming**
23   **home — going to work — coming home — I can't —**
24   **Sometimes in the subway I think I'm going to die —**
25   **sometimes even in the office if something don't**
26   **happen — I got to do something — don't know — it's**
27   **like I'm all tight inside.**
28 **MOTHER: You're crazy.**
29 **YOUNG WOMAN: Oh, Ma!**
30 **MOTHER: You're crazy!**
31 **YOUNG WOMAN: Ma — if you tell me that again I'll kill**
32   **you! I'll kill you!**
33 **MOTHER: If that isn't crazy!**
34 **YOUNG WOMAN: I'll kill you — Maybe I am crazy — I don't**
35   **know. Sometimes I think I am — the thoughts that**

go on in my mind — sometimes I think I am — I can't help it if I am — I do the best I can—I do the best I can and I'm nearly crazy! *(MOTHER rises and sits.)* **Go away! Go away! You don't know anything about anything! And you haven't got any pity — no pity — you just take it for granted that I go to work every day — and come home every night and bring my money every week — you just take it for granted — you'd let me go on forever — and never feel any pity —**

(Offstage radio — a voice singing a sentimental mother song or popular home song. MOTHER begins to cry — crosses to chair left — sits.)

YOUNG WOMAN: **Oh Ma — forgive me! Forgive me!**

MOTHER: **My own child! To be spoken to like that by my own child!**

YOUNG WOMAN: **I didn't mean it, Ma — I didn't mean it!**

(She goes to her mother — crosses to left.)

MOTHER: *(Clinging to her hand)* **You're all I've got in the world — and you don't want me — you want to kill me.**

YOUNG WOMAN: **No — no, I don't, Ma! I just said that!**

MOTHER: **I've worked for you and slaved for you!**

YOUNG WOMAN: **I know, Ma.**

MOTHER: **I brought you into the world.**

YOUNG WOMAN: **I know, Ma.**

MOTHER: **You're flesh of my flesh and —**

YOUNG WOMAN: **I know, Ma, I know.**

MOTHER: **And —**

YOUNG WOMAN: **You rest, now, Ma — you rest —**

MOTHER: *(Struggling)* **I got to do the dishes.**

YOUNG WOMAN: **I'll do the dishes — You listen to the music, Ma — I'll do the dishes.** *(MA sits.)*

(YOUNG WOMAN crosses to behind screen. Takes a pair of rubber gloves and begins to put them on. The MOTHER sees them — they irritate her — there is a return of her characteristic mood.)

1   MOTHER: Those gloves! I've been washing dishes for forty
2   years and I never wore gloves! But my lady's hands!
3   My lady's hands!
4   YOUNG WOMAN: Sometimes you talk to me like you're
5   jealous, Ma.
6   MOTHER: Jealous?
7   YOUNG WOMAN: It's my hands got me a husband.
8   MOTHER: A husband? So you're going to marry him now!
9   YOUNG WOMAN: I suppose so.
10   MOTHER: If you ain't the craziest —
11   *(The scene blacks out. In the darkness, the mother song*
12   *goes into jazz — very faint — as the scene lights into*
13   *[Episode Three.])*
14
15
16
17
18
19
20
21
22
23
24
25
26
27
28
29
30
31
32
33
34
35

SCENE 3: Male Monolog

Husband, no age given

"Episode Three" of the play takes place at the hotel where the Young Woman and her Husband (Mr. Jones, though he is no longer called by that name) go for their honeymoon. No ages are ever given for any of the characters.

"Episode Four" takes place in a hospital where the Young Woman has just had a baby girl. As the scene begins, a nurse is talking to the Young Woman about the baby. The Young Woman indicates that she did not want a child. There is the sound of a riveting machine, which the nurse explains can't be helped because a new wing is being constructed. The Husband enters carrying a large bouquet of flowers. This is what he says then.

1. What is the Husband's attitude to the Young Woman? Explain.

2. Obviously the Husband is being patronizing. Why?

3. Do you think it's logical that he compares his "pulling himself up by the bootstraps" to her situation? Explain.

1   HUSBAND: Better put 'em in water right away. *(Exit*
2   *NURSE.)* **Everything O.K.?** *(YOUNG WOMAN signs "No.")*
3   **Now see here, my dear, you've got to brace up, you**
4   **know! And — and face things! Everybody's got to**
5   **brace up and face things! That's what makes the**
6   **world go round. I know all you've been through but —**
7   *(YOUNG WOMAN signs "No.")* **Oh, yes I do! I know all**
8   **about it! I was right outside all the time!** *(YOUNG*
9   *WOMAN makes violent gesture of "No." Ignoring)* **Oh yes!**
10   **But you've got to brace up now! Make an effort! Pull**
11   **yourself together! Start the uphill climb! Oh I've been**
12   **down — but I haven't stayed down. I've been licked**
13   **but I haven't stayed licked! I've pulled myself up by**
14   **my own bootstraps, and that's what you've got to do!**
15   **Will power! That's what conquers! Look at me! Now**
16   **you've got to brace up! Face the music! Stand the**
17   **gaff! Take life by the horns! Look it in the face! —**
18   **Having a baby's natural! Perfectly natural thing —**
19   **why should** *(YOUNG WOMAN chokes — points wildly to*
20   *door. Enter NURSE with flowers in a vase.)*
21
22
23
24
25
26
27
28
29
30
31
32
33
34
35

SCENE 4: Female Monolog

Young Woman, no age given

After the Husband leaves, a doctor and nurse come in. The Young Woman refuses to nurse her baby. The doctor tells the nurse to bring the baby, but the Young Woman is adamant about not seeing her. The doctor insists, despite the fact that the woman has been gagging. The doctor orders her diet changed from liquids to solids, although the Young Woman has said she can't swallow. When the doctor and nurse leave, this is what the woman says.

1. What do you think the Young Woman means in saying she's submitted to enough?

2. The Young Woman's speech (like the monolog in the second episode) is really stream-of-consciousness, that is, saying anything that comes into her head. What is the main message here? What is the Young Woman saying about her life? Why in particular does she keep saying "it doesn't matter"?

3. Do you think she is losing her mind or that she's just upset? Explain, basing your answer in what you know about her to this point.

1   YOUNG WOMAN: *(Alone)* Let me alone — let me alone — let
2   me alone — I've submitted to enough — I won't
3   submit to any more — crawl off — crawl off in the
4   dark — Vixen crawled under the bed — way back in
5   the corner under the bed — they were all drowned —
6   puppies don't go to heaven — heaven — golden stairs
7   — long   stairs — long — too   long — long   golden
8   stairs — climb those golden stairs — stairs — stairs
9   — climb — tired — too tired — dead — no matter —
10   nothing matters — dead — stairs — long stairs — all
11   the dead going up — going up to be in heaven —
12   heaven — golden stairs — all the children coming
13   down — coming to be born — dead going up — chil-
14   dren coming down — going up — coming down —
15   going up — coming down — going up — coming down
16   — going up — stop — stop — no — no traffic cop —
17   no — no traffic cop in heaven — traffic cop — traffic
18   cop — can't you give us a smile — tired — too tired
19   — no matter — it doesn't matter — St. Peter — St.
20   Peter at the gate — you can't come in — no matter —
21   it doesn't matter — I'll rest — I'll lie down — down —
22   all written down — down in a big book — no matter
23   — it doesn't matter — I'll lie down — it weighs me —
24   it's over me — it weighs — weighs — it's heavy — it's
25   a heavy book — no matter — lie still — don't move —
26   can't move — rest — forget — they say you forget —
27   a girl — aren't you glad it's a girl — a little girl —
28   with no hair — none — little curls all over his head —
29   a little bald girl — curls — curls all over his head —
30   what kind of hair has God? No matter — it doesn't
31   matter — everybody loves God — they've got to —
32   got to — got to love God — God is love — even if he's
33   bad they got to love him — even if he's got fat hands
34   — fat hands — no no — he wouldn't be God — his
35   hands make you well — he lays on his hands — well

— and happy — no matter — doesn't matter — far —
too far — tired — too tired — too tired Vixen crawled
off under bed — eight — there were eight — a woman
crawled off under the bed — a woman has one — two
three four — one two three four — one two three four
— two plus two is four — two times two is four — two
times four is eight Vixen had eight — one two three
four five six seven eight — eight — Puffie had eight
— all drowned — drowned — drowned in blood —
blood — oh God! God — God never had one — Mary
had one — in a manger — the lowly manger — God's
on a high throne — far — too far — no matter — It
doesn't matter — God Mary Mary God Mary — Virgin
Mary — Mary had one — the Holy Ghost — the Holy
Ghost — George H. Jones — oh don't — please don't!
Let me rest — now I can rest — the weight is gone —
inside the weight is gone — it's only outside —
outside — all around — weight — I'm under it —
Vixen crawled under the bed — there were eight —
I'll not submit any more — I'll not submit — I'll not
submit — *(The scene BLACKS OUT.)*

In "Episode Five" the Young Woman meets a man at a restaurant. He talks to her about how he killed someone in Mexico by hitting him over the head with a bottle filled with pebbles. In "Episode Six" she has an affair with this same man. She feels an emotional involvement, but he treats her just as a passing fancy. When she leaves, she asks if she can take a flower he's bought himself. He gives it to her.

"Episode Seven," entitled "Domestic," shows the Young Woman and her Husband at home. He's talking about buying some property; she is not interested and answers him only by rote. The scene ends (probably in her memory and imagination only) with the man she'd met talking about bandits in Mexico and how he filled an empty bottle with stones and killed one of them.

In "Episode Eight" the Young Woman is on trial for killing her husband by hitting him over the head with a bottle filled with pebbles from the flower pot given to her by the other man. In the final episode she is being taken to the electric chair to be executed.

A Man's World

by Rachel Carothers

The most successful woman playwright in America during the early part of this century, Rachel Carothers wrote dozens of plays. An actress and one of the few early women directors, she often both directed and designed her own plays.

In many of her plays Carothers dealt with the problems faced by women. This certainly is true of *A Man's World,* produced in 1909. It dealt with something which, at the time, was very daring. The main character, a woman named Frank Ware, is a successful novelist and a good adoptive mother.

Nearly all her friends are in the arts — writers, musicians, artists. Yet many of them think that for her novels to be so successful they have to have been, at the very least, suggested to her by men. In fact, critics thought her first novel (because of her name) was written by a man.

But more than that, people react to Kiddie, her adopted son, by saying that he must be hers. After all she lived in Paris for a time. When she returned home, it was with the boy.

All of her friends, except one to whom she's told the truth, think that she and Malcolm Gaskell are the boy's parents. (Actually, Frank took in and helped a pregnant woman who died in childbirth.) Malcolm is the man who wants to marry her, and as the play progresses, we discover that she is in love with him. Clara, one of Frank's friends, is a painter of miniature portraits. She says that it's plain that the boy resembles Gaskell.

Frank believes that her friends are gossiping because they think the boy looks like her. When she discovers what they really are saying, she says: "Oh, it can't be. It can't be! Look again." Let it be "any man — any man in the world but Gaskell."

She goes on to say that she's hated the boy's father "all these years...Every time I see a girl who's made a mess of her life because she's loved a man, I think of Kiddie's poor little mother, with the whole burden and disgrace of it — and the man scot-free."

The rest of that same speech is the gist of the whole play: "I tell you it's horrible — the whole thing — the relation between men and women. Women give too much. It's made me afraid to love any man." Her friend Lione points this up by saying: "[Men] take all they can get and don't give any more than they have to. It's a man's world — that's the size of it. What's the use of knocking your head against things you can't change?...Men are men."

Frank replies, "If women decided that men should be equally disgraced for the same sin, they would be."

In other words the play deals with something that's been discussed for years, the double standard. What is okay for a man is taboo for a women.

When Frank talks to Malcolm about Kiddie, he says: "I never thought before that you actually believed things ought to be — the same — for men and women...I see that you believe it so deeply that you think it's a thing to go by — live by." He says he couldn't love a woman who'd been an unwed mother. A woman should be pure.

Malcolm says that people shouldn't continue to think Frank's the mother. She should therefore say who he was and then send the boy away to a boarding school.

Frank asks him if he had known the woman who was the boy's mother; he admits that he is the father, and he does not regret it.

A sub-plot deals with Clara, who lacking in strength, cannot get along financially because she is not trained for anything, not talented enough to succeed as an artist, and not attractive enough to gain a husband.

SCENE 1: Three Males

Fritz, probably 20s

Wells, probably 20s

Emile, probably 20s

There are no ages given for the three men, although they are all fairly young. All are friends of Frank and have gathered in her apartment before she's arrived home. Despite their being her friends, they certainly are male chauvinists.

This scene occurs just a few pages into the play. Kiddie is present, although the dots across the page in the scene indicate anything he says or that is said to him that has been cut.

1. Even though the newspaper's review of Frank is a positive one, it still is sexist. Can you point out the sexist remarks? Why do you think attitudes like this were very prevalent at the time the play was written and are apparent even today?

2. Why do you suppose — even after being friends with Frank — that Wells and Emile feel that she couldn't have written the book on her own?

3. Why does Emile say Frank first of all couldn't write like a man, and second that "no man could write like zat unless she love him?"

4. Do you think there's any validity in Fritz's saying that Frank's a good woman and the others are "too bad in your mind to know wat dot means?"

5. Why do you suppose the three men are talking about Frank so much? Is it any of their business what she does?

6. What do you think Fritz's stand is on the issues the others have brought up about Frank? Which of these three do you like the most? The least? Why?

1   **WELLS: Let me have that paper...Did you see a criticism of**
2   **Frank's book this morning?**
3   **EMILE: Non — I had not ze time. I haf painted all day like**
4   **mad. I have had ze most wonderful —**
5   **WELLS: Here you are.** *(Finding the article)* ***The Beaten Path***
6   **is the strongest thing that Frank Ware has ever done.**
7   **Her first work attracted wide attention when we**
8   **thought Frank Ware was a man, but now that we**
9   **know she is a woman we are more than ever**
10   **impressed by the strength and scope of her work. She**
11   **has laid her scenes this time on the East Side in the**
12   **wretched poverty of the tenement houses, and the**
13   **marvel is that any woman could see and know so**
14   **much and depict crime and degradation so boldly.**
15   **Her great cry is for women — to make them better by**
16   **making them freer. It is decidedly the most striking**
17   **book of the year.** *(KIDDIE with a heavy sigh goes back to*
18   *the window.)* **Bully good criticism.**
19   **FRITZ: It's a bully good book.**
20   **WELLS: You bet it is. Where does she get her stuff, anyway?**
21   **After all, that's the point! How does she get it?**
22   **EMILE: Sere iss only one way.** *(Rising and stretching himself*
23   *complacently, standing with back to fire)* **A woman only**
24   **gets what a man gives her.** *(FRITZ draws KIDDIE away*
25   *from the window and sitting right of desk, takes him on*
26   *his knee.)*
27   **WELLS:** *(Still lying on couch)* **Lione says the man is Gaskell.**
28   **EMILE: Zut! Gaskell has not ze romanse — ze mystery —**
29   **ze charm for a secret love.**
30   **FRITZ:** *(Attracting KIDDIE's attention from the others by*
31   *showing him a trick with his fingers)* **Can you do dot? It**
32   **iss not so easy. Un?**
33   **WELLS: I'm hanged if I can tell whether it** *is Gaskell* **or**
34   **not — but if it is — why the devil won't she marry**
35   **him? I tell you Malcolm Gaskell's going to be a big**

1   man some day. He's got the grip on this newspaper
2   all right, all right, and he's not going to let go till he's
3   got a darned good thing.
4   EMILE: Zat would be nossing to her. She wants ze love of
5   ze poet — ze artist. It is not —
6   FRITZ: Wat are you talking about? It is not dis — it is not
7   dat. It is not nobody.
8   EMILE: Oh, la, la! She is a very brilliant woman, but she
9   cannot do what is impossible. She cannot write like a
10   man unless a man help her — and no man could
11   make her write like zat unless she love him.
12   ***
13   WELLS: *(In a lower voice to EMILE)* You can't see beyond the
14   love idea. Frank isn't a Frenchwoman. What if there is
15   a man helping her — it might be only a business deal.
16   EMILE: Oh — mon enfant!
17   FRITZ: *(Rising quickly as he puts KIDDIE to the floor)* You are
18   two big fools...
19   ***
20   FRITZ: So you — her friends — are talking too.
21   EMILE: Oh — la — la!
22   FRITZ: You have listened to de gossip, de —
23   WELLS: *(Throwing down paper and sitting up)* Oh, come off
24   it, Fritz. Don't get excited. I say I don't know
25   whether it's a love affair or not. *If* it is Gaskell —
26   FRITZ: If — if — if! Why do you always use dot mean little
27   "if"? Are you cowards? Are you afraid to say it is
28   a lie?
29   EMILE: She does not deny it.
30   FRITZ: She would not stoop to deny it.
31   WELLS: I think Frank has had some grand smash up of a
32   love affair sometime. I don't know whether Kiddie's
33   her child or not — don't care — none of my business
34   — but after she's had the courage to adopt the boy,
35   and refuses to explain who he is — after she's made

1   people respect her and accept the situation — I can't
2   see for the life of me, why she lets *another* thing
3   come up for people to talk about.
4 FRITZ: There *is* no other thing! That iss a lie.
5 EMILE: How do you know?
6 FRITZ: *You* know — *you* know it iss a lie! Why don't you
7   kill it?
8 EMILE: How can you kill a lie about a woman?
9 FRITZ: Wid de truth.
10 EMILE: Mais! What is ze truth?
11 FRITZ: De truth iss — that she is a good woman and you
12   are too small, too liddle — too — too — too bad in
13   your mind to know wat dot means.
14 EMILE: *(Following him to center)* Prenez-garde! I am a
15   Frenchman!
16 FRITZ: Yah, dot iss yust it. You don't know a good woman
17   when you see one.
18 EMILE: "Good!" I said nossing about good or bad. It iss you
19   — you who make her bad. You say she must live like
20   zis or like zat — or like one little way *you* think — or
21   she iss bad! Bah! What is bad? She iss good because
22   she has a great heart — a great nature. She is brave
23   enough to keep ziz child wiz her — and snap ze
24   fingers at ze world. She is kind as an angel — she is
25   free — she is not afraid — but she must love because
26   she is too great to live without love. Does zat make
27   her bad? Allons donc! Because she does not tell who
28   ze lover is does zat make her bad? Bah! It is you who
29   are too small — too little, too bete — too German to
30   understand.
31 FRITZ: Oh, yah! yah, yah. You can talk wid your French
32   talk. You mix up de good and de bad like you mix
33   your black and white paint till you get a dirty some-
34   thing and say it iss beautiful. You say — "Oh, yah,
35   she iss a good woman," and you damn her wid dat

1   nasty liddle shrug of dat nasty liddle shoulder.
2   EMILE: Wat do you —
3   FRITZ: You cannot do dat wid me. You are her friend or
4   you are not her friend. You know dat she is what I
5   know she is, and if you don't stop winking and
6   wiggling and smiling — I vill —
7   EMILE: You will? What will you? It is not for you to tell me
8   what I sink of her. You are only jealous. You say zer
9   is no ozzer man because you are crazy wiz ze jealous.
10   Hein! If you was ze man you would not care what I
11   zink — *(FRITZ rushes at EMILE.)*
12   WELLS: *(Springing up from couch and going between them)*
13   Drop it, you fools!
14
15
16
17
18
19
20
21
22
23
24
25
26
27
28
29
30
31
32
33
34
35

SCENE 2: Three Males and Three Females

Lione

Clara, 37

Frank, probably around 30

Wells, probably 20s

Emile, probably 20s

Fritz, probably 20s

Frank arrives home and she and the others talk about their work and so on. Lione arrives. She is a singer who will be giving a concert. Then Clara enters. She's in her mid-thirties and is attempting to make a living painting miniature portraits. Fritz is a musician; Wells a writer, and Emile an artist.

1. Why do you think Lione tells Clara not to be a fool?

2. Clara has no way of living, since she is unmarried. Yet her family objects to her working. If you were she, how would you react to this?

3. Who would you side with, the people who say a person should work for money, or those who say a person should be true to his or her ideals?

1   LIONE: *(Condescendingly)* **Ah, cara mia, where have you**
2   **been all day?**
3   CLARA: **Did you miss me, dearest?**
4   LIONE: **Of course I did. I wanted you to hook my gown.**
5   CLARA: **I am so sorry.**
6   FRANK: **Sit down, child.**
7   CLARA: *(Sitting on the edge of the couch by FRANK)* **I went**
8   **into Cousin Mabel's and she asked me to stay to**
9   **dinner. So I did, of course.**
10   WELLS: **Of course. Don't miss any of Cousin Mabel's**
11   **dinners, Clara.**
12   CLARA: *(Still out of breath)* **She sent me home in the motor.**
13   FRANK: **Too bad she didn't send you all the way upstairs**
14   **in it.**
15   CLARA: **Yes. I ran up three flights I was in such a hurry to**
16   **see you. I have an idea.**
17   LIONE: **Well, sit back and either take your hat off or pin it**
18   **on straight.**
19   CLARA: **Oh, is it crooked?**
20   EMILE: **It make ze whole room crooked — out of drawing.**
21   **I cannot see anything else.**
22   CLARA: *(Struggling with her hat and hair)* **Well — I'm going to**
23   **give an exhibition.**
24   FRITZ: *(From the piano where he is still playing very softly)*
25   **Ach gott!**
26   WELLS: **What?**
27   LIONE: **Now, Clara, don't be a fool.**
28   EMILE: **And what are you going to exhibit?**
29   FRANK: **Be quiet.** *(To CLARA)* **Go on. Why shouldn't you**
30   **give an exhibition? I wish to goodness you'd finish**
31   **that miniature of Kiddie you began about six**
32   **months ago.**
33   CLARA: **I will. I'll get to work at it right away. I'll make it**
34   *the* **important picture of the exhibition.**
35   FRANK: **Kiddie can be there and walk up and down in front**

1   of it to show how good it is.

2   WELLS: I wouldn't run any unnecessary risks, Clara.

3   CLARA: You mean thing!

4   FRANK: Shut up, Wells. *(Throwing a pillow at him)*

5   CLARA: You just wait — you just wait, you people. You

6   don't believe in me. You don't think I am in earnest.

7   I'll show you. I am going to get to work right away.

8   EMILE: Oh, you have some orders, zen?

9   CLARA: No — I didn't mean that. But Cousin Mabel says

10   she'll let me do her miniature.

11   LIONE: Let you? For nothing?

12   CLARA: Well, yes. I don't mind that.

13   WELLS: Good Lord! *(An uproar from the others)*

14   CLARA: Now, listen!

15   FRANK: Listen! Listen! Go on, Clara.

16   CLARA: Then if she likes it, she'll interest other people.

17   That's what I've always wanted her to do, you know.

18   Because if Cousin Mabel really wanted to she could

19   do anything with her social position.

20   LIONE: Your Cousin Mabel and her social position make

21   me sick. Why doesn't she give you an income?

22   CLARA: Oh, I couldn't accept that.

23   WELLS: You couldn't — if you didn't get it.

24   CLARA: You don't understand how conservative my

25   people are.

26   LIONE: How stingy — you mean.

27   EMILE: Why don't you tell them all to go to ze devil?

28   CLARA: Oh, I couldn't do that. I can't afford to cut loose

29   entirely from my family — though of course they

30   object horribly to my working.

31   LIONE: They're a pack of snobs. Why don't they boost you

32   along in society then, if they object to this?

33   CLARA: Well, I really think if I succeeded, they wouldn't

34   mind so much.

35   LIONE: No — you bet. They'd all be running after you then.

1   EMILE: Zat is ze trouble. You are still hanging to ze petti-
2   coats of your fashionable world — and what do it do
3   for you? Look at me — I am alone in a strange
4   country. I have no influence — no rich friends. I am
5   working for ze art — not for ze money.
6   FRITZ: *(Rising, getting pipe from overcoat and going to window)*
7   Dat is a good thing den.
8   EMILE: Bah! What is money?
9   WELLS: Don't ask me.
10   EMILE: Why don't you live for your art — and starve for it
11   if it must be.
12   FRITZ: Yah! And when you are hungry — eat one of your
13   beautiful miniatures.
14   EMILE: Art has nossing to do wiz money.
15   WELLS: No, but money has something to do with art.
16   EMILE: In America, yes. Oui — zat is ze truth — ze sad
17   truth. You have no art in America — and what you
18   have is French. *(A laugh of tolerance from the others)*
19   LIONE: I suppose you'll be swelling it, Frank, now that you
20   don't have to make any sacrifices for the sake of
21   your work.
22   FRANK: I never have made any for it.
23   LIONE: I'd be ashamed to confess it.
24   FRANK: Neither have you — none of you have. We're all
25   working for money. We'd be fools if we didn't.
26   LIONE: Well — really — I thought you had a few ideals.
27   FRANK: Never mind ideals. I've got a little talent and I'm
28   trying to sell it. So are we all — because we haven't
29   got anything else to sell. It's only genius that forgets
30   money. Only the glory of creating that compensates
31   for being hungry. No — no — talent wants three
32   meals a day — genius can live in spite of none.
33   WELLS: Well, by God — I guess you're right. Frank, I want
34   to sell — and I'm going to hang on. I think I've got a
35   chance — not because my plays are any good — but

1   **because other people's are so damned bad.** *(All laugh*
2   *and there is a general movement.)*
3
4
5
6
7
8
9
10
11
12
13
14   ·
15
16
17
18
19
20
21
22
23
24
25
26
27
28
29
30
31
32
33
34
35

SCENE 3: One Male and One Female

Fritz, probably 20s

Frank, probably about 30

When Frank goes to put Kiddie to bed, the others again talk about Frank's supposed lover(s). Lione is sure Kiddie is the son of Frank and Gaskell. Everyone leaves except Fritz.

1. Do you think Frank should be flattered that others think her books are too good to be written by a woman? What would your reaction be to this?

2. Even Fritz, her best friend, is somewhat chauvinistic. How is that apparent in this scene?

3. Frank lived with her father in Paris. Why do you think she says this made her be a "natural" woman? Why does Fritz not agree?

4. Is it logical that Frank brought or was able to bring Kiddie back to the States? Explain.

5. How does Fritz feel about what Frank's done in bringing Kiddie home with her?

1 FRITZ: You are tired tonight, yah? Un?
2 FRANK: A little, Fritz.
3 FRITZ: Und you must work yet?
4 FRANK: I'm going out later.
5 FRITZ: Oh, no. Don't do dot!
6 FRANK: Oh, I must. If I get what I'm after tonight I'll have
7   a fine study. I'm going to have supper with a girl from
8   the East Side.
9 FRITZ: I vill be back. I vill go with you.
10 FRANK: Indeed you won't.
11 FRITZ: But, I don't want you to go — alone — at night.
12 FRANK: Now — now — Fritzie, if you get fidgety —
13 FRITZ: Oh — but de talk — de talk — I can't stand it for
14   you. When you go out like dis people don't believe it
15   is for your work. They say you have a lover — they
16   say he writes your books.
17 FRANK: That's very flattering. It means that they think
18   they are too good for a woman to do.
19 FRITZ: But you see, you make dem talk when you do
20   foolish things.
21 FRANK: Foolish? You mean going out alone? Good
22   heavens! You don't suppose I'm going to give up all
23   my chances of seeing and knowing and under-
24   standing just because a few silly people are talking
25   about me?
26 FRITZ: But you are a woman. You must not expect people
27   to trust you — too much.
28 FRANK: I'm not going to spend my life explaining.
29 FRITZ: *(Sitting at left of desk)* No — but you —
30 FRANK: Oh, Fritz, don't. You've been so nice and so
31   comfortable. And now you're beginning to worry. You
32   see how much better it would have been for both of
33   us if I'd never told you anything about myself and
34   about Kiddie.
35 FRITZ: Don't say that. You have to talk to somebody —

1   sometimes. Don't say you are sorry you told me, dot
2   was de most natural ting I haf ever seen you do.
3   FRANK: Natural? Surely, I am nothing but natural. I'm a
4   natural woman — because I've been a free one. Living
5   alone with my father all those years made me so. He
6   took me with him every possible place.
7   FRITZ: Ah — but he was with you to protect you.
8   FRANK: I didn't need much protection. Dad wanted me to
9   see — to know — to touch all kinds of life — and I
10   surely did. He developed all his stories by telling
11   them aloud to me. He used to walk up and down the
12   little library and talk out his characters. So I began
13   to balance men and women very early — and the
14   more I knew — the more I thought the women had
15   the worst of it.
16 FRITZ: Something has made you bitter to men.
17 FRANK: Kiddie has made me bitter. Poor little nameless
18   fellow! I shall never forget the night his mother came
19   to us. I didn't know her very well — she was only one
20   of the hundreds of American girls studying in Paris —
21   but she came to me because she wanted to get away
22   from her own set. We kept her and she died when
23   Kiddie was born — and then we kept him — because
24   we didn't know what else in God's world to do with
25   him and then we loved him — and after Father died
26   — somehow that poor, little, helpless baby was the
27   greatest comfort in the world to me. I couldn't bear
28   Paris without Dad, so I came back to America. Kiddie
29   was two then, and we set up house in this old place
30   three years ago — and here we are — and it's
31   nobody's business who he is. I don't *know* who his
32   father was; I don't *care* who he was — but my name
33   is better for the boy than his — for mine is honest.
34 FRITZ: I tink it iss a too bad ting to be a woman wid a big
35   mind, a big soul. Yah, I tink it. But I am glad you are

1   one already.

2   FRANK: Dear old Fritz!

3   FRITZ: I only wonder wat vill be de end.

4   FRANK: Kiddie will be the end of everything for me.

5   FRITZ: No — he vill not. Someday you vill lof a strong

6   man—and he vill change it all.

7   FRANK: You don't believe me of course. But, it's Kiddie —

8   Kiddie I am living for. Everything I believe about men

9   and women has been so intensified by him that he

10   has become a sort of symbol to me of what women

11   suffer through men — and he's given me a purpose —

12   something to do.

13 FRITZ: I tink Malcolm Gaskell has cut me out wid — Kiddie.

14 FRANK: Nonsense! Nobody could do that.

15 FRITZ: I am not so sure. I think Gaskell can get most

16   anything he want — if he try.

17 FRANK: Why don't you like him, Fritz?

18 FRITZ: He isn't de kind of a man dot everybody knows all

19   about and can trust de first time you see him.

20 FRANK: Yes, he is. That's just what Gaskell is. Whatever

21   his faults may be, at least they're honest, right out

22   from the shoulder!

23 FRITZ: I am not — so sure. *(A pause)* Don't be sorry tomor-

24   row that you haf talked a liddle tonight. It's gute for

25   you — und don't tink I don't understand. Gute nacht.

26   *(Giving her his hand)*

27 FRANK: **Good night, Fritz.** *(FRITZ goes up to table by piano*

28   *and picks up his violin case and overcoat.)*

29

30

31

32

33

34

35

SCENE 4: One Male and One Female

Frank, probably about 30

Gaskell, about 40

This is the first scene where Gaskell appears. It occurs shortly after the end of the previous scene. Gaskell has asked to borrow a book. Fritz starts to go out when Lione appears. Seeing Gaskell, she obliquely refers to Frank as a "siren." Fritz and Lione leave.

1. What do you think of Gaskell's wanting to borrow a copy of Frank's book because he threw away the copy he bought? What does that tell you about the type of person he is?

2. Gaskell tells Frank a man couldn't have done the book better. If you were playing the role of Frank, how would you deliver the line, "Oh, thank you?"

3. This scene strengthens the major conflict of the play. Can you point that out? What do you think of Gaskell's views on the matter?

4. How do you react to the following statement of Gaskell's? "Man sets the standard for woman. He knows she's better than he is and he demands that she be — and if she isn't she's got to suffer for it. That's the whole business in a nut shell — and you know it."

5. Pick out as many instances as you can of Gaskell's insulting Frank. Why do you suppose he is doing this?

6. Where is the irony in the following statement of Gaskell's? "I don't question you. I take you just as you are."

7. How many ways can you find in this scene that Frank and Gaskell disagree? Explain each instance.

8. How do you react to Gaskell's statement that "love is the only thing that counts much for a woman?"

9. What do you think of Frank's intentions of going to meet the woman and her boyfriend for supper?

10. Do you think Gaskell is a likeable man? Why do you think Frank (as it develops later) is in love with him?

1   **FRANK:** *(Sitting sidewise in the chair at left of desk)* **What did**
2   **you come for?**
3   **GASKELL: Your book. I want to read it again. You haven't**
4   **given me a copy.**
5   **FRANK: Why don't you buy one and help the sale?**
6   **GASKELL: I did buy one — but I threw it away — it irri-**
7   **tated me.**
8   **FRANK: Then you don't need another one.**
9   **GASKELL: No — I don't need it — I admit, but I want it. I**
10   **want to read it again. I want to see why people are**
11   **talking about it.**
12   **FRANK: You don't see then?**
13   **GASKELL: I don't see why they say it's so strong. It's**
14   **clever as the deuce and it's got a lot of you in it —**
15   **but it isn't big. Our paper gave you a darned good**
16   **criticism. Did you see it?** *(Handing her a paper from his*
17   *pocket)*
18   **FRANK:** *(Taking paper and getting scissors from desk she goes*
19   *to couch.)* **Yes, I saw it. Much obliged to your paper.**
20   **GASKELL:** *(Following her)* **Your story's all right — a man**
21   **couldn't have done it any better — your people are**
22   **clean cut as a man's.**
23   **FRANK: Oh, thank you.**
24   **GASKELL:** *(Standing with his back to fire looking down at her)*
25   **But — it's only a story. You haven't got at the social**
26   **evil in the real sense. You couldn't tackle that. It's**
27   **too big for you. You've taken the poverty and the**
28   **wrongs of the woman on the East Side as an effective**
29   **background for your story, and you've let your dare-**
30   **devil profligate girl rail against men and the world.**
31   **She says some darn good things — more or less true**
32   **— but — you don't get** *at* **the thing. You keep banging**
33   **away about woman — woman and what she could do**
34   **for herself if she would. Why — this is a man's world.**
35   **Women'll never change anything.**

1 FRANK: Oh! *(Smiling)*
2 GASKELL: Man sets the standard for woman. He knows
3   she's better than he is and he demands that she be —
4   and if she isn't she's got to suffer for it. That's the
5   whole business in a nut shell — and you know it.
6 FRANK: Oh, don't begin that again. I know your arguments
7   backwards.
8 GASKELL: How did you happen to come here anyway?
9   This isn't a good place for you to live.
10 FRANK: Why did you?
11 GASKELL: Oh, this is all right for a man.
12 FRANK: Rather good for me too. The house is filled with
13   independent women who are making their own living.
14 GASKELL: And you also have a little court of admirers
15   here — all more or less in love with you — all curious
16   — most of them doubting and all of them gossiping
17   about you to beat the band. Don't you know that?
18 FRANK: Let's talk about something else for a change.
19 GASKELL: Hang it! Somebody's got to tell you. You can't
20   live the way you do and do the things you do —
21   without running your head into a noose — just as any
22   other woman would.
23 FRANK: I don't know why you take the trouble to say
24   all this.
25 GASKELL: I don't know why I do myself, for Lord knows, I
26   wouldn't stop you in anything you're trying to do. I
27   like your pluck. I say go on. I understand you — but
28   you needn't think for a moment anybody else does. I
29   don't question you. I take you just as you are. I
30   suppose you think this Dutchman understands you?
31 FRANK: He isn't impertinent to say the least.
32 GASKELL: No, I suppose not. He wouldn't dare to disagree
33   with you.
34 FRANK: Oh, yes he would. Fritz has a mind of his own and
35   a very strong character. He is a genius besides. If he

1 only had a chance to be heard. I wish you'd do some-
2 thing for him, you know so many people. You've got
3 a lot of influence in that direction. Don't you want to?
4 GASKELL: Do you really want me to?
5 FRANK: Oh, awfully. He has the real thing — you know he
6 has. Don't you know it?
7 GASKELL: Oh, I suppose so — the real thing is fiddling —
8 but that's not much for a man.
9 FRANK: He's here without friends — without money. He
10 ought to be heard.
11 GASKELL: What do you want me to do?
12 FRANK: Talk him up to somebody. He can't do that sort of
13 thing for himself. He's too sensitive and too fine.
14 GASKELL: Sensitive and fine — be hanged. That won't get
15 him anywhere.
16 FRANK: *(Rising to go back to desk with the clipping)* I hate you
17 when you say things like that.
18 GASKELL: *(Catching her hand as she passes him)* Do you
19 hate me?! Do you?
20 FRANK: Then don't be so —
21 GASKELL: So what —? Don't you think I'm — What do you
22 think of me? Tell me.
23 FRANK: I think you don't mean half you say.
24 GASKELL: Oh, yes, I do. And a good deal more. You don't
25 mean half *you* say — they're only ideals.
26 FRANK: Oh!
27 GASKELL: You'll acknowledge it someday — when you
28 care for a man. You won't give a hang for anything
29 you ever believed then.
30 FRANK: Oh, yes, I will — and I'll care what he believes.
31 GASKELL: *(Bending close to her)* You'll believe that you've
32 got to live while you are young and you'll believe that
33 love is the only thing that counts much for a woman.
34 FRANK: No — no — no!
35 GASKELL: It is. Women are only meant to be loved — and

1   men have got to take care of them. That's the whole
2   business. You'll acknowledge it some day — when
3   you do — love somebody.
4   FRANK: It would only make me feel more — more than
5   ever the responsibility of love of life. *(She moves back*
6   *from him — looking at him while she speaks.)*
7   GASKELL: *(After a pause)* Come out after awhile and have a
8   bite of supper with me. Will you?
9   FRANK: Oh, couldn't — possibly. *(Sitting at her desk and*
10   *drawing a MS towards her)*
11   GASKELL: Please.
12   FRANK: No — really I can't. I have to work.
13   GASKELL: Well — get to work and I'll come back for you —
14   any time you say.
15   FRANK: Can't. I'm going out at twelve anyway.
16   GASKELL: Oh, that's different — if you're going out to
17   supper anyway.
18   FRANK: I'm going to have supper with a girl from the
19   East Side.
20   GASKELL: Why in the name of heaven are you going at
21   twelve o'clock?
22   FRANK: She is going to bring her sweetheart for me to see
23   and he can't get off any other time.
24   GASKELL: I'll go with you.
25   FRANK: No, you —
26   GASKELL: Yes, I will.
27   FRANK: Indeed you won't. I want them to be natural and
28   talk. She's had a tragic story and this fellow knows
29   all about it and is going to marry her. She is helping
30   me a lot in my club for girls over there — she can get
31   at them because she's been through it all and has
32   come out a fine, decent woman.
33   GASKELL: I can't see for the life of me why you go banging
34   around over there — wasting your time — getting
35   into all sorts of disagreeable things. What's the use?

1   FRANK: What's the use? I call it some use to get hold of
2   about a dozen girls a year and make them want to
3   lead decent lives.
4   GASKELL: *(After a pause)* Are you going to let your Fritz go
5   with you?
6   FRANK: Of course not.
7   GASKELL: Thought perhaps you would. He makes a
8   pretty good watch dog trotting around after you.
9   Doesn't he?
10 FRANK: He makes a pretty good friend. *(Rising)* You must
11   skip now. I've got to get to work!
12 GASKELL: I don't want to go.
13 FRANK: Come on. *(They walk together to door.)*
14 GASKELL: *(Standing in the open door)* You're awfully hard
15   on me.
16 FRANK: Poor you!
17 GASKELL: That's right. You don't know how nice I could
18   be if you didn't fight with me.
19 FRANK: You always begin it.
20 GASKELL: Will you come to dinner tomorrow night and
21   see a show? Will you — will you? *(After a pause she*
22   *nods smilingly.)* Good. *(Taking her hand)* And we won't
23   fight? *(She shakes her head.)* Not a bit?
24 FRANK: *(Drawing her hand away)* Not a bit.
25 GASKELL: If you were only as kind to me as you are to —
26   everybody else — I'd be —
27 FRANK: You wouldn't like me at all.
28 GASKELL: Try it.
29 FRANK: I couldn't. Nobody could get on with you without
30   fighting.
31 GASKELL: Oh, don't say that.
32 FRANK: It's the truth. You're a headstrong, domineering —
33 GASKELL: Just because I don't crawl at your feet the way
34   the other fellows do. Do you hate me?
35 FRANK: You said that before. Skip now. Goodnight.

1 **GASKELL:** *(Taking book out of pocket)* **Are you going to give**
2   **me this?**
3 **FRANK:** I said no.
4 **GASKELL:** But I've got it.
5 **FRANK:** *(Putting her hand on the book)* **But I haven't given it**
6   **to you.**
7 **GASKELL: You'll never give me anything. I'll have to fight**
8   **for it.** *(He snatches her hand and kisses her wrist and*
9   *arm and goes out — closing the door. Hesitating, she puts*
10   *her hand over the arm where he kissed it and puts her*
11   *arm on the door hiding her face in it.)*
12
13
14
15
16
17
18
19
20
21
22
23
24
25
26
27
28
29
30
31
32
33
34
35

SCENE 5: Two Females

Lione, 20s to 30s

Clara, 37

This is the opening of Act II and follows directly after the preceding scene. It's two weeks later. The action occurs in Clara's room in the same building in which Frank lives.

1. Why do you think Lione so strongly dislikes "society women"?

2. Why do you think Lione gossips so much about Frank?

3. Do you like these two women? Can you find anything specific you dislike about them?

1   *(At curtain — LIONE, with the front of her skirt turned up*
2   *and a towel pinned over it as an apron, is sitting on the*
3   *couch down left, polishing a brass candlestick with a*
4   *flannel rag. CLARA wears a skirt and shirtwaist, which*
5   *do not meet in the back, and a much besmeared painting*
6   *apron. The same lock of hair of Act I is constantly falling*
7   *over her face and she mechanically pushes it back.)*
8   **CLARA:** *(Going to take a workbasket from the table to put it on*
9   *bureau at left)* **Oh, dear! I hope it pays for all the**
10   **trouble. Cousin Mabel may have one of her headaches**
11   **at the last minute and not come at all. She's really**
12   **awfully pleased with her miniature. It flatters her**
13   **horribly. I do want to be honest and true in my work,**
14   **but what are you going to do? No woman will accept**
15   **a miniature unless it does flatter her.**
16   **LIONE: I hope to goodness somebody gives you an order**
17   **after this affair. I'm ruining my hands cleaning these**
18   **things.**
19   **CLARA: Don't do them well. We'll never be ready by four**
20   **o'clock. It's two now.** *(Taking hat from armchair and*
21   *dropping on her knees before the couch up right. She*
22   *draws a hatbox from under the bed and puts the hat in it.)*
23   **LIONE: If your cousin doesn't come, I'd never speak to her**
24   **again in all my life, if I were you.**
25   **CLARA:** *(Getting flat on the floor to reach a dress box under the*
26   *bed)* **Oh, pooh! She wouldn't care whether I did or not.**
27   **LIONE: Your cousin Mabel's a damned snob — that's what**
28   **she is.**
29   **CLARA:** *(Taking a shabby afternoon gown from the box)* **Oh,**
30   **she doesn't mean to be. She's just like everybody else**
31   **in her world.** *(Examining the gown)*
32   **LIONE: I hate 'em. Ignorant, idle, society women. That's**
33   **all they are.**
34   **CLARA: You'd give your ears to be one though.**
35   **LIONE:** *(Rising and leaving candles on couch, as she goes to*

1   *look at herself at bureau)* **I wouldn't. I wouldn't give up**
2   **my career for anything on earth.**
3   **CLARA: Yes, that's what I used to think — but somehow,**
4   **I'm not so keen about my — Goodness, this is**
5   **mussed and shabby! Absolutely the only rag I've got**
6   **to wear.** *(Hanging the gown on the chandelier below the*
7   *fireplace she pushes the box back — and arranges the*
8   *cover on couch.)* **Oh, I must get the rest of the minia-**
9   **tures up. Here's Kiddie's picture. Where's the best**
10   **place to put this?**
11 **LIONE: I think Frank's got an awful nerve to let you**
12   **display it at all.**
13 **CLARA: Why?**
14 **LIONE: Why? Because people will ask who he is.**
15 **CLARA: Oh, well, I'll just say he's a little boy that Frank**
16   **Ware adopted.**
17 **LIONE:** *(Going to put a candlestick on mantel)* **Yes, that**
18   **sounds well.**
19 **CLARA: Well, it's plausible.** *(Putting the miniature on the*
20   *screen and standing back to see how it looks)*
21 **LIONE: Not to me. The men say she isn't in love with**
22   **Gaskell. Why, she is, head over heels — and some-**
23   **times I think —**
24 **CLARA: What?**
25 **LIONE: Sometimes — I think —** *(Going to CLARA)* **— he is**
26   **Kiddie's father.**
27 **CLARA: What? Oh, horrible, Lione. She never saw Gaskell**
28   **till she came here.**
29 **LIONE: Yes, so they say. Let me see Kiddie's picture.**
30   **Frank used to live in Paris, and so did Gaskell.**
31 **CLARA: Oh, goodness! I never dreamed of such a thing.**
32 **LIONE:** *(Going to sit at right of table and looking closely at*
33   *miniature)* **Several times I've thought —**
34 **CLARA: You'd better keep on working. The tea table isn't**
35   **ready at all. I hope to goodness nobody looks behind**

1   this screen.
2   **LIONE:** *(Starting as she looks at picture)* **It isn't imagination.**
3   **I do see it — as true as I live.**
4   **CLARA: What's the matter?**
5   **LIONE: Look! Come here.**
6
7
8
9
10
11
12
13
14
15
16
17
18
19
20
21
22
23
24
25
26
27
28
29
30
31
32
33
34
35

SCENE 6: Two Males and Two Females

Clara, 37

Emile, probably 20s

Wells, probably 20s

Lione, 20s-30s

This scene occurs later in Act II while preparations still are being made for Clara's exhibition.

1. Why do you think Lione wants to know if Frank loves Gaskell?

2. The others say Frank is a mystery to them. Lione says she is not one to her. What does she mean by this?

3. Why do you think Lione is so insistent on uncovering something nasty about Frank?

4. Emile accuses the others of being hypocrites. Explain this.

1   CLARA: Frank's a dear. She's got the biggest heart.
2   EMILE: I do not sink Fritz tinks her heart is quite big
3   enough. He would like to get in.
4   WELLS: *(Kicking EMILE and looking at LIONE)* **You don't know**
5   **anything about her heart.**
6   CLARA: I wish I did. I think it would be awfully interesting
7   to know whether she really cares for Gaskell or not.
8   WELLS: Give us more bric-a-brac, Clara, if you want it
9   all up.
10   CLARA: Oh, yes, use it all. *(Giving WELLS another weapon*
11   *from chair)*
12   EMILE: I tell you she loves somebody. Zat iss her charm —
13   her mystery. She could not be what she iss wiz
14   out love.
15   WELLS: She's a mystery to me all right, all right.
16   CLARA: She certainly is to me.
17   LIONE: She certainly is not to me. Look here — all of you.
18   *(Holding out the picture)* **Whom does Kiddie look like?**
19   CLARA: Oh, gracious! What do you mean?
20   LIONE: Simply what I say. Whom does he look like?
21   EMILE: You mean like Frank?
22   LIONE: No, no. Not like Frank. Look now — through the
23   eyes.
24   CLARA: I don't see it — and I ought to if anybody does —
25   I painted it. What do you mean, Lione, anybody we
26   know?
27   WELLS: You couldn't very well see a resemblance to
28   anybody you didn't know.
29   CLARA: Well, dear me. I don't see — through the eyes —
30   Oh, Heaven's — yes — I do.
31   LIONE: You see it! Wait! — Don't say anything.
32   WELLS: Oh, you can imagine anything.
33   LIONE: You can't imagine anything as strong as that.
34   CLARA: Yes — I actually —
35   EMILE: Ah! Mon Dieu! I see what you mean. It is Gaskell.

1   WELLS: What—
2   EMILE: Ah! C'est extraordinaire!
3   LIONE: *(Looking triumphantly at WELLS)* We all see it.
4   WELLS: Rot — rot! Nothing of the sort. I don't see the
5   slightest —
6   LIONE: We see it. All of us.
7   CLARA: I think I do — I did. It sort of comes and goes.
8   WELLS: Especially goes. I don't see it.
9   LIONE: You're blind. Look — it's Gaskell. That child looks
10   like Malcolm Gaskell — and anybody can see it.
11   Unless they don't want to.
12   EMILE: Mais oui! I see it. It is here, the eyes. For *you* —
13   Clara, it iz wonderful — you haf caught ze trick wiz
14   ze eyes.
15   LIONE: Of course it's there.
16   CLARA: Oh my! I think it's awful. What do you mean,
17   Lione? I don't know what you mean.
18   WELLS: Nothing. It doesn't mean anything.
19   LIONE: Oh, no. Nobody means anything — nobody knows
20   anything — nobody says anything — but you all
21   *think* what I do — and you haven't got the courage to
22   say so. I have, you know. I believe in saying what you
23   think — and not pretending to be fooled.
24   WELLS: Well, now, what of it? What if what you imply is
25   true. What of it? What's the good of digging it up?
26   CLARA: Oh, dear! I don't believe it at all.
27   EMILE: I tell you all — all ze time — you are foolish as
28   babies not to understand.
29   WELLS: Oh, yes, you understand a lot, you do. I say,
30   what's the use of talking about it? Let it alone.
31   LIONE: Oh, very well, if that's the sort of thing you accept
32   and believe in — that's your affair — but I don't
33   propose to help a woman of that sort keep up appear-
34   ances by pretending that I don't see what's right
35   under my nose.

1 CLARA: Oh, dear! I never was in anything like this before.
2   I think you have to have strict ideas even if you are
3   broadminded. I do think — Oh, dear! I don't know what
4   to think.
5 EMILE: You amuse me — all. You pretend to live in ze
6   world of art and freedom and yet you make ze grand
7   fight about — about what? What are you talking
8   about? What do you expect — you funny Americans?
9   She is a great woman —she must live and love and —
10 LIONE: You needn't say that to me. I don't — *(FRANK*
11   *knocks and opens the door. LIONE puts the miniature back*
12   *in her blouse. FRANK has taken off her hat and coat. She*
13   *carries a sofa pillow under each arm, and the lace coat.*
14   *She has also the vase and the two framed pictures in*
15   *silver frames in her hands. FRITZ follows with four pillows*
16   *and a rug.)*
17
18
19
20
21
22
23
24
25
26
27
28
29
30
31
32
33
34
35

SCENE 7: One Male and Female

Gaskell, about 40

Frank, probably about 30

This scene occurs just after the opening of Act III.

1. Why does Gaskell say, "It was hell to doubt you, but I couldn't help it?" Do you think this is logical?

2. Why do you think Gaskell doesn't understand what Frank means when she says, "And don't you see why I wanted you — of all people in the world to trust me — in every way?"

3. In what way is Gaskell exhibiting his male chauvinism in this scene?

4. Do you think Frank had valid reasons for not wanting to fall in love? Explain.

5. What do you think Frank and Gaskell's lives together would be like?

1   GASKELL: I've been thinking — since that — since this
2   afternoon. I was a cad. At least that's what I seemed
3   to you. I don't know what those other duffers were
4   driving at — oh, I do know in a way — but — All I
5   mean is that I love you and ask for your — confidence.
6   FRANK: I'm not angry now, but I was then — so horribly
7   angry and hurt. I could tell you who his mother was
8   and prove it in a hundred ways but don't ask me to
9   do that. Oh, Malcolm — You must believe *me* — just
10   me. Look at me. I give you the one love of my life.
11 GASKELL: *(Catching her in his arms)* **Frank!**
12 FRANK: I love you. I love you.
13 GASKELL: My darling! It was hell to doubt you, but I
14   couldn't help it, dear. It was only because I love you
15   so. Because I want you to be the most perfect woman
16   in the world. Do you understand?
17 FRANK: And don't you see why I wanted you — of all
18   people in the world to trust me — in every way?
19   Don't you understand?
20 GASKELL: No, not quite. *(Sitting beside her)* When will you
21   marry me?
22 FRANK: Oh, I don't know.
23 GASKELL: I want to take care of you. You need it as much
24   as any woman does. Do you love me?
25 FRANK: I've tried — not to.
26 GASKELL: Don't say that. Why?
27 FRANK: I haven't wanted to love anybody — and when I
28   knew I was beginning to care — I didn't want to.
29 GASKELL: When did you know you — cared?
30 FRANK: Oh — When I began to fight with you. You made
31   me so awfully angry — and then I was always
32   wretched until we made up. I began to know your
33   step in the hall, and when you opened the door and
34   stood there I knew something strong and sweet,
35   something stronger than myself was coming in.

1   GASKELL: I'm a beast in lots of ways and stubborn as a mule

2   — but I can take care of you and I'll be good to you.

3   FRANK: When did you first know you cared?

4   GASKELL: From the first minute I saw you.

5   FRANK: Oh, every man says that. You know that isn't true.

6   I wouldn't want it to be. I'll tell you when I first knew

7   you cared.

8   GASKELL: When?

9   FRANK: Do you remember that day — it was — it was

10   Sunday evening about three months ago. You were

11   here and Fritz came in with some roses for me and

12   you didn't look at me for the rest of the evening. You

13   talked to Clara every minute.

14   GASKELL: Oh, come, I wasn't quite such an ass as that.

15   FRANK: You were. You were just as silly as you could be,

16   and perfectly adorable. When you'd gone I —

17   GASKELL: You what —

18   FRANK: I won't tell you.

19   GASKELL: Oh, please tell me.

20   FRANK: No.

21   GASKELL: Oh, please. What did you do when I'd gone?

22   FRANK: I won't tell.

23   GASKELL: I don't believe you love me at all. Do you?

24   FRANK: Um — you haven't the faintest idea how much.

25   GASKELL: Well — tell me — tell me how much.

26   FRANK: I never can. You don't know what it means for a

27   woman to love only one man in all her life.

28   GASKELL: Oh, now, Frank —

29   FRANK: It's true. You're the one man, Malcolm. That's

30   why I've tried to resist it, because it means so terribly

31   much to me. My life has been filled with other things

32   you know — with Kiddie — and my work. They

33   absorbed me and satisfied me; and when you — when

34   love began to crowd in — to overpower me — I was

35   afraid. It seemed almost like being a traitor to

1   myself. Oh, it means such a — such an overwhelming
2   thing for a woman to give up to love after she's —
3   she's been —
4 GASKELL: After she's been as strong and independent as
5   you have been. I'm the luckiest dog on earth. I don't
6   see how I got you.
7 FRANK: Just because you are you. Oh, don't ever disap-
8   point me. Be big and fine and honest always — let me
9   lean on you and worship you.
10 GASKELL: **Kiss me.** *(She puts her head back and he bends*
11   *over her kissing her. KIDDIE opens the door and comes in,*
12   *standing amazed.)*
13
14
15
16
17
18
19
20
21
22
23
24
25
26
27
28
29
30
31
32
33
34
35

Mightier Than the Sword

by Nirmala Moorthy

Nirmala Moorthy, now a resident of the United States, originally is from India. A former journalist who worked for the *Times of India* (where the play originally was published in excerpted form), Moorthy has lived in various countries, all of which become settings for her writing. A novelist and short story writer, Moorthy also has written a book on Japanese flower arrangements.

The play essentially is a one-character piece, and the central character is Walter Whittaker. Here's how Moorthy describes him: "It is an established fact that every club has a resident bore. Years of practice and effort have elevated Walter Whittaker to that position...and enabled him to hold it for ten straight years... [A] widower, his only daughter happily married and settled in New York, Walter is a man who lives in the past. And he keeps it alive by constant repetition."

Former "overseas manager of an oil company, Walter has spent most of his life in Africa." He tells stories well, but after the third or fourth hearing, people tire of them. Therefore, he corners whomever he can.

Only one scene from the play follows. It's essentially a monolog in which Walter latches onto an unsuspecting young man.

If you wish, you can eliminate the part of Bill.

SCENE 1: two males

Bill, about 20

Walter, 64

The scene, which occurs near the beginning of the play, takes place in a country club bar where the young man is waiting for friends to finish a round of golf. He takes a seat near Walter.

1. Why do you think Moorthy wrote a play such as this? What is its purpose, its central idea?

2. Do you like the character of Walter? Do you think you'd like such a person in real life?

3. Why do you suppose Walter has such a need to tell stories about his life in Africa?

4. Do you think Walter is a good storyteller? Why?

5. If you were to play the part of Walter, what would you most want to reveal about his character? Why?

6. Is there anything you do not like about this play? Why?

1 WALTER: *(Puts out his hand.)* **I'm Walt Whittaker.**

2 BILL: **Bill Steadman.**

3 WALTER: **Welcome to the club, Bill.** *(Indicating the other*

4 *patrons)* **I was just telling my friends here about my life**

5 **in West Africa.** *(He bears down on the kid with the finesse*

6 *of a ten-ton diesel truck.)* **Ever been to Nigeria, Bill?**

7 BILL: No, sir.

8 WALTER: No? Well, let me tell you about it. It was way

9 back in '78 that I was assigned to Lagos. The country

10 was still reeling from the civil war — you remember

11 the Biafran war? It was a baptism in blood and fire.

12 The situation worsened when the war ended. Whole

13 regiments of disbanded soldiers wandered around,

14 armed to the teeth, bent on revenge...soldiers who

15 had gotten used to killing for a living.

16   Nobody wanted a posting in Lagos. And I was the

17 one to get it. But Walt Whittaker is not a man you can

18 scare. Turned out to be a good life, and I'm not

19 complaining. The country's rich — the land gushes

20 oil at the touch of a drill. It has gorgeous beaches,

21 and some of the best boating and water-skiing you

22 can get anywhere. I had my own speedboat. Most of

23 the foreigners did. *(He picks up his glass and swishes a*

24 *mouthful across his tongue and exhales through his teeth.)*

25   We had a good time. I remember it like yesterday

26 — afternoons of sun on lawns scented with jasmine

27 and plumeria; barbecue lunches by the swimming

28 pool; Sunday-morning tennis and brunch at the club.

29 We had two gardeners working all day, and my wife

30 bagged prizes at the flower show. We had a chauffeur,

31 a cook, and a house-boy. My daughter Lisa went to

32 the American School — she really loved it there. *(His*

33 *voice deepens with nostalgia.)*

34   But fear was the price we had to pay — mind-

35 numbing, gut-twisting fear. Armed robbery was the

1   order of the day. They attacked you on the street if
2   you walked in lonely places — even in broad daylight.
3   And they came to stand over your bed at night and
4   take away everything you had — in a truck. Every
5   house was barred like a fortress. We were boxed in by
6   guards, burglar alarms, and dogs that were trained to
7   kill on command. Would you believe, a lot of people
8   kept cash in the house just to give to robbers? Those
9   devils could turn nasty if you had nothing to offer
10   them. But put out a television, a stereo, and a thou-
11   sand Naira cash downstairs in your living room and
12   they wouldn't bother to climb upstairs to look for you.
13   *(WALTER chews for a moment on the straggly ends of his*
14   *sandy moustache.)*
15   We used to hear some gruesome stories of rapes
16   and tortures and mutilations. But we never heard of
17   children being killed or hurt. Africans love children.
18   There was a man who was macheted to death in his
19   car — the victim of a personal vendetta. He had his
20   ten-year-old son with him at the time, but they never
21   laid a finger on the boy. Warmhearted killers, don't
22   you agree? They left a witness to the murder because
23   they could not bring themselves to kill a child. Or
24   was it because they did not fear the police? They
25   could certainly afford to grease the right palms. Put
26   a man in a cage and he turns into a beast. What
27   happens if you put a monkey in a palace? I often
28   wondered about this.
29   Moneybags or skid-row bum, nobody was safe.
30   There was a friend of mine, a little Italian guy, a
31   "keep-fit" nut, who used to go out jogging. He liked
32   to jog at five o'clock every morning. We tried to warn
33   him, but he wouldn't listen. He went out dressed in a
34   T-shirt and shorts, and left his watch and wallet at
35   home. "How can they rob me," he said, "when I have

1   nothing for them to rob?" Well, one day they caught
2   him. Since they had nothing else to take, they took
3   his shirt and shorts, and sent him streaking home.
4   And so we settled down to our life in Lagos — Lisa,
5   my wife Jane, and I... *(He fixes BILL with a piercing stare.)*
6   A lot of our friends fled the country at the first
7   opportunity. They couldn't take the tension, the
8   constant fear of visitors in the night. But not me! I
9   knew what to do, and so did my wife. Christ, she was
10   a plucky one all right. But she knew she could count
11   on me. Mind you, I'm no Chuck Norris. Karate is not
12   my bag, and guns were never my style. I don't
13   approve of violence, never have and never will.
14   There's nothing that can't be settled by negotiation
15   — a little bit of give and take. Believe me, my boy...
16   *(He leans over and practically whispers the last words*
17   *into BILL's ear.)* **The tongue is mightier than the sword.**
18   *(He pauses for effect.)*
19   One night they came to my house — about ten of
20   them, in an Isuzu station wagon. I'm a light sleeper
21   and I heard them coming. They had killed the dog,
22   tied up the guard, and cut the telephone cable. I saw
23   it all from my upstairs window. I woke up my wife
24   and told her to go to Lisa's room.
25   "Shhh...quiet!" I whispered, "Hide under the bed and
26   don't worry. I'll make sure those devils don't find you."
27   I went downstairs and opened the front door. They
28   were all out there, getting ready to break it down.
29   They were armed with guns, rifles, knives, and even
30   a machete. Some of them were ragged and bare-foot.
31   Others wore designer clothes. All were black, fierce
32   and dangerous. The leader was tall and boney, with a
33   broken nose and an air of authority. He was dressed
34   in casual splendor: blue Jordache jeans, a dark
35   striped T-shirt, and black crocodile skin shoes. He

1   had a red silk scarf tied around his neck. I wished
2   them "good evening" and invited them in. I told
3   them that they were welcome to take anything from
4   the house, and I would help in every way. I said I had
5   four air conditioners, one television, two video
6   recorders, a refrigerator, and a music system. I
7   showed them the assorted pieces of silverware in the
8   dining room. I offered to pack up each article in its
9   respective carton, now stored in the garage, and load
10   it into their station wagon.
11   "You certainly are a pleasant fellow, my friend,"
12   said the leader of the gang. "We don't usually meet
13   such intelligent and understanding people in our
14   trade."
15   "We're hungry!" they said. "Get us something to
16   eat." My wife, bless her soul, always kept the freezer
17   well-stocked. One of those bearded, bare-foot jocks
18   turned out to be an excellent cook. "Chicken legs,"
19   he said, rubbing his hands and picking up the kitchen
20   knife. I brought out half a dozen bottles of nicely
21   chilled Chablis from the cellar. We had a feast. Some
22   of the punks were sprawled on the floor as they ate.
23   "I have some fine Napoleon brandy," I said, when
24   dinner was over. By this time quite a few of my guests
25   were asleep on the carpet.
26   "My name," said the leader, as he savoured the
27   aroma of the brandy, "is Charles Augustine
28   Chukueke. But you may call me Chuck." It was
29   nearing dawn when they finally left. "Thank you, my
30   friend," said Chuck, "for a truly memorable evening.
31   I wish there were more people like you in this world."
32   They left without taking anything, not even the
33   antique silver tea pot that sat on the buffet.
34   *(BILL gets up to go.)*
35 WALTER: Wait! Don't go! There's just a little more to my

1 story. The next morning I was arrested by the police.
2 You see, those blasted devils had stopped at my
3 neighbor's on their way home, and relieved him of
4 about ten thousand dollars' worth of jewelry and elec-
5 trical goods. And my good neighbor told the police
6 that this was after attending a long and noisy party
7 at my place. Unfortunately, there was no room for
8 negotiation at the police station. I had to pay an
9 expensive lawyer to do it for me.
10
11
12
13
14
15
16
17
18
19
20
21
22
23
24
25
26
27
28
29
30
31
32
33
34
35

Miss Lulu Bett

by Zona Gale

A champion of women's rights, Zona Gale often wrote about mid-American towns, which she exposed as dull and petty. Many of her plays were developed from her novels, as is the case with *Miss Lulu Bett*, which was awarded a Pulitzer Prize.

The plot is a simple one in which Lulu lives in a household composed of her sister's family and her mother. She does all the housework and cooking and receives almost no compensation for it. Although she works very hard, her sister and brother-in-law insist that she is too weak to work outside the home. Dwight often makes jokes at her expense and Ina, the sister, is so selfish she orders Lulu to cater to almost any whim.

Lulu has no life of her own; she has never received a compliment except on her cooking, and she never goes anywhere. That is, until Ninian arrives in town. Dwight's brother, he is a romantic, moving from place to place, not taking life seriously.

While in town, Ninian invites Dwight, Ina (Lulu's sister) and Lulu to go to the theatre with him. Lulu has nothing appropriate to wear and puts together what she considers a mismatched, inappropriate outfit.

Ninian doesn't care; he's attracted to her. As a joke, he starts saying the wedding ceremony: "I, Ninian, take thee, Lulu, to be my wedded wife." Lulu answers in kind, and Dwight says that civil weddings are legal in their state and he is empowered to conduct them. So as it turns out, Ninian and Lulu are married.

Lulu goes off with Ninian but returns shortly thereafter saying Ninian was already married. Lulu is taken back by the family and once more treated like a slave.

There were two endings, both different from the novel in which she marries a man who has recently moved to town. In the first ending, performed for the original 1920 production, the new man does ask Lulu to marry him. Instead, she says she may do that, but first she has to "see out of her own eyes." This ending was not well-accepted in New York, though it was on tour. In the new ending, Ninian discovers his first wife, whom he hasn't seen in many years, died long ago. He comes back for Lulu.

SCENE 1: One Male and One Female

Lulu, 33

Ninian, probably a few years older

Monona, a young child

    The following scene occurs part of the way into Act I, Scene 2, the first time Lulu and Ninian talk. Ninian has arrived in town a few days earlier. If you wish, you just skip Monona's speech.

1. What are some of the things about Lulu that Ninian finds attractive? Point this out in the dialog.

2. Why do you suppose Lulu has pretty much accepted as her lot in life that she has to take care of her sister's family? Is this logical? Why?

3. What provides humor in this scene?

4. Do you think Lulu is happy? Satisfied with her life? Why? Back up what you say by finding supporting material in the dialog.

5. Why do you suppose Lulu has trouble accepting that Ninian finds her attractive?

6. How do Ninian and Lulu view life differently?

1   LULU: I — I think I was wondering what kind of pies you
2   like best.
3   NINIAN: That's easy. I like your kind of pies best. The best
4   ever. Every day since I've been here I've seen you
5   baking, Mrs. Bett.
6   LULU: Yes, I — bake. What did you call me then?
7   NINIAN: Mrs. Bett — isn't it? Every one says just Lulu, but
8   I took it for granted...Well, now — is it Mrs.? Or Miss
9   Lulu Bett?
10 LULU: It's Miss...From choice.
11 NINIAN: You bet! Oh, you bet! Never doubted that.
12 LULU: What kind of a Mr. are you?
13 NINIAN: Never give myself away. Say, by George, I never
14   thought of that before. There's no telling whether a
15   man's married or not, by his name.
16 LULU: It doesn't matter.
17 NINIAN: Why?
18 LULU: Not so many people want to know.
19 NINIAN: Say, you're pretty good, aren't you?
20 LULU: If I am it never took me very far.
21 NINIAN: Where you been mostly?
22 LULU: Here. I've always been here. Fifteen years with Ina.
23   Before that we lived in the country.
24 NINIAN: Never been anywhere much?
25 LULU: Never been anywhere at all.
26 NINIAN: Hmmm. Well, I want to tell you something about
27   yourself.
28 LULU: About me?
29 NINIAN: Something that I'll bet you don't even know. It's
30   this: I think you have it pretty hard around here.
31 LULU: Oh, no!
32 NINIAN: See here. Do you have to work like this all the
33   time? I guess you won't mind my asking.
34 LULU: But I ought to work. I have a home with them.
35   Mother, too.

1   NINIAN: But glory! You ought to have some kind of a life
2   of your own.
3   LULU: How could I do that?
4   NINIAN: A man don't even know what he's like till he's
5   roamed around on his own...Roamed around on his
6   own. Course a woman don't understand that.
7   LULU: Why don't she? Why don't she?
8   NINIAN: Do you? *(LULU nods.)* I've had twenty-five years
9   galloping about — Brazil, Mexico, Panama.
10   LULU: My!
11   NINIAN: It's the life.
12   LULU: Must be. I —
13   NINIAN: Yes, you. Why, you've never had a thing! I guess
14   you don't know how it seems to me, coming along —
15   a stranger so. I don't like it.
16   LULU: They're very good to me.
17   NINIAN: Do you know why you think that? Because you've
18   never had anybody really be good to you. That's why.
19   LULU: But they treat me good.
20   NINIAN: They make a slavey of you. Regular slavey.
21   Damned shame *I* call it.
22   LULU: But we have our whole living —
23   NINIAN: And you earn it. I been watching you ever since
24   I've been here. Don't you ever go anywhere?
25   LULU: Oh, no, I don't go anywhere. I —
26   NINIAN: Lord! Don't you want to? Of course you do.
27   LULU: Of course I'd like to get clear away — or I used to
28   want to.
29   NINIAN: Say — you've been a blamed fine-looking woman.
30   LULU: You must have been a good-looking man once
31   yourself.
32   NINIAN: You're pretty good. I don't see how you do it,
33   darned if I do.
34   LULU: How I do what?
35   NINIAN: Why come back, quick like that, with what you

1   say. You don't look it.
2   LULU: It must be my grand education.
3   NINIAN: Education: I ain't never had it and I ain't never
4   missed it.
5   LULU: Most folks are happy without an education.
6   NINIAN: You're not very happy, though.
7   LULU: Oh, no.
8   NINIAN: Well you ought to get up and get out of here —
9   find — find some work you *like* to do.
10   LULU: But, you see, I can't do any other work — that's the
11   trouble — women like me can't do any other work.
12   NINIAN: But you make this whole house go round.
13   LULU: If I do, nobody knows it.
14   NINIAN: I know it. I hadn't been in the house twenty-four
15   hours till I knew it.
16   LULU: You did? You thought that...Yes, well if I do I hate
17   making it go round.
18   NINIAN: See here — couldn't you tell me a little bit about
19   — what you'd *like* to do? If you had your own way?
20   LULU: I don't know — now.
21   NINIAN: What did you ever think you'd like to do?
22   LULU: Take care of folks that needed me. I — I mean sick
23   folks or old folks or — like that. Take care of them.
24   Have them — have them want me.
25   NINIAN: By George! You're a wonder.
26   LULU: Am I? Ask Dwight.
27   NINIAN: Dwight. I could knock the top of his head off the
28   way he speaks to you. I'd like to see you get out of
29   this, I certainly would.
30   LULU: I can't get out. I'll never get out — now.
31   NINIAN: Don't keep saying "now" like that. You — you put
32   me out of business, darned if you don't.
33   LULU: Oh, I don't mean to feel sorry for myself — you stop
34   making me feel sorry for myself!
35   NINIAN: I know one thing — I'm going to give Dwight

1   Deacon a chunk of my mind.

2   LULU: Oh, no! no! no! I wouldn't want you to do that.

3   Thank you.

4   NINIAN: Well, somebody ought to do something. See here

5   — while I'm staying around you know you've got a

6   friend in me, don't you?

7   LULU: Do I?

8   NINIAN: You bet you do.

9   LULU: Not just my cooking?

10   NINIAN: Oh, come now — why, I liked you the first moment

11   I saw you.

12   LULU: Honest?

13   NINIAN: Go on — go on. Did you like me?

14   LULU: Now you're just being polite.

15   NINIAN: Say, I wish there was some way —

16   LULU: Don't you bother about me.

17   NINIAN: I wish there was some way —

18   *(MONONA's voice chants. Enter MONONA.)*

19   MONONA: You've had him long enough, Aunt Lulu — Can't

20   you pay me some 'tention?

21   NINIAN: Come here. Give us a kiss. My stars, what a great

22   big tall girl! Have to put a board on her head to stop

23   this growing.

24   MONONA: *(Seeing diamond)* What's that?

25   NINIAN: That diamond came from Santa Claus. He has a

26   jewelry shop in heaven. I have twenty others like this

27   one. I keep the others to wear on the Sundays when

28   the sun comes up in the west.

29   MONONA: Does the sun ever come up in the west?

30   NINIAN: Sure — on my honor. Some day I'm going to melt

31   a diamond and eat it. Then you sparkle all over in the

32   dark, ever after. I'm going to plant one too, some day.

33   Then you can grow a diamond vine. Yes, on my honor.

34   LULU: Don't do that — don't do that.

35   NINIAN: What?

1   LULU: To her. That's lying.

2   NINIAN: Oh, no. That's not lying. That's just drama.

3   Drama. Do you like going to a good show?

4   LULU: I've never been to any; only those that come here.

5   NINIAN: Think of that now. Don't you ever go to the city?

6   LULU: I haven't been in six years and over.

7   NINIAN: Well, sir, I'll tell you what I'm going to do with

8   you. While I'm here I'm going to take you and Ina and

9   Dwight up to the city, to see a show.

10   LULU: Oh, you don't want me to go.

11   NINIAN: Yes, sir, I'll give you one good time. Dinner and a

12   show.

13   LULU: Ina and Dwight do that sometimes. I can't imagine

14   me.

15   NINIAN: Well, you're coming with me. I'll look up some-

16   thing good. And you tell me just what you like to eat

17   and we'll order it —

18   LULU: It's been years since I've eaten anything that I

19   haven't cooked myself.

20   NINIAN: It has. Say, by George! Why shouldn't we go to the

21   city *tonight*.

22   LULU: Tonight?

23   NINIAN: Yes. If Dwight and Ina will. It's early yet. What do

24   you say?

25   LULU: You sure you want me to go? Why — I don't know

26   whether I've got anything I could wear.

27   NINIAN: Sure you have.

28   LULU: I — yes, I have. I could wear the waist I always

29   thought they'd use — if I died.

30   NINIAN: Sure you could wear that. Just the thing. And

31   throw some things in a bag — it'll be too late to come

32   back tonight. Now don't you back out...

33   LULU: Oh, the pies —

34   NINIAN: Forget the pies — well, no, I wouldn't say that.

35   But hustle them up.

1   **LULU: Oh, maybe Ina won't go...**
2   **NINIAN: Leave Ina to me.**
3
4
5
6
7
8
9
10
11
12
13
14
15
16
17
18
19
20
21
22
23
24
25
26
27
28
29
30
31
32
33
34
35

SCENE 2: Two Females and One Male

Ina, 30s

Dwight, a little older

Lulu, 33

This scene occurs a few minutes into Act II. Lulu has gone off with Ninian and now has returned home after discovering that Ninian already was married to someone else.

If you wish you can cut the dialog pertaining to what Mrs. Bett says, that is, both her speeches and the responses to it. The scene still will have continuity.

1. What does Dwight mean by saying, "That's a pretty story"?

2. Why does Lulu say she wishes Ninian hadn't told her about his first marriage until they'd reached Oregon?

3. What provides the conflict in this scene? Point it out in the dialog.

4. What is Dwight's major concern about what has happened? What does this say about the type of person he is?

5. Why does Ina say "Why, Lulu, anyone would think you loved him"? What is she implying here?

6. What do you think Dwight is implying when he asks if Ninian gave Lulu any proof of his first marriage?

7. What emotions would Lulu be feeling in this scene? How might you portray them for an audience?

8. In what way is Dwight's final speech in this scene ironic?

1   INA: Mercy, think of anything like that in our family.
2   DWIGHT: Well, go on — go on. Tell us about it.
3   LULU: We were going to Oregon. First down to New Orleans
4   and then out to California and up the coast...Well,
5   then at Savannah, Georgia, he said he thought I
6   better know first. So then he told me.
7   DWIGHT: Yes — well, what did he say?
8   LULU: Cora Waters. Cora Waters. She married him down in
9   San Diego eighteen years ago. She went to South
10   America with him.
11   DWIGHT: Well, he never let us know of it, if she did.
12   LULU: No. She married him just before he went. Then in
13   South America, after two years, she ran away. That's
14   all he knows.
15   DWIGHT: That's a pretty story.
16   LULU: He says if she was alive she'd be after him for a
17   divorce. And she never has been so he thinks she
18   must be dead. The trouble is he wasn't sure. And I
19   had to be sure.
20   INA: Well, but mercy! Couldn't he find out now?
21   LULU: It might take a long time and I didn't want to stay
22   and not know.
23   INA: Well, then, why didn't he say so here?
24   LULU: He would have. But you know how sudden every-
25   thing was. He said he thought about telling us right
26   here that afternoon when — when it happened but, of
27   course, that'd been hard, wouldn't it? And then he
28   felt so sure she was dead.
29   INA: Why did he tell you at all then?
30   DWIGHT: Yes. Why indeed?
31   LULU: I thought that just at first but only just at first. Of
32   course that wouldn't have been right. And then you
33   see he gave me my choice.
34   DWIGHT: Gave you your choice?
35   LULU: Yes. About going on and taking the chances. He

1   **gave me my choice when he told me, there in**

2   **Savannah, Georgia.**

3   **DWIGHT: What made him conclude by then that you ought**

4   **to be told?**

5   **LULU: Why, he'd got to thinking about it.** *(A silence)* **The**

6   **only thing, as long as it happened, I kind of wish he**

7   **hadn't told me till we got to Oregon.**

8   **INA: Lulu! Oh, you poor, poor thing...**

9   *(MRS. BETT suddenly joins INA in tears, rocking her body.)*

10   **LULU: Don't, mother. Oh, Ina, don't...He felt bad too.**

11   **DWIGHT: He! He must have.**

12   **INA: It's you. It's you.** *My* **sister!**

13   **LULU: I never thought of it making you both feel bad. I**

14   **knew it would make Dwight feel bad. I mean, it was**

15   **his brother —**

16   **INA: Thank goodness! Nobody need know about it.**

17   **LULU: Oh, yes. People will have to know.**

18   **DWIGHT: I do not see the necessity.**

19   **LULU: Why, what would they think?**

20   **DWIGHT: What difference does it make what they think?**

21   **LULU: Why, I shouldn't like — you see they might — why,**

22   **Dwight, I think we'll have to tell them.**

23   **DWIGHT: You do. You think the disgrace of bigamy in this**

24   **family is something the whole town will have to know**

25   **about.**

26   **LULU: Say. I never thought about it being that.**

27   **DWIGHT: What did you think it was? And whose disgrace**

28   **is it, pray?**

29   **LULU: Mine. And Ninian's.**

30   **DWIGHT: Ninian's. Well, he's gone. But you're here. And**

31   **I'm here — and my family. Folks'll feel sorry for you.**

32   **But the disgrace, that would reflect on me.**

33   **LULU: But if we don't tell what'll they think?**

34   **DWIGHT: They'll think what they always think when a**

35   **wife leaves her husband. They'll think you couldn't**

1   get along. That's all.

2 LULU: I should hate that. I wouldn't want them to think I

3   hadn't been a good wife to Ninian.

4 DWIGHT: Wife? You never were his wife. That's just the

5   point.

6 LULU: Oh!

7 DWIGHT: Don't you realize the position he's in?...See here

8   — do you intend — Are you going to sue Ninian?

9 LULU: Oh! No! No! No!

10 INA: Why, Lulu, anyone would think you loved him.

11 LULU: I do love him. And he loved me. Don't you think I

12   know? He loved me.

13 INA: Lulu.

14 LULU: I love him — I do, and I'm not ashamed to tell you.

15 MRS. BETT: Lulie, Lulie, was his other wife — was she

16   there?

17 LULU: No, no, Mother. She wasn't there.

18 MRS. BETT: Then it ain't so bad. I was afraid maybe she

19   turned you out.

20 LULU: No, no. It wasn't that bad, Mother.

21 DWIGHT: In fact, I simply will not have it, Lulu. You

22   expect, I take it, to make your home with us in the

23   future on the old terms.

24 LULU: Well —

25 DWIGHT: I mean, did Ninian give you any money?

26 LULU: No. He didn't give me any money — only enough to

27   get home on. And I kept my suit and the other dress

28   — why! I wouldn't have taken any money.

29 DWIGHT: That means that you will have to continue to

30   live here on the old terms and, of course, I'm quite

31   willing that you should. Let me tell you, however,

32   that this is on condition — on condition that this

33   disgraceful business is kept to ourselves.

34 INA: Truly, Lulu, wouldn't that be best? They'll talk

35   anyway. But this way they'll only talk about you and

1   the other way it'll be about all of us.

2 LULU: But the other way would be the truth.

3 DWIGHT: My dear Lulu, are you sure of that?

4 LULU: Sure?

5 DWIGHT: Yes. Did he give you any proofs?

6 LULU: Proofs?

7 DWIGHT: Letter — documents of any sort? Any sort of

8   assurance that he was speaking the truth?

9 LULU: Why — no. Proofs — no. He told me.

10 DWIGHT: He told you!

11 LULU: That was hard enough to have to do. It was terrible

12   for him to have to do. What proofs —

13 DWIGHT: I may as well tell you that I myself have no idea

14   that Ninian told you the truth. He was always imag-

15   ining things, inventing things — you must have seen

16   that. I know him pretty well — have been in touch

17   with him more or less the whole time. In short, I

18   haven't the least idea he was ever married before.

19 LULU: I never thought of that.

20 DWIGHT: Look here — hadn't you and he had some little

21   tiff when he told you?

22 LULU: No — no! Not once. He was very good to me. This

23   dress — and my shoes — and my hat. And another

24   dress, too. *(She takes off her hat.)* He liked the red wing —

25   I wanted black — oh, Dwight! He did tell me the truth!

26 DWIGHT: As long as there's any doubt about it — and I feel

27   the gravest doubts — I desire that you should keep

28   silent and protect my family from this scandal. I have

29   taken you into my confidence about these doubts for

30   your own profit.

31 LULU: My own profit! *(Moves toward the door.)*

32 INA: Lulu — you see! We just couldn't have this known

33   about Dwight's own brother, could we now?

34 DWIGHT: You have it in your own hands to repay me, Lulu,

35   for anything that you feel I may have done for you in

1   the past. You also have it in your hands to decide
2   whether your home here continues. This is not a
3   pleasant position for me to find myself in. In fact, it
4   is distinctly unpleasant I may say. But you see for
5   yourself. *(Lulu goes into the house.)*
6
7
8
9
10
11
12
13
14
15
16
17
18
19
20
21
22
23
24
25
26
27
28
29
30
31
32
33
34
35

SCENE 3: Two Females

Lulu Bett, 33

Di, about 16

Di, a high school girl, is Lulu's niece. Throughout the play there has been a secondary plot about her relationship with Bobby Larkin. Dwight and Ina are out of town when the following occurs.

1. Di and Bobby's relationship in a way parallels that of Lulu and Ninian. Yet there are a lot of differences in the two situations. Can you explain what they are?

2. Di says that Lulu doesn't know what it's like to be laughed at and not paid attention to. Yet this is exactly how Dwight and Ina treat Lulu. Why do you suppose Di doesn't see this? How would Di's speech affect Lulu, do you think?

3. Do you think Di would be happier running off with Bobby? Explain.

1   LULU: Di! Why, Di! What does this mean? Where were you
2   going? Why, Mama won't like your carrying her nice
3   new satchel...
4   DI: Aunt Lulu — the idea. What right have you to interfere
5   with me like this?
6   LULU: Di, you must explain to me what this means...Di,
7   where can you be going with a satchel this time of
8   the night? Di Deacon, are you running away with
9   somebody?
10 DI: You have no right to ask me questions, Aunt Lulu.
11 LULU: Di, you're going off with Bobby Larkin. Aren't you?
12   Aren't you?
13 DI: If I am it's entirely our own affair.
14 LULU: Why, Di. If you and Bobby want to be married why
15   not let us get you up a nice wedding here at home —
16 DI: Aunt Lulu, you're a funny person to be telling me what
17   to do.
18 LULU: I love you just as much as if I was married happy,
19   in a home.
20 DI: Well, you aren't. And I'm going to do just as I think
21   best. Bobby and I are the ones most concerned in
22   this, Aunt Lulu.
23 LULU: But — but getting married is for your whole life!
24 DI: Yours wasn't.
25 LULU: Di, my dear little girl, you must wait at least till
26   Mama and Papa get home.
27 DI: That's likely. They say I'm not to be married till I'm
28   twenty-one.
29 LULU: Well, but how young that is.
30 DI: It is to you. It isn't young to me, remember, Aunt Lulu.
31 LULU: But this is wrong — it is wrong!
32 DI: There's nothing wrong about getting married if you
33   stay married.
34 LULU: Well, then it can't be wrong to let your mother and
35   father know.

1   DI: It isn't. But they'd treat me wrong. Mama'd cry and say
2   I was disgracing *her*. And Papa — first he'd scold me
3   and then he'd joke me about it. He'd joke me about
4   it every day for weeks, every morning at breakfast,
5   every night here on the porch — he'd joke me.
6   LULU: Why, Di! Do you feel that way, too?
7   DI: You don't know what it is to be laughed at or paid no
8   attention to, everything you say.
9   LULU: Don't I? Don't I? Is that why you're going?
10   DI: Well, it's one reason.
11   LULU: But, Di, do you love Bobby Larkin?
12   DI: Well...I could love almost anybody real nice that was
13   nice to me.
14   LULU: Di...Di...
15   DI: It's true. *(BOBBY enters.)* You ought to know that...You
16   did it. Mama said so.
17   LULU: Don't you think that I don't know...
18
19
20
21
22
23
24
25
26
27
28
29
30
31
32
33
34
35

Painting Churches

by Tina Howe

Painting Churches, a portrait of the three members of the Church family, opened in New York in 1983 where it won a number of awards. The three characters, though tied by blood and feelings, nevertheless exist in their own worlds. In effect, this is a family on its way to being totally dysfunctional. This is seen in several ways. Gardner, the father, a well-known and highly respected poet, now lives in his own world, probably experiencing the beginning stages of Alzheimer's disease or some other sort of senility. Whereas, while his wife Fanny seems indiscriminately to dislike any existing condition or state, Gardner goes to opposite extremes in liking everything.

Fanny creates her own world in which she amuses herself by buying hats in thrift shops and ignoring or pushing away the seriousness of her husband's mental state. In fact, she even goes so far as to laugh at him and mock the things he does. Although he is a distinguished writer, she treats his books and manuscripts as meaningless, mere toys with which to amuse himself.

The daughter, Mags, a painter and painting instructor, seems to be concerned with her parents. Yet the play reveals that she is more interested in painting a portrait of them and having them accept it as good. It is a sad play in which the family's entire existence is changing as symbolized in Fanny and Gardner's move from a large house to a beach cottage. Their life is going from something grand to something humble.

The play occurs in a short space of time in which Mags has returned home to paint the portrait. Although she wants to preserve their likenesses on canvas, she refuses to see them realistically.

Tina Howe is the author of a number of plays. An instructor at Hunter College and New York University, she has served as a council member of the Dramatists Guild.

The play occurs in the "living room of the Churches' townhouse on Beacon Hill" "several years ago." Howe describes the place as being, at first glance, "like any other discreet Boston interior." Yet a closer look shows "a certain flamboyance. Oddities from secondhand stores are mixed in with fine old furniture, and exotic handmade curios vie with tasteful family objets d'art." The room, however, is made "remarkable" through "the play of light that pours through three soaring arched windows. At one hour it's hard-edged and brilliant; the next, it's dappled and yielding. It transforms whatever it touches, giving the room a distinct feeling of unreality."

SCENE 1: One Male and One Female

Fanny Sedgwick Church, 60s

Gardner Church, her husband, 70s

The scene occurs a minute or two after the play has opened when Fanny has been examining her mother's old silver and remarking on how she can never let it go, no matter how desperate things become. She calls to Gardner to come and guess how much her hat costs. He thinks she's calling to say that Mags has arrived. He is carrying typing paper which he continues to drop while Fanny insists he look at and comment on the hat she is wearing.

1. Although this is rather a static scene, that is, it doesn't seem to move the action forward, there is underlying tension and conflict. This is shown in the dialog between the two characters. What do you think is at the basis of the conflict? Point to specific lines that back up what you say.

2. Why do you think the hat is so important to Fanny, and why is she so concerned about convincing Gardner that it has a Lily Daché label? Why does she want Gardner to guess how much it is, and why is it so important to her that he guess high? Why does she not want to admit that Gardner's bathrobe also was designed by Daché?

3. Which of the two characters is more likeable? Why do you think so? Do you see any familiar traits that they possess? Explain.

4. If you examine the dialog, you can see that both Gardner and Fanny are immersed in their own little worlds, their own perceptions of reality. From what you can see in the lines and action, what can you tell about each of these worlds? Is one or the other more realistic? Explain.

5. Judging only from this scene, can you speculate as to why this play was so successful?

1   FANNY: *(Gets to them first.)* **It's all right, I've got them, I've**
2   **got them.** *(She hands them to him.)*
3   GARDNER: **You'd think they had wings on them...**
4   FANNY: **Here you go...**   GARDNER:**...damned things**
5   **won't hold still!**
6   FANNY: **Gar...?**
7   GARDNER: *(Engrossed in one of the pages)* **Mmmm?**
8   FANNY: **HELLO?**
9   GARDNER: *(Startled)* **What's that?**
10 FANNY: *(In a whisper)* **My hat. Guess how much it cost.**
11 GARDNER: **Oh, yes. Let's see...ten dollars?**
12 FANNY: **Ten dollars...IS THAT ALL?**
13 GARDNER: **Twenty?**
14 FANNY: **GARDNER, THIS HAPPENS TO BE A DESIGNER**
15   **HAT! DESIGNER HATS START AT FIFTY DOL-**
16   **LARS...SEVENTY-FIVE!**
17 GARDNER: *(Jumps.)* **Was that the doorbell?**
18 FANNY: **No, it wasn't the doorbell. Though it's high time**
19   **Mags were here. She was probably in a train wreck!**
20 GARDNER: *(Looking through his papers)* **I'm beginning to get**
21   **fond of Wallace Stevens again.**
22 FANNY: **This damned move is going to kill me! Send me**
23   **straight to my grave!**
24 GARDNER: *(Reading from a page)*
25   **"The mules that angels ride come slowly down**
26   **The blazing passes, from beyond the sun.**
27   **Descensions of their tinkling bells arrive.**
28   **These muleteers are dainty of their way..."**
29   *(Pause)* **Don't you love that! "These muleteers are**
30   *dainty* **of their way"!?**
31 FANNY: **Gar, the hat. How much?** *(GARDNER sighs.)*
32   **Darling ...?**
33 GARDNER: **Oh, yes. Let's see...fifty dollars? Seventy-five?**
34 FANNY: **It's French.**
35 GARDNER: **Three hundred!**

1   FANNY: *(Triumphant)* **No, eighty-five cents.**

2   GARDNER: **Eighty-five cents!...I thought you said...**

3   FANNY: **That's right...eighty...five...*cents!***

4   GARDNER: **Well, you sure had me fooled!**

5   FANNY: **I found it at the thrift shop.**

6   GARDNER: **I thought it cost at least fifty dollars or**

7   **seventy-five. You know, designer hats are very**

8   **expensive!**

9   FANNY: **It was on the markdown table.** *(She takes it off and*

10   *shows him the label.)* **See that? Lily Daché! When I saw**

11   **that label, I nearly keeled over right into the fur coats!**

12   GARDNER: *(Handling it)* **Well, what do you know, that's the**

13   **same label that's in my bathrobe.**

14   FANNY: **Darling, Lily Daché designed hats, not men's**

15   **bathrobes!**

16   GARDNER: **Yup...Lily Daché...same name...**

17   FANNY: **If you look again, I'm sure you'll see...**

18   GARDNER: **...same script, same color, same size. I'll show**

19   **you.** *(He exits.)*

20   FANNY: **Poor lamb can't keep anything straight anymore.**

21   *(Looks at herself in the tray again.)* **God, this is a good-**

22   **looking hat!**

23   GARDNER: *(Returns with a nondescript plaid bathrobe. He*

24   *points to the label.)* **See that?...What does it say?**

25   FANNY: *(Refusing to look at it)* **Lily Daché was a hat designer!**

26   **She designed ladies' hats!**

27   GARDNER: **What...does...it...say?**

28   FANNY: **Gardner, you're being ridiculous.**

29   GARDNER: *(Forcing it on her)* **Read...the label!**

30   FANNY: **Lily Daché did not design this bathrobe, I don't**

31   **care what the label says!**

32   GARDNER: **READ!** *(FANNY reads it.)* **ALL RIGHT, NOW WHAT**

33   **DOES IT SAY?**

34   FANNY: *(Chagrined)* **Lily Daché.**

35   GARDNER: **I told you!**

1   **FANNY: Wait a minute, let me look at that again.** *(She does;*
2   *then throws the robe at him in disgust.)* **Gar, Lily Daché**
3   **never designed a bathrobe in her life! Someone obvi-**
4   **ously ripped the label off one of her hats and then**
5   **sewed it into the robe.**
6   **GARDNER:** *(Puts it on over his jacket.)* **It's damned good-**
7   **looking. I've always loved this robe. I think you gave**
8   **it to me...Well, I've got to get back to work.** *(He*
9   *abruptly exits.)*
10 **FANNY: Where did you get that robe anyway?...I didn't**
11   **give it to you, did I...?**
12
13
14
15
16
17
18
19
20
21
22
23
24
25
26
27
28
29
30
31
32
33
34
35

SCENE 2: Two Females and One Male

Mags, early 30s

Fanny, 60s

Gardner, 70s

There is only an intervening monolog and a few short speeches between the last scene and this one.

1. What can you tell in this scene about the relationship Mags has with Fanny? With Gardner? Explain.

2. Why do you suppose Fanny says it's "so typical" that her zipper has broken? Why do you suppose both she and Mags are so flustered? What does this say about their relationship? What makes you think so?

3. First Fanny "staggers around blindly" and then Gardner lurches "around in circles" with Mags' luggage. What could this symbolize? Explain. What is symbolic about Gardner's white hair? How does Mags see his becoming gray differently from the way Fanny does? Why do you suppose Fanny objects to Mags' changing her hair color while Gardner says it's "damned attractive"?

4. Why do you suppose Mags says that she doesn't want her parents to move? Would you feel the same way? If you already have experienced a move or moves, how did this make you feel? Can you identify with Mags' feelings? Is she being realistic about it? Explain.

5. Why do you suppose that Mags at this particular time, when her parents are in the midst of packing to move, has decided that no matter what, she wants to paint their portraits?

6. Why do you think Mags says Fanny is exaggerating about Gardner's going into the wrong house? Which of the two would you believe in this regard? Explain. Remembering that Gardner is an eminent poet, why do you suppose Fanny makes fun of his writing literary criticism by saying "his mind is a complete jumble and always has been"?

1   MAGS: I'm sorry...I'm sorry I'm so late...Everything went
2   wrong! A passenger had a heart attack outside of New
3   London and we had to stop...It was terrifying! All
4   these medics and policemen came swarming onto the
5   train and the conductor kept running up and down
6   the aisles telling everyone not to leave their seats
7   under any circumstances...Then the New London fire
8   department came screeching down to the tracks,
9   sirens blaring, lights whirling, and all these men in
10   black rubber suits started pouring through the
11   doors...That took two hours...
12 FANNY: *(Offstage)* DARLING...DARLING...WHERE ARE YOU?
13 MAGS: *Then*, I couldn't get a cab at the station. There just
14   weren't any! I must have circled the block fifteen
15   times. Finally, I just stepped out into the traffic with
16   my thumb out, but no one would pick me up...so I
17   walked...
18 FANNY: *(Offstage)* Damned zipper's stuck...
19 GARDNER: You walked all the way from the South Station?
20 MAGS: Well actually, I ran...
21 GARDNER: You had poor Mum scared to death.
22 MAGS: *(Finally puts the bags down with a deep sigh.)* I'm
23   sorry...I'm really sorry. It was a nightmare.
24   *(FANNY re-enters the room, her dress over her head. The*
25   *zipper's stuck; she staggers around blindly.)*
26 FANNY: Damned zipper! Gar, will you please help me with
27   this?
28 MAGS: I sprinted all the way up Beacon Hill.
29 GARDNER: *(Opening his arms wide)* Well come here and let's
30   get a look at you. *(He hugs her.)* Mags!
31 MAGS: *(Squeezing him tight)* Oh, Daddy...Daddy!
32 GARDNER: My Mags!
33 MAGS: I never thought I'd get here!...Oh, you look
34   wonderful!
35 GARDNER: Well, you don't look so bad yourself!

1   MAGS: I love your hair. It's gotten so...white!
2   FANNY: (Still lost in her dress, struggling with the zipper) **This**
3   **is so typical...just as Mags arrives, my zipper has to**
4   **break!** (She grunts and struggles.)
5   MAGS: (Waves at her.) **Hi, Mum...**
6   FANNY: **Just a minute, dear, my zipper's...**
7   GARDNER: (Picks up MAGS' bags.) **Well, sit down and take a**
8   **load off your feet...**
9   MAGS: **I was so afraid I'd never make it...**
10 GARDNER: (Staggering under the weight of the bags) **What**
11   **have you got in here? Lead weights?**
12 MAGS: **I can't believe you're finally letting me do you.**
13   (FANNY flings her arms around MAGS, practically
14   knocking her over.)
15 FANNY: OH, DARLING...   GARDNER: (Lurching around in
16   MY PRECIOUS MAGS,   circles) **Now let's see...**
17   YOU'RE HERE AT   **Where should I put these?**
18   LAST.
19 FANNY: **I was sure your train had derailed and you were**
20   **lying dead in some ditch!**
21 MAGS: (Pulls away from FANNY to come to GARDNER's rescue.)
22   **Daddy, please, let me...these are much too heavy.**
23 FANNY: (Finally noticing MAGS) **GOOD LORD, WHAT HAVE**
24   **YOU DONE TO YOUR HAIR?!**
25 MAGS: (Struggling to take the bags from GARDNER) **Come on,**
26   **give them to me...please?** (She sets them down by the
27   sofa.)
28 FANNY: (As her dress starts to slide off one shoulder) **Oh, not**
29   **again!...Gar, would you give me a hand and see what's**
30   **wrong with this zipper? One minute it's stuck, the**
31   **next it's falling to pieces.**
32   (GARDNER goes to her and starts fussing with it.)
33 MAGS: (Pacing) **I don't know, it's been crazy all week.**
34   **Monday, I forgot to keep an appointment I'd made**
35   **with a new model...Tuesday, I overslept and stood up**

1   my advanced painting students...Wednesday, the day

2   of my meeting with Max Zoll, I forgot to put on my

3   underpants...

4   FANNY: GODDAMMIT, GAR, CAN'T YOU DO ANYTHING

5   ABOUT THIS ZIPPER?!

6   MAGS: I mean, there I was, racing down Broome Street in

7   this gauzy Tibetan skirt when I tripped and fell right

8   at his feet...SPLATTT! My skirt goes flying over my

9   head and there I am...everything staring him in the

10   face...

11   FANNY: COME ON, GAR, USE A LITTLE MUSCLE!

12   MAGS: *(Laughing)* Oh, well, all that matters is that I finally

13   got here...I mean...there you are...

14   GARDNER: *(Struggling with the zipper)* I can't see it, it's

15   too small!

16   FANNY: *(Whirls away from GARDNER, pulling her dress off*

17   *altogether.)* OH, FORGET IT! JUST FORGET IT! The

18   trolley's probably missing half its teeth, just like

19   someone else I know. *(To MAGS)* I grind my teeth in

20   my sleep now, I've worn them all down to stubs. Look

21   at that! *(She flings open her mouth and points.)* Nothing

22   left but the gums!

23   GARDNER: I never hear you grind your teeth...

24   FANNY: That's because I'm snoring so loud. How could

25   you hear anything through all that racket? It even

26   wakes me up. It's no wonder poor Daddy has to sleep

27   downstairs.

28   MAGS: *(Looking around)* Jeez, look at the place! So, you're

29   finally doing it...selling the house and moving to

30   Cotuit year round. I don't believe it. I just don't

31   believe it!

32   GARDNER: Well, how about a drink to celebrate Mags'

33   arrival?

34   MAGS: You've been here so long. Why move now?

35   FANNY: Gardner, what are you wearing that bathrobe for?

1   MAGS: You can't move. I won't let you!

2   FANNY: *(Softly to GARDNER)* **Really, darling, you ought to**

3   **pay more attention to your appearance.**

4   MAGS: You love this house. *I* love this house...the

5   room...the light.

6   GARDNER: So, Mags, how about a little... *(He drinks from an*

7   *imaginary glass)* **to wet your whistle?**

8   FANNY: We can't start drinking now, it isn't even noon yet!

9   MAGS: I'm starving. I've got to get something to eat before

10   I collapse! *(She exits towards the kitchen.)*

11   FANNY: What *have* you done to your hair, dear? The

12   color's so queer and all your nice curl is gone.

13   GARDNER: It looks to me as if she dyed it.

14   FANNY: Yes, that's it. You're absolutely right! It's a

15   completely different color. She dyed it bright red!

16   *(MAGS can be heard thumping and thudding through the*

17   *icebox.)*

18   FANNY: NOW, MAGS, I DON'T WANT YOU FILLING UP ON

19   SNACKS...I'VE MADE A PERFECTLY BEAUTIFUL LEG

20   OF LAMB FOR LUNCH!...HELLO?...DO YOU HEAR

21   ME?... *(To GARDNER)* **No one in our family has *ever***

22   had red hair, it's so common looking.

23   GARDNER: I like it. It brings out her eyes.

24   FANNY: WHY ON EARTH DID YOU DYE YOUR HAIR *RED*,

25   OF ALL COLORS?!

26   MAGS: *(Returns, eating Saltines out of the box.)* **I didn't dye**

27   my hair, I just added some highlight.

28   FANNY: I suppose that's what your arty friends in New

29   York do...dye their hair all the colors of the rainbow!

30   GARDNER: Well, it's damned attractive if you asked me...

31   damned attractive!

32   *(MAGS unzips her duffel bag and rummages around in it*

33   *while eating the Saltines.)*

34   FANNY: Darling, I told you not to bring a lot of stuff with

35   you. We're trying to get rid of things.

1   **MAGS:** *(Pulls out a folding easel and starts setting it up)*
2   **AAAHHH, here it is. Isn't it a beauty? I bought it just**
3   **for you!**
4   **FANNY: Please don't get crumbs all over the floor. Crystal**
5   **was just here yesterday. It was her last time before**
6   **we move.**
7   **MAGS:** *(At her easel)* **God, I can hardly wait! I can't believe**
8   **you're finally letting me do you.**
9   **FANNY: Do us?...What *are* you talking about?**
10   **GARDNER:** *(Reaching for the Saltines)* **Hey, Mags, could I**
11   **have a couple of those?**
12   **MAGS:** *(Tosses him the box.)* **Sure!** *(To FANNY)* **Your portrait.**
13   **GARDNER: Thanks. (***He starts munching on a handful.***)**
14   **FANNY: You're planning to paint our portrait now? While**
15   **we're trying to move...?**
16   **GARDNER:** *(Sputtering Saltines)* **Mmmm, I'd forgotten just**
17   **how delicious Saltines are!**
18   **MAGS: It's a perfect opportunity. There'll be no distrac-**
19   **tions; you'll be completely at my mercy. Also, you**
20   **promised.**
21   **FANNY: I did?**
22   **MAGS: Yes, you did.**
23   **FANNY: Well, I must have been off my rocker.**
24   **MAGS: No, you said, "You can paint us, you can dip us in**
25   **concrete, you can do anything you want with us just**
26   **so long as you help us get out of here!"**
27   **GARDNER:** *(Offering the box of Saltines to FANNY)* **You really**
28   **ought to try some of these, Fan, they're absolutely**
29   **delicious!**
30   **FANNY:** *(Taking a few)* **Why, thank you.**
31   **MAGS: I figure we'll pack in the mornings and you'll pose**
32   **in the afternoons. It'll be a nice diversion.**
33   **FANNY: These *are* good!**
34   **GARDNER: Here, dig in...take some more.**
35   **MAGS: I have some wonderful news...amazing news! I**

1   **wanted to wait till I got here to tell you.**
2   *(GARDNER and FANNY eat their Saltines, passing the box*
3   *back and forth as MAGS speaks.)*
4   **MAGS: You'll die! Just fall over into the packing cartons**
5   **and die! Are you ready?...BRACE YOURSELVES...**
6   **OKAY, HERE GOES...I'm being given a one-woman**
7   **show at one of the most important galleries in New**
8   **York this fall. Me, Margaret Church, exhibited at**
9   **Castelli's, 420 West Broadway...Can you believe it?!**
10   **...MY PORTRAITS HANGING IN THE SAME ROOMS**
11   **THAT HAVE SHOWN RAUSCHENBERG, JOHNS,**
12   **WARHOL, KELLY, LICHTENSTEIN, STELLA, SERRA,**
13   **ALL THE HEAVIES...It's incredible, beyond belief...I**
14   **mean, at my age...Do you know how good you have to**
15   **be to get in there? It's a miracle...an honest-to-God,**
16   **star-spangled miracle!** *(Pause)*
17   **FANNY:** *(Mouth full)* **Oh,**   **GARDNER:** *(Mouth full)* **No one**
18   **darling, that's wonder-**   **deserves it more, no**
19   **ful. We're so happy for**   **one deserves it more!**
20   **you!**
21   **MAGS: Through some fluke, some of Castelli's people**
22   **showed up at our last faculty show at Pratt and were**
23   **knocked out...**
24   **FANNY:** *(Reaching for the box of Saltines)* **More, more...**
25   **MAGS: They said they hadn't seen anyone handle light**
26   **like me since the French Impressionists. They said I**
27   **was this weird blend of Pierre Bonnard, Mary Cassatt**
28   **and David Hockney ...**
29   **GARDNER:** *(Swallowing his mouthful)* **I told you they were**
30   **good.**
31   **MAGS: Also, no one's doing portraits these days. They're**
32   **considered passé. I'm so out of it, I'm in.**
33   **GARDNER: Well, you're loaded with talent and always have**
34   **been.**
35   **FANNY: She gets it all from Mama, you know. Her miniature**

1   of Henry James is still one of the main attractions at

2   the Atheneum. Of course no woman of breeding could

3   be a professional artist in her day. It simply wasn't

4   done. But talk about talent...that woman had talent

5   to burn!

6 MAGS: I want to do one of you for the show.

7 FANNY: Oh, do Daddy, he's the famous one.

8 MAGS: No, I want to do you both. I've always wanted to do

9   you and now I've finally got a good excuse.

10 FANNY: It's high time somebody painted Daddy again! I'm

11   sick to death of that dreadful portrait of him in the

12   National Gallery they keep reproducing. He looks like

13   an undertaker!

14 GARDNER: Well, I think you should just do Mum. She's

15   never looked handsomer.

16 FANNY: Oh, come on, I'm a perfect fright and you know it.

17 MAGS: I want to do you both. Side by side. In this room.

18   Something really classy. You look so great. Mum with

19   her crazy hats and everything and you with that face.

20   If I could just get you to hold still long enough and

21   actually pose.

22 GARDNER: *(Walking around, distracted)* Where are those

23   papers I just had? Goddammit, Fanny...

24 MAGS: I have the feeling it's either now or never.

25 GARDNER: I can't hold on to anything around here. *(He*

26   *exits to his study.)*

27 MAGS: I've always wanted to do you. It would be such a

28   challenge.

29 FANNY: *(Pulling MAGS onto the sofa next to her)* I'm so glad

30   you're finally here, Mags. I'm very worried about

31   Daddy.

32 MAGS: Mummy, please. I just got here.

33 FANNY: He's getting quite gaga.

34 MAGS: Mummy...!

35 FANNY: You haven't seen him in almost a year. Two weeks

1   ago he walked through the front door of the
2   Codman's house, kissed Emily on the cheek and
3   settled down in the maid's room, thinking he was
4   home!
5 MAGS: Oh, come on, you're exaggerating.
6 FANNY: He's as mad as a hatter and getting worse every
7   day! It's this damned new book of his. He works on it
8   around the clock. I've read some of it, and it doesn't
9   make one word of sense, it's all at sixes and sevens...
10 GARDNER: *(Pokes his head back in the room, spies some of his*
11   *papers on a table and grabs them.)* **Ahhh, here they are.**
12   *(He exits.)*
13 FANNY: *(Voice lowered)* Ever since this dry spell with his
14   poetry, he's been frantic, absolutely...frantic!
15 MAGS: I hate it when you do this.
16 FANNY: I'm just trying to get you to face the facts around
17   here.
18 MAGS: There's nothing wrong with him! He's just as sane
19   as the next man. Even saner, if you ask me.
20 FANNY: You know what he's doing now? You couldn't
21   guess in a million years!...He's writing criticism!
22   Daddy! *(She laughs.)* Can you believe it? The man
23   doesn't have one analytic bone in his body. His mind
24   is a complete jumble and always has been!
25
26
27
28
29
30
31
32
33
34
35

SCENE 3: Two Females and One Male

Mags, early 30s

Gardner, 70s

Fanny, 60s

After the preceding scene, Fanny shows Mags a lampshade she has made, showing a scene in Venice. The three characters discuss the portrait Mags wants to do. At first, Fanny says she wants only Gardner to be in it. She and Gardner clown around taking different poses, while Mags says "It's not a game."

Gardner and Fanny discuss friends who are ill with various diseases, all the while Mags is trying to arrange things for painting the portrait. Mags feels that Fanny and Gardner think her portraits (her specialty) are "ridiculous." She tells about the time they completely embarrassed her at a showing of her and others' art.

The next segment of the play occurs two days later when Fanny and Gardner are going through their clothes, deciding what to take with them on the move. Mags takes a Polaroid shot which startles them. Gardner keeps making a tangled mess of his clothing while Fanny nags Mags about how forlorn she looks, telling her that if she continues not to care about her appearance she'll never get a husband. They discuss, while Mags makes fun of, her old boyfriends. Mags is getting things all arranged now for the portrait. That's where this scene begins. It continues to the end of Act I.

1. What do you think are Mags' feelings about her "great masterpiece" and what happened to it? Point to specific lines that back up what you say. Do you think the masterpiece should have been destroyed?

2. If you were to act in or direct this scene, what is the most important mood or feeling you would want to convey to an audience? Why?

3. Why do you suppose Fanny says she doesn't remember the things Mags describes doing as a child? Why do you suppose Gardner discusses in detail Mags' playing with her food and squirting it through her teeth? Why does Fanny not want her to discuss this? Would you feel the same way about discussing it? Why?

4. Why is and was the masterpiece so important to Mags? What can you deduce from this scene about the type of child Mags might have been? Can you understand or empathize with her feelings then? Now? Why?

5. Would you have let Mags keep her masterpiece? Why?

1   MAGS: *(Walking over to her easel)* **The great thing about**
2   **being a portrait painter, you see, is it's the** *other* **guy**
3   **that's exposed; you're safely hidden behind the**
4   **canvas and easel.** *(Standing behind it)* **You can be as**
5   **plain as a pitchfork, as inarticulate as mud, but it**
6   **doesn't matter because you're completely concealed:**
7   **your body, your face, your intentions. Just as you**
8   **make your most intimate move, throw open your**
9   **soul...they stretch and yawn, remembering the dog**
10   **has to be let out at five...To be so invisible while so**
11   **enthralled...it takes your breath away!**
12 GARDNER: Well put, Mags. Awfully well put!
13 MAGS: That's why I've always wanted to paint you, to see
14   if I'm up to it. It's quite a risk. Remember what I
15   went through as a child with my great master-
16   piece...?
17 FANNY: You painted a masterpiece when you were a
18   child...?
19 MAGS: Well, it was a masterpiece to me.
20 FANNY: I had no idea you were precocious as a child.
21   Gardner, do you remember Mags painting a master-
22   piece as a child?
23 MAGS: I didn't paint it. It was something I made!
24 FANNY: Well, this is all news to me! Gar, do get me another
25   drink! I haven't had this much fun in years! *(She*
26   *hands him her glass and reaches for MAGS'.)* **Come on,**
27   **darling, join me...**
28 MAGS: No, no more, thanks. I don't really like the taste.
29 FANNY: Oh, come on, kick up your heels for once!
30 MAGS: No, nothing...really.
31 FANNY: Please? Pretty please?...To keep me company?!
32 MAGS: *(Hands GARDNER her glass.)* **Oh, all right, what the**
33   **hell...**
34 FANNY: That's a good girl! GARDNER: *(Exiting)* **Coming**
35   **right up, coming right up.**

1   FANNY: *(Yelling after GARDNER)* **DON'T GIVE ME TOO MUCH**
2   **NOW. THE LAST ONE WAS AWFULLY STRONG...AND**
3   **HURRY BACK SO YOU DON'T MISS ANYTHING!...**
4   **Daddy's so cunning, I don't know what I'd do without**
5   **him. If anything should happen to him, I'd just...**
6   MAGS: **Mummy, nothing's going to happen to him...**
7   FANNY: **Well, wait till you're our age, it's no garden party.**
8   **Now...where were we...?**
9   MAGS: **My first masterpiece...**
10   FANNY: **Oh, yes, but do wait till Daddy gets back so he can**
11   **hear it too...YOO-HOO...GARRRDNERRR?... ARE YOU**
12   **COMING?** *(Silence)* **Go and check on him will you?**
13   *(GARDNER enters with both drinks. He's very shaken.)*
14   GARDNER: **I couldn't find the ice.**
15   FANNY: **Well, *finally!***
16   GARDNER: **It just up and disappeared...***(Hands FANNY her*
17   *drink.)* **There you go.** *(FANNY kisses her fingers and*
18   *takes a hefty swig.)* **Mags.** *(He hands MAGS her drink.)*
19   MAGS: **Thanks, Daddy.**
20   GARDNER: **Sorry about the ice.**
21   MAGS: **No problem, no problem.**
22   *(GARDNER sits down; silence.)*
23   FANNY: *(To MAGS)* **Well, drink up, drink up!** *(MAGS downs it*
24   *in one gulp.)* **GOOD GIRL!...Now, what's all this about**
25   **a masterpiece...?**
26   MAGS: **I did it during that winter you sent me away from**
27   **the dinner table. I was about nine years old.**
28   FANNY: **We sent you from the dinner table?**
29   MAGS: **I was banished for six months.**
30   FANNY: **You *were*?...How extraordinary!**
31   MAGS: **Yes, it *was* rather extraordinary!**
32   FANNY: **But why?**
33   MAGS: **Because I played with my food.**
34   FANNY: **You did?**
35   MAGS: **I used to squirt it out between my front teeth.**

1　FANNY: Oh, I remember that! God, it used to drive me
2　　　crazy, absolutely...crazy! *(Pause)* "MARGARET, STOP
3　　　THAT OOZING RIGHT THIS MINUTE, YOU ARE NOT A
4　　　TUBE OF TOOTHPASTE!"
5　GARDNER: Oh, yes...
6　FANNY: It was perfectly disgusting!
7　GARDNER: I remember. She used to lean over her plate
8　　　and squirt it out in long runny ribbons...
9　FANNY: That's enough, dear.
10　GARDNER: They were quite colorful, actually; decorative,
11　　　almost. She made the most intricate designs. They
12　　　looked rather like small, moist Oriental rugs...
13　FANNY: *(To MAGS)* But why, darling? What on earth
14　　　possessed you to do it?
15　MAGS: I couldn't swallow anything. My throat just closed
16　　　up. I don't know, I must have been afraid of choking
17　　　or something.
18　GARDNER: I remember one in particular. We'd had chicken
19　　　fricassee and spinach...She made the most extraordi-
20　　　nary —
21　FANNY: *(To GARDNER)* WILL YOU PLEASE SHUT UP?!
22　　　*(Pause)* Mags, what *are* you talking about? You never
23　　　choked in your entire life! This is the most
24　　　distressing conversation I've ever had. Don't you
25　　　think it's distressing, Gar?
26　GARDNER: Well, that's not quite the word I'd use.
27　FANNY: What word would you use, then?
28　GARDNER: I don't know right off the bat, I'd have to think
29　　　about it.
30　FANNY: THEN, THINK ABOUT IT! *(Silence)*
31　MAGS: I guess I was afraid of making a mess. I don't
32　　　know; you were awfully strict about table manners.
33　　　I was always afraid of losing control. What if I started
34　　　to choke and began spitting up over every-
35　　　thing...?

1   FANNY: All right, dear, that's enough.

2   MAGS: No, I was really terrified about making a mess; you
3   always got so mad whenever I spilled. If I just got rid
4   of everything in neat little curlicues beforehand, you
5   see...

6   FANNY: I SAID: THAT'S ENOUGH! *(Silence)*

7   MAGS: I thought it was quite ingenious, but you didn't see
8   it that way. You finally sent me from the table with,
9   "When you're ready to eat like a human being, you
10   can come back and join us!"...So, it was off to my
11   room with a tray. But I couldn't seem to eat there
12   either. I mean, it was so strange settling down to
13   dinner in my *bedroom*...So I just flushed everything
14   down the toilet and sat on my bed listening to you:
15   clinkity-clink, clatter clatter, slurp, slurp...but that
16   got pretty boring after a while, so I looked around for
17   something to do. It was wintertime, because I noticed
18   I'd left some crayons on top of my radiator and they'd
19   melted down into these beautiful shimmering globs,
20   like spilled jello, trembling and pulsing...

21   GARDNER: *(Overlapping; eyes closed)*
22   "This luscious and impeccable fruit of life
23   Falls, it appears, of its own weight to earth..."

24   MAGS: Naturally, I wanted to try it myself, so I grabbed a
25   red one and pressed it down against the hissing lid.
26   It oozed and bubbled like raspberry jam!

27   GARDNER:
28   "When you were Eve, its acrid juice was sweet,
29   Untasted, in its heavenly, orchard air..."

30   MAGS: I mean, that radiator was really hot! It took
31   incredible will power not to let go, but I held on,
32   whispering, "Mags, if you let go of this crayon, you'll
33   be run over by a truck on Newberry Street, so help
34   you God!" So I pressed down harder, my fingers
35   steaming and blistering...

1   FANNY: I had no idea about any of this, did you, Gar?

2   MAGS: Once I'd melted one, I was hooked! I finished off
3   my entire supply in one night, mixing color over
4   color until my head swam!...The heat, the smell, the
5   brilliance that sank and rose...I'd never felt such
6   exhilaration...Every week I spent my allowance on
7   crayons. I must have cleared out every box of
8   Crayolas in the city!

9   GARDNER: *(Gazing at MAGS)* You know, I don't think I've
10   ever seen you looking prettier! You're awfully attrac-
11   tive when you get going!

12 FANNY: Why, what a lovely thing to say.

13 MAGS: AFTER THREE MONTHS THAT RADIATOR
14   WAS...SPECTACULAR! I MEAN, IT LOOKED LIKE
15   SOME COLOSSAL FRUITCAKE, FIVE FEET TALL.

16 FANNY: It sounds perfectly hideous.

17 MAGS: It was a knockout; shimmering with pinks and
18   blues, lavenders and maroons, turquoise and golds,
19   oranges and creams...For every color, I imagined a
20   taste...YELLOW: lemon curls dipped in sugar...RED:
21   glazed cherries laced with rum...GREEN: tiny pepper-
22   mint leaves veined with chocolate...PURPLE: —

23 FANNY: That's quite enough!

24 MAGS: And then the frosting...ahhh, the frosting! A satiny
25   mix of white and silver...I kept it hidden under blan-
26   kets during the day...My huge... *(She starts laughing)*
27   looming... teetering sweet —

28 FANNY: I ASKED YOU TO STOP! GARDNER, WILL YOU
29   PLEASE GET HER TO STOP!

30 GARDNER: See here, Mags, Mum asked you to —

31 MAGS: I was so...*hungry*...losing weight every week. I
32   looked like a scarecrow what with the bags under my
33   eyes and bits of crayon wrapper leaking out of my
34   clothes. It's a wonder you didn't notice. But finally
35   you came to my rescue...if you could call what

1   happened rescue. It was more a like a rout!
2   FANNY: Darling...please!   GARDNER: Now look, young
3   *please!*   lady —
4   MAGS: The winter was almost over...It was very late at
5   night...I must have been having a nightmare because
6   suddenly you and Daddy were at my bed, shaking
7   me...I quickly glanced towards the radiator to see if
8   it was covered...It *wasn't!* It glittered and towered in
9   the moonlight like some...gigantic Viennese pastry!
10   You followed my gaze and saw it. Mummy screamed
11   ..."WHAT HAVE YOU GOT IN HERE?...MAGS, WHAT
12   HAVE YOU BEEN DOING?"...She crept forward and
13   touched it, and then jumped back. "IT'S FOOD!" she
14   cried..."IT'S ALL THE FOOD SHE'S BEEN SPITTING
15   OUT! OH, GARDNER, IT'S A MOUNTAIN OF ROTTING
16   GARBAGE!"
17   FANNY: *(Softly)* Yes...it's coming back...it's coming back...
18   MAGS: Daddy exited as usual; left the premises. He
19   fainted, just keeled over onto the floor...
20   GARDNER: Gosh, I don't remember any of this...
21   MAGS: My heart stopped! I mean, I knew it was all over.
22   My lovely creation didn't have a chance. Sure enough
23   ...out came the blowtorch. Well, it couldn't have
24   *really* been a blowtorch, I mean, where would you
25   have ever gotten a blowtorch?...I just have this very
26   strong memory of you standing over my bed, your
27   hair streaming around your face, aiming this...flame
28   thrower at my confection...my cake...my tart...my
29   strudel..."IT'S GOT TO BE DESTROYED IMMEDI-
30   ATELY! THE THING'S ALIVE WITH VERMIN!...JUST
31   LOOK AT IT!...IT'S PRACTICALLY CRAWLING
32   ACROSS THE ROOM!"...Of course, in a sense you
33   were right. It *was* a monument of my castoff dinners,
34   only I hadn't built it with food...I found my own
35   materials. I was languishing with hunger, but oh, dear

1   Mother...I FOUND MY OWN MATERIALS...
2 FANNY: Darling...please?!
3 MAGS: I tried to stop you, but you wouldn't listen...OUT
4   SHOT THE FLAME!...I remember these waves of wax
5   rolling across the room and Daddy coming to,
6   wondering what on earth was going on...Well, what
7   did you know about my abilities?...You see, I had...I
8   mean, I have abilities... *(Struggling to say it)* I have
9   abilities. I have strong abilities. I have...very strong
10   abilities. They are very strong...very, very strong...
11   *(MAGS rises and runs out of the room overcome as FANNY*
12   *and GARDNER watch, speechless.)*
13
14
15
16
17
18
19
20
21
22
23
24
25
26
27
28
29
30
31
32
33
34
35

SCENE 4: Male Monolog

Gardner, 7Os

This monolog is taken from the first part of Act II, which is a great deal shorter than Act I. The act opens with Gardner's reciting poetry while Mags is painting his and Fanny's portrait. Fanny says it's "like a Chinese water torture" to keep holding the pose, and besides she has to finish packing — particularly the things in Gardner's study. Just before this monolog, Fanny goes to the study and returns with an armload of books, which she drops with a crash. She's done this despite Gardner's saying he doesn't want anyone touching his stuff. He says he doesn't know if he "can take this," and Mags agrees that "moving is awful." The monolog follows directly after that.

As you see, there are other lines interspersed here. If you wish, you can skip over them or have other actors deliver them.

1. Do you think Gardner's dreams have significance? Why? Why do you suppose he dreams himself a child again? Do you suppose this is symbolic in any way? Discuss this with the rest of the class.

2. Why do you think Gardner is telling all this to Mags?

3. Why do you suppose all the furniture in the dream is familiar to Gardner? Does this say anything about his situation? Explain.

4. What do you think it means when Gardner says he isn't in his bed and can't get into it?

1   **GARDNER:** *(Settling back into his pose)* **Ever since Mum**
2   **began tearing the house apart, I've been having these**
3   **dreams...I'm a child again back at 16 Louisberg**
4   **Square...and this stream of moving men is carrying**
5   **furniture into our house...van after van of tables and**
6   **chairs, sofas and love seats, desks and bureaus...**
7   **rugs, bathtubs, mirrors, chiming clocks, pianos,**
8   **iceboxes, china cabinets...but what's amazing is that**
9   **all of it is familiar...**
10   *(FANNY comes in with another load, which she drops on*
11   *the floor. She exits for more.)*
12   **GARDNER: No matter how many items appear, I've seen**
13   **every one of them before. Since my mother is**
14   **standing in the midst of it directing traffic, I ask her**
15   **where it's all coming from, but she doesn't hear me**
16   **because of the racket...so finally I just scream out...**
17   **"WHERE IS ALL THIS FURNITURE COMING FROM?"**
18   **...Just as a moving man is carrying Toots into the**
19   **room, she looks at me and says, "Why, from the land**
20   **of Skye!" The next thing I know, *people* are being**
21   **carried in along with it...**
22   *(FANNY enters with her next load; drops it and exits.)*
23   **GARDNER: People I've never seen before are sitting**
24   **around our dining-room table. A group of foreigners is**
25   **going through my books, chattering in a language**
26   **I've never heard before. A man is playing a Chopin**
27   **polonaise on Aunt Alice's piano. Several children are**
28   **taking baths in our tubs from Cotuit...**
29   **MAGS: It sounds marvelous.**
30   **GARDNER: Well, it isn't marvelous at all because all of**
31   **these perfect strangers have taken over our things...**
32   *(FANNY enters, hurls down another load and exits.)*
33   **MAGS: How odd...**
34   **GARDNER: Well, it is odd, but then something even odder**
35   **happens...**

1   **MAGS:** *(Sketching away)* **Tell me, tell me!**

2   **GARDNER: Well, our beds are carried in. They're all made**

3   **up with sheets and everything, but instead of all**

4   **these strange people in them, *we're* in them...**

5   **MAGS: What's so odd about that?**

6   **GARDNER: Well, you and Mum are brought in, both**

7   **sleeping like angels...Mum snoring away to beat the**

8   **band...**

9   **MAGS: Yes...**

10   *(FANNY enters with another load, lets it fall.)*

11   **GARDNER: But there's no one in mine. It's completely**

12   **empty, never even been slept in! It's as if I were dead**

13   **or had never even existed...**

14   *(FANNY exits.)*

15   **GARDNER: "HEY...WAIT UP!" I yell to the moving men...**

16   **"THAT'S MY BED YOU'VE GOT THERE!" But they**

17   **don't stop; they don't even acknowledge me..."HEY,**

18   **COME BACK HERE...I WANT TO GET INTO MY BED!"**

19   **I cry again and I start running after them...down the**

20   **hall, through the dining room, past the library...**

21   **Finally I catch up to them and hurl myself right into**

22   **the center of the pillow. Just as I'm about to land,**

23   **the bed suddenly vanishes and I go crashing down to**

24   **the floor like some insect that's been hit by a fly**

25   **swatter!**

26   *(FANNY staggers in with her final load; she drops it with*

27   *a crash and then collapses in her posing chair.)*

28

29

30

31

32

33

34

35

SCENE 5: Female Monolog

Fanny, 60s

Gardner forgets why they're moving and so has to be reminded that it's because they cannot afford to keep their house anymore. They do have savings but don't want to touch them. Fanny says she would be perfectly willing to shoot herself instead of moving. Then she recalls someone who did commit suicide.

Gardner, in the meantime, is bringing onstage the contents of his study. However, he becomes engrossed in them, rather than packing. Fanny then brings in his books, arranging them according to color. She wants to discard those that don't look good, no matter what they are. One, for instance, is inscribed to Gardner by Robert Frost.

Next Fanny, disregarding the fact that the papers are part of Gardner's book manuscript, dumps them haphazardly into a cardboard box. Gardner becomes very upset at this. Mags tried to help him keep the papers in order but discovers they are not numbered. She then discovers that what her mother has said is true. "It doesn't make sense. It's just fragments...pieces of poems."

Gardner again begins to read poetry printed on the papers, but one of the poems is cut off at the end of a page. At this point, Fanny begins to laugh at him, saying he does not have control over bodily functions.

Mags becomes upset at her laughter. At the same time Gardner cannot remember what he's looking for, the rest of his manuscript. At this point, Fanny starts making a game of dropping papers into a box. "BOMBS AWAY...This is fun," she says. Gardner becomes involved in the game. Mags is furious at Fanny for treating Gardner as a "dimwitted serving boy," "an amusement." The monolog is Fanny's response.

1. Do you think life really is as bleak as Fanny paints it to be in this monolog? Explain.

2. Obviously, neither Fanny nor Mags behaves ideally toward Gardner. Who do you think is most at fault in their views and in their treatment of him? Why?

3. What does Fanny mean when she says Mags should paint her

and Gardner as they really are?

4. Do you like this play? Why?

5. What is the significance of the play's title?

1 **FANNY:** *(Fatigue has finally overtaken her. She's calm, almost*
2 *serene.)* **And to you who see him once a year, if that...**
3 **what is he to you?...I mean, what do you give him**
4 **from yourself that costs you something?... Hmmm?**
5 **...***(Imitating MAGS)* **"Oh, hi Daddy, it's great to see you**
6 **again. How have you been?...Gee, I love your hair. It's**
7 **gotten so** *white!"* **...What color do you expect it to get**
8 **when he's this age? I mean, if you care so much how**
9 **he looks, why don't you come and see him once in a**
10 **while?...But oh, no...you have your paintings to do**
11 **and your shows to put on. You just come and see us**
12 **when the whim strikes.** *(Imitating MAGS)* **"Hey, you**
13 **know what would be really great?...To do a portrait of**
14 **you! I've always wanted to paint you, you're such**
15 **great subjects!"...***Paint* **us?!...What about opening**
16 **your eyes and really** *seeing* **us?...Noticing what's**
17 **going on around here for a change! It's all over for**
18 **Daddy and me. This is it! "Finita la commedia!"...All**
19 **I'm trying to do is exit with a little flourish; have**
20 **some fun...What's so terrible about that?...It can get**
21 **pretty grim around here, in case you haven't noticed**
22 **...Daddy, tap-tap-tapping out his nonsense all day;**
23 **me traipsing around to the thrift shops trying to**
24 **amuse myself...He never keeps me company**
25 **anymore; never takes me out anywhere...I'd put a**
26 **bullet through my head in a minute, but then who'd**
27 **look after him? ... What do you think we're moving to**
28 **the cottage for?...So I can watch him like a hawk and**
29 **make sure he doesn't get lost. Do you think that's**
30 **anything to look forward to?...Being Daddy's nurse-**
31 **maid out in the middle of nowhere? I'd much rather**
32 **stay here in Boston with the few friends I have left,**
33 **but you can't always do what you want in this world!**
34 **"L'homme propose, Dieu dispose!"...If you want to**
35 **paint us so badly, you ought to paint us as we really**

1   **are. There's your picture."**
2   *(FANNY points to GARDNER, who's quietly playing with a*
3   *paper glide.)*
4   **FANNY: Daddy spread out on the floor with all his toys and**
5   **me hovering over him to make sure he doesn't hurt**
6   **himself!** *(She goes over to him.)* **Yoo-HOO...GAR?...**
7   **HELLO?**
8
9
10
11
12
13
14
15
16
17
18
19
20
21
22
23
24
25
26
27
28
29
30
31
32
33
34
35

Such Things Are

by Mary Inchbald

Written in 1787, *Such Things Are* is a comedy, although it is a little heavy-handed on moralizing and sentimentality.

Inchbald, who lived from 1753-1821, was considered a "beautiful and spirited" woman, who followed a brother George into acting, although she apparently had a speech impediment, which she worked hard to correct.

Despite having played some good roles in the English provinces, such as Cordelia in Shakespeare's King Lear and later having appeared at London's most famous theatre, Covent Garden, she retired from acting in 1789 without having made much of a mark. She did, however, become a successful playwright, one of very few up until this point in history. Despite prejudice against her because of her sex, she edited three volumes of plays.

Her comedies in large part are adaptations of French and German models.

Such Things Are deals with the theme of hypocrisy. Although humorous mainly due to the foibles of several characters and the bickering between a husband, Sir Luke, and his wife, Lady Tremor, the plot is highly contrived and unbelievable, with a lot of moralizing and characters who either are too shallow or too morally good to be true, making the play highly melodramatic. Some of the happenings also rely on coincidence.

SCENE 1: One Male and One Female

Sir Luke Tremor, probably in his 40s

Lady Tremor, 32

The following scene, except for a prologue, opens the play. The action is set in "a parlor at Sir Luke Tremor's" in India.

1. What sorts of people are the Tremors? Point to lines in the text that make you think so.

2. A lot of exposition or background information is presented in this scene. With the rest of the class, pick out as many instances of this as you can and then discuss why you think this information may be important to the rest of the play.

3. Why do you suppose Lady Tremor is so against admitting her age? Do you think this is logical or believable? Why?

4. What sort of feelings do the Tremors have in regard to Lord Flint? How can you tell?

1   *(Enter SIR LUKE, followed by LADY TREMOR.)*

2   SIR LUKE: I tell you, madam, you are two and thirty.

3   LADY TREMOR: I tell you, sir, you are mistaken.

4   SIR LUKE: Why, did not you come over from England

5   exactly sixteen years ago?

6   LADY TREMOR: Not so long.

7   SIR LUKE: Have not we been married, the tenth of next

8   April, sixteen years?

9   LADY TREMOR: Not so long.

10 SIR LUKE: Did you not come over the year of the great

11   eclipse? — Answer me that.

12 LADY TREMOR: I don't remember it.

13 SIR LUKE: But I do — and shall remember it as long as I live.

14   — The first time I saw you was in the garden of the

15   Dutch envoy: you were looking through a glass at the

16   sun — I immediately began to make love to you, and

17   the whole affair was settled while the eclipse lasted —

18   just one hour, eleven minutes, and three seconds.

19 LADY TREMOR: But what is all this to my age?

20 SIR LUKE: Because I know you were at that time near

21   seventeen, and without one qualification except your

22   youth, and your fine clothes.

23 LADY TREMOR: Sir Luke, Sir Luke, this is not to be borne.

24 SIR LUKE: Oh! Yes — I forgot — you had two letters of

25   recommendation from two great families in England.

26 LADY TREMOR: Letters of recommendation!

27 SIR LUKE: Yes; your character — that you know, is all the

28   fortune we poor Englishmen, situated in India,

29   expect with a wife, who crosses the sea at the hazard

30   of her life, to make us happy.

31 LADY TREMOR: And what but our characters would you

32   have us bring? — Do you suppose any lady ever came

33   to India, who brought along with her friends or

34   fortune?

35 SIR LUKE: No, my dear: and what is worse, she seldom

1   leaves them behind.
2 LADY TREMOR: No matter, Sir Luke: but if I delivered to
3   you a good character —
4 SIR LUKE: Yes, my dear, you did: and if you were to ask
5   me for it again, I can't say I could give it you.
6 LADY TREMOR: How uncivil! How unlike are your
7   manners to the manners of my Lord Flint!
8 SIR LUKE: Ay, you are never so happy as when you have
9   an opportunity of expressing your admiration of him.
10   — A disagreeable, nay, a very dangerous man — one
11   is never sure of one's self in his presence — he
12   carries every thing he hears to the ministers of our
13   suspicious Sultan — and I feel my head shake when-
14   ever I am in his company.
15 LADY TREMOR: How different does his lordship appear to
16   me! — To me he is all *politesse.*
17 SIR LUKE: *Politesse!* How should you understand what is
18   real *politesse*? You know your education was very
19   much confined.
20 LADY TREMOR: And if it *was* confined? — I beg, Sir Luke,
21   you will cease these reflections; you know they are
22   what I can't bear! *(Walks about in a passion.)* — **Pray,**
23   does not his lordship continually assure me, I might
24   be taken for a countess, were it not for a certain little
25   grovelling toss I have caught with my head, and a
26   certain little confined hitch in my walk; both which
27   I learnt of you — learnt by looking so much at you.
28 SIR LUKE: And now, if you don't take care, by looking so
29   much at his lordship, you may catch some of his
30   defects.
31 LADY TREMOR: I know of very few he has.
32 SIR LUKE: I know of many — besides those he assumes.
33 LADY TREMOR: Assumes.
34 SIR LUKE: Yes: Do you suppose he is as forgetful as he
35   pretends to be? — No, no; but because he is a favorite

1   with the Sultan, and all our great men, he thinks it
2   genteel or convenient to have no memory; and yet,
3   I'll answer for it, he has one of the best in the
4   universe.
5   LADY TREMOR: I don't believe your charge.
6   SIR LUKE: Why, though he forgets his appointments with
7   his tradesmen, did you ever hear of his forgetting to
8   go to court when a place was to be disposed of? Did
9   he ever make a blunder, and send a bribe to a man out
10   of power? Did he ever forget to kneel before the
11   prince of this island, or to look in his highness's pres-
12   ence like the statue of patient resignation, in humble
13   expectation?
14   LADY TREMOR: Dear, Sir Luke —
15   SIR LUKE: Sent from his own country in his very infancy,
16   and brought up in the different courts of petty arbi-
17   trary princes here in Asia, he is the slave of every
18   rich man, and the tyrant of every poor one.
19   LADY TREMOR: "Petty princes!" — 'Tis well his highness,
20   our Sultan, does not hear you.
21   SIR LUKE: 'Tis well he does not — don't you repeat what I
22   say: but you know how all this fine country is
23   harassed and laid waste by a set of princes —
24   Sultans, as they style themselves, and I know not
25   what — who are for ever calling out to each other,
26   "That's mine," and "That's mine"; — and "You have
27   no business here," and "You have no business there";
28   — and "I have business everywhere." *(Strutting)* Then,
29   "Give *me* this," and "Give me that"; and — "Take
30   this," and "Take that." *(Makes signs of fighting.)*
31   LADY TREMOR: A very elegant description, truly.
32   SIR LUKE: Why, you know 'tis all matter of fact: and Lord
33   Flint, brought up from his youth among these people,
34   has not one trait of an Englishman about him: he has
35   imbibed all this country's cruelty; and I dare say

would mind no more seeing me hung up by my
thumbs, or made to dance upon a red hot gridiron —
LADY TREMOR: That is one of the tortures I never heard
of! — O! I should like to see that of all things!
SIR LUKE: Yes, by keeping this man's company, you'll
soon be as cruel as he is: he will teach you every vice.
A consequential, grave, dull — and yet with that
degree of levity which dares to pay addresses to a
woman, even before her husband's face.
LADY TREMOR: Did you not declare, this minute, his lordship had not a trait of his own country about him?
SIR LUKE: Well, well — as you say, that last is a trait of his
own country.

SCENE 2: Two Males and One Female

Lady Tremor, 32

Sir Luke Tremor, probably 40s

Lord Flint, probably early 40s

This scene follows directly after the preceding, except that Flint is introduced by a servant.

1. What is your opinion of Lord Flint? What in the script makes you think this?
2. What sort of relationship do the Tremors have? Explain.
3. Why does Lady Tremor insist that she tell Lord Flint what she and her husband have been saying about him?
4. Why does Lord Flint have or pretend to have such a bad memory?
5. Some of the lines are meant to be funny. Do you see humor in this scene? Explain.

1   LADY TREMOR: My lord, I am extremely glad to see you:
2   we were just mentioning your name.
3   LORD FLINT: Were you, indeed, madam? You do me great
4   honor.
5   SIR LUKE: No, my lord — no great honor.
6   LORD FLINT: Pardon me, Sir Luke.
7   SIR LUKE: But, I assure you, my lord, in what I said I did
8   myself a great deal.
9   LADY TREMOR: Yes, my lord; and I'll acquaint your lord-
10   ship what it was. *(Going up to him)*
11   SIR LUKE: *(Pulling her aside)* Why, you would not inform
12   against me, sure! Do you know what would be the
13   consequence? My head must answer it. *(Frightened)*
14   LORD FLINT: Nay, Sir Luke, I insist upon knowing.
15   SIR LUKE: *(To her)* Hush! hush! — No, my lord, pray excuse
16   me: your lordship, perhaps, may think what I said did
17   not come from my heart; and I assure you, upon my
18   honor, it did.
19   LADY TREMOR: O, yes — that I am sure it did.
20   LORD FLINT: I am extremely obliged to *you*. *(Bowing)*
21   SIR LUKE: O, no, my lord, not at all — not at all. *(Aside to*
22   *her)* I'll be extremely obliged to you, if you will hold
23   your tongue. Pray, my lord, are you engaged out to
24   dinner to-day? For her ladyship and I are.
25   LADY TREMOR: Yes, my lord, and we should be happy to
26   find your lordship of the party.
27   LORD FLINT: "Engaged out to dinner"? — Egad, very likely
28   — very likely: but if I am, I have positively forgotten
29   where.
30   LADY TREMOR: We are going to —
31   LORD FLINT: No — I think, now you put me in mind of it
32   — I think I have company to dine with me. I am
33   either going out to dinner, or have company to dine
34   with me; but I really can't tell which: however, my
35   people know — but I can't recollect.

1   SIR LUKE: Perhaps your lordship has dined: can you
2   recollect that?
3   LORD FLINT: No, no — I have not dined — What's o'clock?
4   LADY TREMOR: Perhaps, my lord, you have not break-
5   fasted?
6   LORD FLINT: O, yes; I've breakfasted — I think so — but,
7   upon my word these things are very difficult to
8   remember.
9   SIR LUKE: They are, indeed, my lord — and I wish all my
10   family would entirely forget them.
11   LORD FLINT: What did your ladyship say was o'clock?
12   LADY TREMOR: Exactly twelve, my lord.
13   LORD FLINT: Bless me! I ought to have been somewhere
14   else then — an absolute engagement. — I have broke
15   my word — a positive appointment.
16   LADY TREMOR: Shall I send a servant?
17   LORD FLINT: No, no, no, no — by no means — it can't be
18   helped now; And they know my unfortunate failing:
19   besides, I'll beg their pardon, and I trust, that will be
20   ample satisfaction.
21   LADY TREMOR: You are very good, my lord, not to leave
22   us.
23   LORD FLINT: I could not think of leaving you so soon —
24   the happiness I enjoy in your society is so extreme —
25   SIR LUKE: That were your lordship to go away now, you
26   might never remember to come again.
27
28
29
30
31
32
33
34
35

SCENE 3: Two Males

Twineall, probably 30s

Meanwright, probably somewhat older

As the last scene ends, a servant announces that a gentleman has landed from an English ship and has letters to present to Sir Luke. Mr. Twineall, wearing informal clothes, probably to appear foppish, enters and hands over three letters from friends of Sir Luke, who invites him to be his and Lady Tremor's house guest. There is a lot of byplay about Twineall's apparel.

This leads to a discussion of the "fashion" of words with Twineall explaining that to appear astute a gentleman says things like, "Really it appears to me ee-e-e-e — (Mutters and shrugs) — that is-mo-mo-mo-mo-mo — (Mutters) if you see the thing — for my part te-te-te-te — and that's all I can tell about it at present."

Just after this Mr. Haswell enters, and they discuss Twineall's relatives in Parliament. There is mention of the Sultan who has had many people sold into slavery and many others sent to prison. Haswell will see the Sultan later in the day.

The following scene occurs near the beginning of Act II just after Twineall has gone to visit an old acquaintance, Meanwright, whose help Twineall asks in making sure that Sir Luke and Lady Tremor think him "*very* clever."

1. Why do you suppose Twineall wants the others to think well of him? Explain.

2. What does Meanwright mean by, "Why, such a man as you ought to have made your fortune in England"?

3. Do you see any humor in this scene? Explain.

4. What sort of person is Meanwright? What makes you think so?

1   TWINEALL: But my dear friend, you must help me to make
2   them think better of me still — and when my fortune
3   is made, I'll make — for when I once become
4   acquainted with people's dispositions, their little
5   weaknesses, foibles, and faults, I can wind, twist,
6   twine, and get into the corner of everyone's heart,
7   and lie so snug, they can't know I'm there till they
8   want to pull me out, and find 'tis impossible.
9   MEANWRIGHT: Excellent talent!
10   TWINEALL: Is not it? — And now, my dear friend, do you
11   inform me of the secret dispositions and propensities
12   of every one in this family, and that of all their
13   connections? — What lady values herself upon one
14   qualification, and what lady upon another? — What
15   gentleman will like to be told of his accomplish-
16   ments, or what man would rather hear of his wife's or
17   his daughter's? — Or of his horse's, or of his dog's?
18   — Now, my dear Ned, acquaint me with all this; and,
19   within a fortnight, I will become the most necessary
20   rascal — not a creature shall know how to exist
21   without me.
22   MEANWRIGHT: Why, such a man as you ought to have
23   made your fortune in England.
24   TWINEALL: No; there — my father and my three uncles
25   monopolized all the great men themselves, and
26   would never introduce me where I was likely to
27   become their rival. — This, this is the very spot for
28   me to display my genius — But then I must first
29   penetrate the people, unless you will kindly save me
30   that trouble. — Come, give me all their characters —
31   all their little propensities — all their whims — in
32   short, all I am to praise, and all I am to avoid
33   praising, in order to endear myself to them. *(Takes*
34   *out tablets.)* Come — begin with Sir Luke.
35   MEANWRIGHT: Sir Luke values himself more upon

255

1   **personal bravery, than upon any thing.**
2   TWINEALL: Thank you, my dear friend — thank you.
3   *(Writes.)* **Was he ever in the army?**
4   MEANWRIGHT: Oh, yes, besieged a capital fortress a few
5   years ago: and now the very name of a battle, or a
6   great general tickles his vanity; and he takes all the
7   praises you can lavish upon the subject as compli-
8   ments to himself.
9   TWINEALL: Thank you — thank you, a thousand times.
10   *(Writes.)* **I'll mention a battle very soon.**
11   MEANWRIGHT: Not directly.
12   TWINEALL: Oh, no — let me alone for time and place. —
13   Go on, my friend — go on — her ladyship —
14   MEANWRIGHT: Descended from the ancient kings of
15   Scotland.
16   TWINEALL: You don't say so!
17   MEANWRIGHT: And though she is so nicely scrupulous as
18   never to mention the word genealogy, yet I have seen
19   her agitation so great, when the advantages of high
20   birth have been extolled, that she could scarcely
21   withhold her sentiments of triumph; which, in order
22   to disguise, she has assumed a disdain for all "vain
23   titles, empty sounds, and idle pomp."
24   TWINEALL: Thank you — thank you: this is a most excel-
25   lent trait of the lady's. *(Writes.)* **"Pedigree of the kings**
26   **of Scotland"?** — Oh, I have her at once.
27   MEANWRIGHT: Yet do it nicely; — oblique touches, rather
28   than open explanations.
29   TWINEALL: Let me alone for that.
30   MEANWRIGHT: She has, I know, in her possession — but I
31   dare say she would not show it you; nay, on the
32   contrary, would affect to be highly offended, were
33   you to mention it; — and yet it certainly would
34   flatter her to know you were acquainted with her
35   having it.

1   TWINEALL: What — what — what is it?

2   MEANWRIGHT: A large old-fashioned wig — which

3   Malcolm the third or fourth, her great ancestor, wore

4   when he was crowned at Scone, in the year —

5   TWINEALL: I'll mention it.

6   MEANWRIGHT: Take care.

7   TWINEALL: O, let me alone for the manner.

8   MEANWRIGHT: She'll pretend to be angry.

9   TWINEALL: That I am prepared for. — Pray, who is my

10   Lord Flint?

11   MEANWRIGHT: A deep man — and a great favorite at court.

12   TWINEALL: Indeed! — How am I to please him?

13   MEANWRIGHT: By insinuations against the present

14   Sultan.

15   TWINEALL: Indeed!

16   MEANWRIGHT: With all his pretended attachment, his

17   heart —

18   TWINEALL: Are you sure of it?

19   MEANWRIGHT: Sure: — he blinds Sir Luke, who by the bye

20   is no great politician — but I know his lordship; and

21   if he thought he was certain of his ground — and he

22   thinks, he shall be soon — then —

23   TWINEALL: I'll insinuate myself, and join his party; but, in

24   the meantime, preserve good terms with Sir Luke, in

25   case anything should fall in my way there. — Who is

26   Mr. Haswell?

27   MEANWRIGHT: He pretends to be a man of principle and

28   sentiment; flatter him on that.

29   TWINEALL: The easiest thing in the world — no characters

30   love flattery better than such as those: they will bear

31   even to hear their vices praised. — I will myself,

32   undertake to praise the vices of a man of sentiment,

33   (Sensitive moral feelings) till he shall think them so

34   many virtues. — You have mentioned no ladies yet,

35   but the lady of the house.

1   MEANWRIGHT: I know little about any other, except a
2   pretty girl who came over from England, about two
3   years ago, for a husband; and, not succeeding in a
4   distant part of the country, was recommended to this
5   house; and has been here three or four months.
6   TWINEALL: Let me alone to please her.
7   MEANWRIGHT: Yes — I believe you are skilled.
8   TWINEALL: In the art of flattery, no one more.
9   MEANWRIGHT: But, damn it, it is not a liberal art.
10 TWINEALL: It is a great science, notwithstanding — and
11   studied, at present, by all wise men. — Zounds! I
12   have stayed a long time — I can't attend to anymore
13   characters at present — Sir Luke and his lady will
14   think me inattentive, if I don't join them. — Shall I
15   see you again? If not, I wish you a pleasant voyage —
16   I'll make the most of what you have told me — you'll
17   hear I'm a great man. — Heaven bless you! — Good-
18   bye! — You'll hear I'm a great man. *(Exit)*
19
20
21
22
23
24
25
26
27
28
29
30
31
32
33
34
35

SCENE 4: Male Monolog

Meanwright, probably 30s

This speech follows directly after Twineall exits, and, of course, gives us a better look at Meanwright's feelings.

1. Why do you suppose Meanwright tells Twineall the exact opposite of the truth?

2. What can you tell about Meanwright by what he says in this monolog?

1 MEANWRIGHT: And, if I am not mistaken, I shall hear you
2 are turned out of this house before tomorrow
3 morning. O, Twineall! Exactly the reverse of every
4 character have you now before you. — The greatest
5 misfortune in the life of Sir Luke has been flying from
6 his regiment in the midst of an engagement, and a
7 most humiliating degradation in consequence; which
8 makes him so feelingly alive on the subject of a
9 battle, that nothing but his want of courage can
10 secure my friend Twineall's life for venturing to
11 name the subject. Then my Lord Flint, firmly
12 attached to the interest of the Sultan, will be all on
13 fire when he hears of open disaffection. — But most
14 of all, Lady Tremor! Whose father was a grocer, and
15 uncle a noted advertising "Periwig-maker on a new
16 construction." She will run mad to hear of births,
17 titles, and long pedigrees. — Poor Twineall! Little
18 dost thou think what is prepared for thee. — There is
19 Mr. Haswell too! But to him have I sent you to be
20 reclaimed — to him, who, free from faults, or even
21 foibles, of his own, has yet more potently received
22 the blessing — of pity for his neighbors.
23
24
25
26
27
28
29
30
31
32
33
34
35

SCENE 5: One Male and One Female

Prisoner, probably late 30s

Haswell, probably late 30s

The next scene opens in a prison which Haswell is visiting. One of the prisoners, an Indian named Zedan, picks his pocket, stealing his wallet. A guard mentions a young man, Elvirus, who constantly keeps watch on his father, a prisoner who is very ill. The young man has filed pleas with the Sultan to have his father released and that he will become a prisoner in his place or serve as a soldier. He has received no answer. The guard says there never is an answer.

Next the guard takes Haswell to an area where female prisoners are kept. He meets one woman "who appears faint and as if the light affected her eyes." She tells Haswell she has never sought to be released.

This is what follows. If you wish, you can simply skip the Keeper or guard's line.

1. Do you find that the Prisoner is a believable character? Why?

2. Why do you suppose Haswell says he will have the woman released?

3. Do you find the dialog believable, realistic? Why?

4. What is the mood of this scene? Explain.

1   PRISONER: Forgive me — I am mild with all these people
2   but — from a countenance like yours — I could not
3   bear reproach.
4   HASWELL: You flatter me.
5   PRISONER: Alas! Sir, and what have I to hope from such a
6   meanness? — You do not come to ransom me.
7   HASWELL: Perhaps I do.
8   PRISONER: Oh! Do not say so — unless — unless — I am
9   not to be deceived. Pardon in your turn this suspi-
10   cion: but when I have so much to hope for — when
11   the sun, the air, fields, woods, and all that wondrous
12   world wherein I have been so happy, is in prospect —
13   forgive me, if the vast hope makes me fear.
14   HASWELL: Unless your ransom is fixed at something
15   beyond my power to give, I *will* release you.
16   PRISONER: Release me! — Benevolent!
17   HASWELL: How shall I mark you down in my petition?
18   *(Takes out his book.)* What name?
19   PRISONER: 'Tis almost blotted from my memory. *(Weeping)*
20   [KEEP: It is of little note — a female prisoner, taken with
21   the rebel party, and in these cells confined for fifteen
22   years.]
23   PRISONER: During which time I have demeaned myself
24   with all humility to my governors: neither have I
25   distracted my fellow prisoners with a complaint that
26   might recall to their memory their own unhappy fate.
27   I have been obedient, patient; and cherished hope to
28   cheer me with vain dreams, while despair possessed
29   my reason.
30   HASWELL: Retire — I will present the picture you have
31   given.
32   PRISONER: And be successful — or, never let me see you
33   more. *(She goes up the stage.)*
34   HASWELL: So it shall be.
35   PRISONER: *(Returns.)* Or, if you should miscarry in your

1   views — for who forms plans that do not sometimes
2   fall? — I will not reproach you, even to myself. — No
3   — nor will I suffer much from the disappointment —
4   merely that you may not have what I suffer, to
5   account for. *(Exit to her cell)*
6   HASWELL: Excellent mind!
7
8
9
10
11
12
13
14
15
16
17
18
19
20
21
22
23
24
25
26
27
28
29
30
31
32
33
34
35

SCENE 6: Three Males and Two Females

Sir Luke Tremor, probably 40s

Lady Tremor, 32

Aurelia, probably early 20s

Twineall, probably 30s

Lord Flint, probably early 40s

When Zedan discovers that Haswell is a good man, he returns his wallet, thus ending Act II. Act III opens in "an apartment at Sir Luke Tremor's." This is at the very beginning.

1. What is the significance of the opening dialog between Sir Luke and Aurelia? Can you see the attempts at humor here? What feelings do you think the two characters have in responding to each other? Why?

2. Do you think the relationship between Sir Luke and Lady Tremor is believable in this scene? Is it logical for a wife to act this way when her husband has been scalded? What does the reaction she had then show about her feelings for Sir Luke?

3. What does Sir Luke mean by the line: "That day, in particular, we did not; for I remember you had been no less than three hours at your toilet?"

4. Why do Sir Luke and Lady Tremor insult each other so much, particularly in front of others? Is this logical? Believable? Humorous? Explain.

5. What is humorous about Twineall's dialog? Explain.

6. Do you think Sir Luke agrees with Lord Flint or with what Twineall says about the Sultan? Why?

7. How does Lord Flint view Twineall? What are his feelings about the man? Explain.

1   *(Enter SIR LUKE and AURELIA.)*

2   SIR LUKE: Why, then, Aurelia, (Though I never mentioned

3   it to my Lady Tremor) my friend wrote me word he

4   had reason to suppose your affections were improp-

5   erly fixed upon a young gentleman in that

6   neighborhood; and this was his reason for wishing

7   you to leave that place to come hither; and this

8   continual dejection convinces me my friend was not

9   mistaken. — Answer me — can you say he was?

10 AURELIA: Sir Luke, candidly to confess —

11 SIR LUKE: Nay, no tears — why in tears? For a husband?

12   — be comforted — we'll get you one ere long, I

13   warrant.

14 AURELIA: Dear Sir Luke, how can you imagine I am in

15   tears because I have not a husband, while you see

16   Lady Tremor every day in tears for the very opposite

17   cause?

18 SIR LUKE: No matter; women like to have a husband

19   through pride; and I have known a woman marry,

20   from that very motive, even a man she has been

21   ashamed of.

22 AURELIA: Perhaps Lady Tremor married from pride.

23 SIR LUKE: Yes — and I'll let her know that pride is painful.

24 AURELIA: But, sir, her ladyship's philosophy —

25 SIR LUKE: She has no philosophy.

26   *(Enter LADY TREMOR and TWINEALL.)*

27 SIR LUKE: Where is my Lord Flint? What have you done

28   with him?

29 LADY TREMOR: He's speaking a word to Mr. Meanwright,

30   about his passport to England — Did you mean me, Sir

31   Luke, who has no philosophy? — I protest, I have a

32   great deal.

33 SIR LUKE: When did you show it?

34 LADY TREMOR: When the servant at my Lady Grissell's

35   threw a whole urn of boiling water upon your legs. —

1   Did I then give any proofs of female weakness? Did I
2   faint, scream, or even shed a tear?
3 SIR LUKE: No, very true; and while I lay sprawling on the
4   carpet, I could see you holding a smelling bottle to
5   the lady of the house, begging of her not to make
6   herself uneasy, "for that the accident was of no
7   manner of consequence."
8 AURELIA: Dear sir, don't be angry: I am sure her ladyship
9   spoke as she thought.
10 SIR LUKE: I suppose she did, miss.
11 AURELIA: I mean — she thought the accident might be
12   easily — She thought you might be easily recovered.
13 LADY TREMOR: No, indeed, I did not: but I thought Sir
14   Luke had frequently charged me with the want of
15   patience; and, that moment, the very thing in the
16   world I could have wished occurred, on purpose to
17   give me an opportunity to prove his accusation false.
18 SIR LUKE: Very well, Madam — but did not the whole
19   company censure your behavior? Did not they say, it
20   was not the conduct of a wife?
21 LADY TREMOR: Only our particular acquaintance could
22   say so; for the rest of the company, I am sure, did not
23   take me to be your wife. — Thank Heaven, our
24   appearance never betrays that secret. Do you think
25   we look like the same flesh and blood?
26 SIR LUKE: That day, in particular, we did not; for I
27   remember you had been no less than three hours at
28   your toilet.
29 LADY TREMOR: And indeed, Sir Luke, if you were to use
30   milk of roses, and several other things of the same
31   kind, you can't think how much more like a fine
32   gentleman you would look. — Such things as those
33   make, almost, all the difference between you and
34   such a man as Mr. Twineall.
35 TWINEALL: No, pardon me, Madam — a face like mine may

1   use those things; but in Sir Luke's they would entirely

2   destroy that fine martial appearance — *(SIR LUKE looks*

3   *confounded.)* — which women, as well as men, admire

4   — for, as valor is the first ornament of our sex —

5   LADY TREMOR: What are you saying, Mr. Twineall? —

6   *(Aside)* I'll keep on this subject if I can.

7   TWINEALL: I was going to observe, Madam, that the repu-

8   tation of a general — which puts me in mind, Sir

9   Luke, of an account I read of a battle — *(He crosses*

10   *over to SIR LUKE, who turns up the stage, in the utmost*

11   *confusion, and steals out of the room.)*

12   LADY TREMOR: Well, sir — go on, go on — you were going

13   to introduce —

14   TWINEALL: A battle, Madam — but Sir Luke is gone!

15   LADY TREMOR: Never mind that, sir: he generally runs

16   away on these occasions.

17   SIR LUKE: *(Coming back)* What were you saying, Aurelia,

18   about a husband?

19   LADY TREMOR: She did not speak.

20   SIR LUKE: To be sure, ladies in India do get husbands very

21   soon.

22   TWINEALL: Not always, I am told, Sir Luke — women of

23   family, *(Fixing his eyes steadfastly on LADY TREMOR)*

24   indeed, may soon enter into the matrimonial state —

25   but the rich men in India, we are told in England, are

26   grown of late very cautious with whom they marry;

27   and there is not a man of any repute that will now

28   look upon a woman as a wife, unless she is descended

29   from a good family. *(Looking at LADY TREMOR, who*

30   *walks up the stage, and steals out of the room, just as SIR*

31   *LUKE had done before.)*

32   SIR LUKE: I am very sorry — very sorry to say, Mr.

33   Twineall, that has not been always the case.

34   TWINEALL: Then I am very sorry, too, Sir Luke; for it is as

35   much impossible that a woman, who is not born of an

1   **ancient family, can be —** *(LADY TREMOR returns.)*
2 **SIR LUKE: That is just what I say — they** *cannot* **be —**
3 **LADY TREMOR: Sir Luke, let me tell** *you* **—**
4 **SIR LUKE: It does not signify telling, my dear — you have**
5   **proved it.**
6 **LADY TREMOR:** *(To TWINEALL)* **Sir, let me tell** *you.*
7 **TWINEALL: O! O! my dear Madam, 'tis all in vain — there**
8   **is no such thing — it can't be — there is no pleading**
9   **against convictions — a person of low birth must, in**
10   **every particular, be a terrible creature.**
11 **SIR LUKE:** *(Going to her)* **A terrible creature! A terrible**
12   **creature!**
13 **LADY TREMOR: Here comes my Lord Flint — I'll appeal to**
14   **him.**
15   *(Enter LORD FLINT.)*
16 **SIR LUKE:** *(Going to him)* **My lord, I was saying, as a proof**
17   **that our great Sultan, who now fills this throne, is no**
18   **imposter, as the rebel party would insinuate, no low-**
19   **born man, but of the royal stock, his conduct**
20   **palpably evinces — for, had he not been nobly born,**
21   **we should have beheld the plebeian bursting forth**
22   **upon all occasions —** *(Looking at LADY TREMOR)* **—**
23   **and plebeian manners who can support.**
24 **LADY TREMOR: Provoking!** *(Goes up the stage.)*
25 **LORD FLINT: Sir Luke, is there a doubt of the Emperor's**
26   **birth and title? — He is the real Sultan, depend upon**
27   **it: it surprises me to hear you talk with the smallest**
28   **uncertainty.**
29 **TWINEALL: Indeed, Sir Luke, I wonder at it too:** *(Aside to*
30   *LORD FLINT)* **and yet, damn me, my lord, if I have not**
31   **my doubts.** *(LORD FLINT starts.)*
32 **SIR LUKE:** *I,* **my Lord? Far be it from me! I was only saying**
33   **what other people have said; for my part, I never**
34   **harbored a doubt of the kind. —** *(Aside)* **My head begins**
35   **to nod, only for that word — Pray heaven, I may die**

1   with it on! — I should not like to lose my head; nor
2   should I like to die by a bullet — nor by a sword; and
3   a cannonball would be as disagreeable as any thing I
4   know. — It is very strange that I never yet could make
5   up my mind in what manner I should like to go out
6   of the world. *(During this speech, TWINEALL is paying*
7   *court to LORD FLINT — they come forward and SIR LUKE*
8   *retires.)*
9   LORD FLINT: Your temerity astonishes me!
10   TWINEALL: I must own, my lord, I feel somewhat awkward
11   in saying it to your lordship — but my own heart, my
12   own conscience, my own sentiments — they *are* my
13   own; and they are dear to me. — So it is — the Sultan
14   does not appear to me — *(With significance)* — that
15   great man some people think him.
16   LORD FLINT: Sir, you astonish me — Pray, what is your
17   name? I have forgotten it.
18   TWINEALL: Twineall, my lord — the Honorable Henry
19   Twineall — your lordship does me great honor to ask.
20   — Landed this morning from England, as your lord-
21   ship may remember, in the ship Mercury, my lord;
22   and all the officers on board speaking with the
23   highest admiration and warmest terms of your lord-
24   ship's official character.
25   LORD FLINT: Why, then, Mr. Twineall, I am very sorry —
26   TWINEALL: And so am I, my lord, that your sentiments
27   and mine should so far disagree, as I know they do.
28   — I am not unacquainted with your firm adherence
29   to the Sultan, but I am unused to disguise my
30   thoughts — I could not, if I would. I have no little
31   views, no sinister motives, no plots, no intrigues, no
32   schemes of preferment; and I verily believe, that, if a
33   pistol was now directed to my heart, or a large
34   pension directed to my pocket (in the first case at
35   least), I should speak my mind.

1   **LORD FLINT:** *(Aside)* **A dangerous young man this! And I**
2   **may make something of the discovery.**
3   **TWINEALL:** *(Aside)* **It tickles him to the soul I find. — My**
4   **lord, now I begin to be warm on the subject, I feel**
5   **myself quite agitated; and, from the intelligence**
6   **which I have heard, even when I was in England —**
7   **there is every reason to suppose — exm — exm —**
8   **exm** *(Mutters —)*
9   **LORD FLINT: What, sir? What?**
10   **TWINEALL: You understand me.**
11   **LORD FLINT: No — explain.**
12   **TWINEALL: Why, then, there is every reason to suppose —**
13   **some people are not what they should be — pardon**
14   **my suspicions, if they are wrong.**
15   **LORD FLINT: I *do* pardon your thoughts, with all my heart**
16   **— but your words young man, you must answer for.**
17
18
19
20
21
22
23
24
25
26
27
28
29
30
31
32
33
34
35

SCENE 7: Two Males

Sultan, probably 4Os

Haswell, probably late 3Os

The previous scene continues with Lady Tremor inviting Lord Flint, who is very angry with Twineall, to spend the evening. As the others exit, Twineall is pleased with himself at having made such a "good" impression on the others. He says it is thanks to Meanwright — yet, he could have done it without Meanwright. So actually he owes him no obligation. This leads directly into the following scene, which ends Act 3 (out of five acts).

1. More of Haswell's character is revealed in this scene. What sort of person is he? What are his main personality traits? Is he a believable character? Why?

2. What is your opinion of the Sultan? He says he is a Christian, yet he has kept a lot of people in prison. Do you think this is a contradiction or not? Explain.

3. Haswell obviously could be putting himself in danger in arguing with the Sultan about releasing prisoners. Why do you suppose he disregards this fact?

4. Inchbald has been accused of over sentimentalizing her plays. Can you find evidence of this here? Explain.

5. The scene, in places, also is overly melodramatic. Can you find instances of this? Do you suppose Inchbald intended the audience to take this seriously? Explain.

6. How does Haswell propose to cure the "mind's disease" the Sultan is experiencing? Is this logical? What is this disease to which Haswell is referring?

7. Do you think it is logical that the Sultan agrees to do what Haswell asks? Why?

1 SULTAN: Sir, you were invited hither to receive public
2   thanks for our troops restored to health by your
3   prescriptions. — Ask a reward adequate to your
4   services.
5 HASWELL: Sultan, the reward I ask, is to preserve more of
6   your people still.
7 SULTAN: How! More! My subjects are in health: no conta-
8   gion visits them.
9 HASWELL: The prisoner is your subject. There, misery,
10   more contagious than disease, preys on the lives of
11   hundreds: sentenced but to confinement, their doom
12   is death. Immured in damp and dreary vaults, they
13   daily perish; and who can tell but that, among these
14   many hapless sufferers, there may be hearts bent
15   down with penitence to heaven and you for every —
16   slight offence — there may be some, among the
17   wretched multitude, even innocent victims. Let me
18   seek them out — let me save them and you.
19 SULTAN: Amazement! Retract your application: curb this
20   weak pity; and receive our thanks.
21 HASWELL: Restrain my pity! — And what can I receive in
22   recompense for that soft bond which links me to the
23   wretched? And, while it soothes their sorrow, repays
24   me more than all the gifts an empire could bestow. —
25   But, if repugnant to your plan of government, I apply
26   not in the name of pity, but of justice.
27 SULTAN: Justice!
28 HASWELL: The justice which forbids all, but the worst of
29   criminals, to be denied that wholesome air the very
30   brute creation freely takes.
31 SULTAN: Consider for whom you plead — for men (if not
32   base culprits) so misled, so depraved, they are
33   dangerous to our state, and deserve none of its
34   blessings.
35 HASWELL: If not upon the undeserving — if not upon the

1   hapless wanderer from the paths of rectitude, where

2   shall the sun diffuse his light, or the clouds distill

3   their dew? Where shall spring breathe fragrance, or

4   autumn pour its plenty?

5 SULTAN: Sir, your sentiments, still more your character,

6   excite my curiosity. They tell me, that in our camps

7   you visited each sick man's bed, administered your-

8   self the healing draught, encouraged our savages

9   with the hope of life, or pointed out their better hope

10   in death. — The widow speaks your charities, the

11   orphan lisps your bounties, and the rough Indian

12   melts in tears to bless you. — I wish to ask why you

13   have done all this? — What is it which prompts you

14   thus to befriend the wretched and forlorn?

15 HASWELL: In vain for me to explain: — the time it would

16   take to reveal to you —

17 SULTAN: Satisfy my curiosity in writing then.

18 HASWELL: Nay, if you will read, I'll send a book in which

19   is already written why I act thus.

20 SULTAN: What book? — What is it called?

21 HASWELL: "The Christian Doctrine." *(HASWELL bows here*

22   *with the utmost reverence.)* There you will find — all I

23   have done was but my duty.

24 SULTAN: *(To the guards)* Retire, and leave me alone with

25   the stranger. *(All retire except HASWELL and the SULTAN*

26   *— they come forward.)* Your words recall reflections

27   that distract me; nor can I bear the pressure on my

28   mind, without confessing — I am a Christian.

29 HASWELL: A Christian! — What makes you thus assume

30   the apostate?

31 SULTAN: Misery and despair.

32 HASWELL: What made you a Christian?

33 SULTAN: My Arabella, a lovely European, sent hither in her

34   youth, by her mercenary parents, to sell herself to

35   the prince of all these territories. But 'twas my happy

1 lot, in humble life, to win her love, snatch her from
2 his expecting arms, and bear her far away; where, in
3 peaceful solitude we lived, till, in the heat of the
4 rebellion against the late Sultan, I was forced from
5 my happy home to take a part. — I chose the
6 imputed rebels' side, and fought for the young
7 aspirer. — An arrow, in the midst of the engagement,
8 pierced his heart; and his officers, alarmed at the
9 terror this stroke of fate might cause among their
10 troops, urged me (as I bore a strong resemblance to
11 him) to counterfeit a greater still, and show myself to
12 the soldiers as their king recovered. I yielded to their
13 suit, because it gave me ample power to avenge the
14 loss of my Arabella, who had been taken from her
15 home by the merciless foe, and barbarously
16 murdered.
17 HASWELL: Murdered!
18 SULTAN: I learnt so, and my fruitless search to find her
19   has confirmed the intelligence. Frantic for her loss, I
20   joyfully embraced a scheme which promised
21   vengeance on the enemy: — it prospered; and I
22   revenged my wrongs and hers with such unsparing
23   justice on the opposite army and their king, that
24   even the men, who made me what I am, trembled to
25   reveal their imposition; and for their interest still
26   continue it.
27 HASWELL: Amazement!
28 SULTAN: Nay, they fill my prisons every day with
29   wretches, who but whisper I am not their real Sultan.
30   The secret, therefore, I myself boldly relate in
31   private: the danger is to him who speaks it again;
32   and, with this caution, I trust it is safe with you.
33 HASWELL: It was, without that caution. — Now hear my
34   answer to your tale: — Involved in deeds, in cruel-
35   ties, at which your better thoughts revolt, the

1   meanest wretch your camps or prisons hold, claims
2   not half the compassion you have excited. Permit
3   me, then, to be your comforter.
4 SULTAN: Impossible!
5 HASWELL: In the most fatal symptoms, I have undertaken
6   the body's cure. The mind's disease, perhaps, I am
7   not less a stranger to. Oh! Trust the noble patient to
8   my care.
9 SULTAN: What medicine will you apply?
10 HASWELL: Lead you to behold the wretched in their
11   misery, and then show you yourself in their deliverer.
12   — 'tis this: — give me the liberty of six whom I shall
13   name, now in confinement, and be yourself a witness
14   of their enlargement. — See joy lighted in the coun-
15   tenance where sorrow still has left its rough remains
16   — behold the tear of rapture chase away that of
17   anguish — hear the faltering voice, long used to
18   lamentation, in broken accents, utter thanks and
19   blessings! Behold this scene, and if you find the
20   prescription ineffectual, dishonor your physician.
21 SULTAN: I will make trial of it.
22 HASWELL: Come, then, to the governor's house this very
23   night, — into that council — room so often perverted
24   to the use of the torture; and there (unknown to
25   those, I shall release, as their king) you will be
26   witness to all the grateful heart can dictate, and feel
27   all that benevolence can taste.
28 SULTAN: I will meet you there.
29 HASWELL: In the evening?
30 SULTAN: At ten precisely. — Guards, conduct the stranger
31   from the palace.
32 HASWELL: Thus far advanced, what changes may not be
33   hoped for!
34
35

SCENE 8: One Male and One Female

Sir Luke, probably 40s

Lady Tremor, 32

This scene switches back to "an apartment at Sir Luke Tremor's" and occurs near the beginning of Act IV. The scene actually opens with Elvirus visiting Aurelia; they are in love. He has disguised himself in a "habit" and said he's just arrived from England, so no one will see who he is. Sir Luke enters, followed by Lady Tremor.

1. Lady Tremor wants Sir Luke to kick out Twineall. Why?

2. Sir Luke refuses his wife's request, saying, "I make it a rule never to quarrel in my own house, a friend's house, in a tavern or in the streets." What does this tell us about his character? Is this logical? Believable? Explain.

1   SIR LUKE: I am out of all patience, and all temper — did
2   you ever hear of such a complete impertinent
3   coxcomb? Talk, talk, talk, continually! And referring
4   to me on all occasions! "Such a man was a brave
5   general — another a great admiral"; and then he
6   must tell a long story about a siege, and ask me if it
7   did not make my bosom glow!
8   LADY TREMOR: It had not that effect upon your face, for
9   you were as white as ashes.
10   SIR LUKE: But you did not see yourself while he was
11   talking of grandfathers and great grandfathers; — If
12   you had —
13   LADY TREMOR: I was not white, I protest.
14   SIR LUKE: No — but you were as red as scarlet.
15   LADY TREMOR: And you ought to have resented the
16   insult, if you saw me affected by it. — Oh! Some men
17   would have given him such a dressing! (A pun on
18   friseur, which means hairdresser.)
19   SIR LUKE: Yes, my dear, if your uncle the friseur had
20   been alive, he would have given him a "dressing," I
21   dare say.
22   LADY TREMOR: Sir Luke, none of your impertinence: you
23   know I can't, I won't bear it — neither will I wait for
24   Lord Flint's resentment on Mr. Twineall. — No, I
25   desire you will tell him to quit this roof immediately.
26   SIR LUKE: My dear, you must excuse me — I can't think of
27   quarreling with a gentleman in my own house.
28   LADY TREMOR: Was it your own house today at dinner
29   when he insulted us? And would you quarrel then?
30   SIR LUKE: No; that was a friend's house — and I make it a
31   rule never to quarrel in my own house, a friend's
32   house, in a tavern, or in the streets.
33   LADY TREMOR: Well, then, I would quarrel in my own
34   house, a friend's house, a tavern, or in the street, if
35   anyone offended me.

1   SIR LUKE: O, my dear, I have no doubt of it — no doubt,
2   in the least.
3   LADY TREMOR: But, at present, it shall be in my own
4   house: and I will desire Mr. Twineall to quit it
5   immediately.
6   SIR LUKE: Very well, my dear — pray do.
7   LADY TREMOR: I suppose, however, I may tell him, I have
8   your authority to bid him go?
9   SIR LUKE: Tell him I have no authority — none in the
10   world over you — but that you will do as you please.
11   LADY TREMOR: I can't tell him — so he won't believe it.
12   SIR LUKE: Why not? — You tell me so, and make me
13   believe it too.
14   LADY TREMOR: Here the gentleman comes — Go away for
15   a moment.
16   SIR LUKE: With all my heart, my dear. *(Going in a hurry)*
17   LADY TREMOR: I'll give him a few hints, that he must
18   either change his mode of behavior, or leave us.
19   SIR LUKE: That's right — but don't be too warm: or if he
20   should be very impertinent, or insolent — I hear
21   Aurelia's's voice in the next room — call *her*, and I
22   dare say she'll come and take your part.
23
24
25
26
27
28
29
30
31
32
33
34
35

SCENE 9: One Male and One Female

Twineall, probably 30s

Lady Tremor, 32

> At this point Sir Luke exits, and Twineall enters.
>
> This scene follows directly afterward.

1. Why do you suppose Inchbald included this scene? Do you like it? In your opinion, does it add anything to the play?

2. Do you think Lady Tremor's reactions are logical? Humorous? Explain.

1　TWINEALL: I positively could pass a whole day upon that
2　　　staircase — those reverend faces! — I presume they
3　　　are the portraits of some of your ladyship's illus-
4　　　trious ancestors?
5　LADY TREMOR: Sir! Mr. Twineall — give me leave to tell
6　　　you — *(In a violent passion)*
7　TWINEALL: The word illustrious, I find, displeases you.
8　　　Pardon me, I did not mean to make use of so forcible
9　　　an epithet. I know the delicacy of sentiment, which
10　　　cannot bear the reflection that a few centuries only
11　　　should reduce from royalty, one whose dignified
12　　　deportment seems to have been formed for that
13　　　resplendent station.
14　LADY TREMOR: The man is certainly mad! — Mr. Twineall —
15　TWINEALL: Pardon me, Madam; I own I am an enthusiast
16　　　on these occasions. The dignity of blood —
17　LADY TREMOR: You have too much, I am sure — do have
18　　　a little taken from you.
19　TWINEALL: Gladly would I lose every drop that fills these
20　　　plebeian veins, to be ennobled by the smallest —
21　LADY TREMOR: Pray, sir, take up your abode in some
22　　　other place.
23　TWINEALL: Madam? *(Surprised)*
24　LADY TREMOR: Your behavior, sir —
25　TWINEALL: If my friend had not given me the hint, damn
26　　　me if I should not think her downright angry. *(Aside)*
27　LADY TREMOR: I can scarcely contain my rage at being so
28　　　laughed at. *(Aside)*
29　TWINEALL: I'll mention the wig: this is the time — *(Aside)*
30　　　— Perhaps you may resent it, Madam: but there is a
31　　　favor —
32　LADY TREMOR: A favor, sir! Is this a time to ask a favor?
33　TWINEALL: To an admirer of antiquity, as I am —
34　LADY TREMOR: Antiquity again!
35　TWINEALL: I beg pardon — but — a wig —

1   **LADY TREMOR: A what?** *(Petrified)*

2   **TWINEALL: A wig.** *(Bowing)*

3   **LADY TREMOR: Oh! Oh! Oh!** *(Choking)* **This is not to be**

4   **borne — this is too much — ah! Ah!** *(Sitting down and*

5   *going into fits)* **A direct, plain, palpable, and unequiv-**

6   **ocal attack upon my family, without evasion or**

7   **palliative. — I can't bear it any longer. — Oh! Oh! —**

8   *(Shrieking)*

9

10

11

12

13

14

15

16

17

18

19

20

21

22

23

24

25

26

27

28

29

30

31

32

33

34

35

SCENE 1O: One Male and One Female

Haswell, probably 3Os

Prisoner, probably late 3Os

The following scene skips to the beginning of Act 5. In the meantime, Sir Luke still will not provoke a quarrel with Twineall. However, Lord Flint enters and says he has informed against Twineall in his condemnation of the Sultan, and so he will be arrested.

Haswell enters and is introduced to Elvirus in the guise of "Glanmore," the man just arrived from England and supposedly a relative of Aurelia. Twineall insists he did not see Glanmore on the English vessel. Haswell has recognized Elvirus as the man who would trade places with his father in prison. Yet Elvirus does not recognize Haswell and treats him rudely when Haswell asks if he's an imposter.

Haswell informs Lady Tremor that the Sultan has said he can have six prisoners released. Elvirus then apologizes profusely.

Sir Luke, Twineall and Lady Tremor step outside into the garden, and guards arrive and arrest Twineall for treason.

The following opens with Haswell back at the prison.

1. Do you believe it logical that the Prisoner, upon reflection, would not want to be released? Explain.

2. Point out the overly melodramatic and overly sentimental lines in this scene. Do you think they accomplish the playwright's intended purpose? Explain.

3. Do you think it logical that the Prisoner was left here for fourteen years — particularly in view of the sort of man the Sultan says he is? Explain.

4. What role does coincidence play in this scene? Is it believable? Explain.

5. Do you like this scene? Why or why not?

6. The play is called a comedy. Do you believe it is? Why?

1   *(HASWELL and the Female PRISONER discovered)*

2   HASWELL: Rather remain in this loathsome prison! —

3   Refuse the blessing offered you! The blessing your

4   pleased fancy formed so precious, that you durst not

5   even trust its reality?

6   PRISONER: While my pleased fancy only saw the prospect, I

7   own it was delightful: but now reason beholds it, the

8   view is changed; and what, in the gay dream of fond

9   delirium, seemed a blessing, in my waking hours of sad

10   reflection, would prove the most severe of punishments.

11   HASWELL: Explain — what is the cause that makes you

12   think thus?

13   PRISONER: A cause, that has alone for fourteen years

14   made me resigned to a fate like this. — When you

15   first mentioned my release from this dark dreary

16   place, my wild ideas included, with the light, all that

17   had ever made the light a blessing. — 'Twas not the

18   sun I saw in my mad transport, but a husband filled

19   — my imagination — 'twas his idea, that gave the

20   colors of the world their beauty, and made me fondly

21   hope to be cheered by its brightness.

22   HASWELL: A husband!

23   PRISONER: But the world that I was wont to enjoy with

24   him — to see again without him; every well-known

25   object would wound my mind with dear delights

26   forever lost, and make my freedom torture —

27   HASWELL: But yet —

28   PRISONER: Oh! On my knees a thousand times I have

29   thanked heaven that he partook not of this dire

30   abode — that he shared not with me my hard

31   bondage; a greater blessing I possessed from that

32   reflection, than all his loved society could have

33   given. — But in a happy world, where smiling nature

34   pours her boundless gifts! Oh! There his loss would be

35   insupportable.

1   HASWELL: Do you lament him dead?
2   PRISONER: Yes — or, like me, a prisoner — else he would
3   have sought me out — have sought his Arabella! —
4   *(HASWELL starts.)* Why do you start?
5   HASWELL: Are you a Christian? An European?
6   ARABELLA: I am.
7   HASWELL: The name made me suppose it. — I am shocked
8   that — the Christian's sufferings — *(Trying to conceal*
9   *his surprise)* But were you made a prisoner in the
10   present Sultan's reign?
11   ARABELLA: I was — or I had been set free on his ascent to
12   the throne; for he of course gave pardon to all the
13   enemies of the slain monarch, among whom I and my
14   husband were reckoned: but I was taken in a vessel,
15   where I was hurried in the heat of the battle with
16   a party of the late emperor's friends; and all these
17   prisoners were, by the officers of the present Sultan,
18   sent to slavery, or confined, as I have been, in hopes
19   of ransom.
20   HASWELL: And did never intelligence or inquiry reach you
21   from your husband?
22   ARABELLA: Never.
23   HASWELL: Never?
24   ARABELLA: I was once informed of a large reward offered
25   for the discovery of a female Christian, and, with
26   boundless hopes, I asked an interview with the
27   messenger, — but found, on questioning him, *I* could
28   not answer his description; as he secretly informed
29   me, it was the Sultan who had caused the search, for
30   one, *himself* had known, and dearly loved.
31   HASWELL: Good heaven! *(Aside)* You then conclude your
32   husband dead?
33   ARABELLA: I do; or, like me, by some mischance, taken
34   with the other party: and having no friend to plead
35   his cause before the emperor whom he served —

284

1   HASWELL: I will plead it, should I ever chance to find him:
2   but, ere we can hope for other kindness, you must
3   appear before the Sultan, to thank him for the favor
4   which you now decline, and to tell the cause why you
5   cannot accept it.
6   ARABELLA: Alas! Almost worn out with sorrow — an
7   object of affliction as I am — in pity excuse me.
8   Present my acknowledgments — my humble grati-
9   tude — but pardon my attendance.
10   HASWELL: Nay; you must go — it is necessary. I will
11   accompany you to his presence. — Retire a moment;
12   but when I send, be ready.
13   ARABELLA: I shall obey. *(She bows obediently and exits.)*
14
15
16
17
18
19
20
21
22
23
24
25
26
27
28
29
30
31
32
33
34
35

The play ends happily, with Arabella and the Sultan united, the prisoners released, Aurelia and Elvirus united, and Sir Luke, Lord Flint and Lady Tremor deciding that they have dealt too harshly with Twineall, that he does not deserve to be punished, if he refrains henceforth from trying to flatter others. He agrees.

The Universal Wolf

(A Vicious New Version of *Little Red Riding Hood*)

by Joan M. Schenkar

There have been many retellings of the *Little Red Riding Hood* story from various versions of the fairy tale to this one by Joan Schenkar. As the subtitle suggests, this retelling is one of the most violent. Yet the story is told very theatrically. Even the directions at the beginning suggest this: "a little proscenium stage with red velvet curtains. It sits on the larger stage like a telephone booth or a police box — and carries with it the same sense of isolation."

The play is not at all realistic, a concept that is reinforced throughout. At various points the "stagehands" (see the playwright's note below) complain and, at one point, even get into an argument. A "Playwright's Note" explains that "The READER will read all the stage directions that the actors can't, won't or don't do (indicated by indented material). The READER will also create the voices of the structuralists, the bird, the post-structuralists, the audience, the stagehands, and Little Red Riding Hood's mother."

Schenkar, the author of a number of plays, has won numerous grants and awards for her work. She once said that *The Universal Wolf* is a play about appetite, with the hungriest character the Grandmother. The idea is that women, as well as men, have strong appetites.

SCENE 1: Male Monolog

M. Woolf, no age given

The play opens with Little Red Riding Hood "on the stage apron in a field of wild flowers, carrying a wicker basket." Since the play has not yet begun, her presence "is a little insubstantial."

Little Red is collecting items for her grandmother's basket. She spies a little bird, catches it and wrings its neck. "The house lights go down. A hairy paw parts the tiny velvet curtains. Voilà! The head of a wolf emerges! Authentic teeth, authentic fur, authentic everything. Except the accent, which is the accent of Maurice Chevalier."

287

In performing the monolog, you can elect — if you wish — to eliminate the lines of the Reader.

1. The play is largely for fun, and so can be highly exaggerated. What are some things you could do to try to exaggerate the character of M. Woolf?

2. Would you enjoy playing this sort of role? Why?

3. What provides the humor in this monolog? As a performer, what are some things you could do to point it up?

1   M. WOOLF: Bon soir, mesdames and messieurs. Bon soir.
2   *(Sings.)*
3   I am ze Wolf Aoow Aoww
4   I am ze Wolf Aoow Aooow
5   I am ze 'orrible terrible
6   Creature zat lurks in your
7   Dreams when you scream
8   In your bed are you dead?
9   I am ze Wolf
10 Aowww Aowww
11   Bon soir. I am M. Woolf, at votre service. *(Snarrl,*
12 *yeowll, snap, snap, drool)* Oh, excusez-moi, pardon,
13 pardon. Forgive me, mesdames et messieurs. I 'ave a
14 'ard time to keep control when it comes to ze saying
15 of my last name. Wiz your permission I will try it
16 anozzer time. Woo...Wooo...Woooo...Woooolff! *(Snarrl,*
17 *yowl, yeeowll)* A thousand pardons again, good people.
18 [a silk handkerchief dries the jaw] It is such an
19 inflammatory last name, non? So, 'ow do you say,
20 provocatif? But it 'as a certaine ring, do you not
21 agree? A résonnance of long white teeth and croque
22 — messieurs made wiz ze fingers of five-year-old
23 cheeldren. *(Snarrrl, arrrl, arrrl snap!)* Nom de dieu! I see
24 I can keep nozzing from you tonight, good people. [a
25 toothy grin, a resettling of intentions] Mesdames et
26 messieurs. A small confession. I love to devour leetle
27 cheeldren. *(Smack, smack, drool)* Oui, monsieur, I
28 assure you I speak only ze truth. Devouring leetle
29 cheeldren is my mission in life. Mon destin. I do not
30 choose it, it chooses me. For petit déjeuner, I like ze
31 five-year-olds, *(Smack, smack)* for lunch ze nine to
32 twelves, and for mon diner ze teenagers are always
33 appropriate. And because, like all ze moderne French
34 [left paw on hip] I am structuraliste, ze meaning of
35 my obsession wiz cheeldren 'as no meaning for me. I

1   eat cheeldren raw and I eat zem cooked. Ça y est.
2   The image of Claude Levi-Strauss appears behind
3   M. WOOLF. It holds up an enormous carte de visite
4   labelled MYTHS ABOUT THE ORIGINS OF COOKING,
5   then gently fades away.
6   I can substitute one child for anozzer, I can change
7   *zere* names, I can change *my* name. *(A graceful shrug*
8   *of lupine shoulders)* It is all ze same to me, so long as
9   I 'ave my leetle collation.
10   The image of Roland Barthes appears in an
11   armchair, deliberately crosses its legs and says:
12   "An eminently structural object is created by two
13   modest actions: substitution [one part replaces
14   another as in a paradigm] and nomination [the
15   name is in no way linked to the stability of the
16   parts]." The image uncrosses its legs and is
17   instantly replaced by the velvet curtain.
18   You see good people. It is merely a question of
19   application. Ze right part for ze right part. Ze bon
20   dieu gave me zees lovely teeth — ze better to eat
21   leetle limbs wiz — and [a hairy paw taps a canine]
22   Aowww! Oh zat hurrts! Pardon! Aooowww!
23   Aooowwrrr! Zis tooth must be replaced! [the silk
24   handkerchief comes out and dries the jaw] To
25   continue, bon gens. You are 'ere tonight to witness
26   the re-enactment of a leetle meet. Mit? Meeth? I
27   *cannot* say zis word but you understand me, non? I
28   come to you in a mytology. Zere are many people in
29   zis room right now who think zey know how my small
30   story will end. Eh? Am I right? Of course I am right.
31   You see [mouths the words, he's not going to lose
32   control] M. Woolf, you think fairy tale. And zen you
33   think of ze Little Red Riding Hood wiz 'er cape and 'er
34   basket and 'er benign grandmozzer in bed. Suddenly
35   ze image of M. Woolf wis 'is teeth [a coy display of

dentition] appears on ze screen of memory. Quel horreur! Eh? And zen you remember ze 'appy ending of your violent American childhoods. Ze brave Woodsman comes wiz 'is gleaming axe and commits an 'orrible vivisection upon ze suffering protagonist. Well *zat* was ze version of ze Brothers Grimm. Ze *German* version. Germans love to — 'ow you say — compensate for zere national crimes and terrible cameras wiz 'eroic avoidances of ze *real*. But we French — anozzer style entirely. We French always — 'ow do your American gangsters call it — face ze musique.

The image of Alain Robbe-Grillet appears looking thru a pair of binoculars. It says: "Metaphor is never an innocent figure of speech," then drops its binoculars and vanishes.

And so tonight, good people, you will see ze French version of ze Little Red One. Tonight we will remove entirely ze concept of ze Woodsman from ze narratif and — 'ow do your American landlords call it — *reno-vate* zis little story. For wizout ze Woodsman, wizout ze 'eroic male, zis simple tale returns to its sixteenth century spirit — bestiale, brutale, and trés, trés primitif. Tonight, mesdames et messieurs [flourish of an imaginary cape] M. Woolf *(Snarrrl, yowl, owl, howwwll)* will be ze only male on ze stage!

The image of Julia Kristeva appears holding a glass of chartreuse. It sips and says: "Narrative is, in sum, the most elaborate attempts of the speaking subject to situate his or herself among his or her desires or taboos, that is at the interior of the Oedipal triangle...oooops!" The glass falls to the floor, the image disappears. The velvet curtains fold around M. WOOLF and, in the place where his teeth just were, the charm-

1   ing face of a charming LITTLE RED RIDING
2   HOOD appears. Curls, big eyes, dimpled cheeks,
3   cupid's mouth, cleft chin, the works. The face is
4   framed by a red velvet hood and smiles insup-
5   portably.
6
7
8
9
10
11
12
13
14
15
16
17
18
19
20
21
22
23
24
25
26
27
28
29
30
31
32
33
34
35

SCENE 2: Female Monolog

Little Red, no age given

Although there is no age given for Little Red, the actress probably would be a teenager or adult rather than a little girl.

This monolog follows directly after the one delivered by M. Woolf.

1. Why do you suppose Little Red insults the audience about having only one language while she has two? How does this go along with the rest of her character?

2. In what way does Little Red's speech about how unusual she and her grandmother are, prepare you for what is to follow? How can you try to point this up for an audience?

3. In what way would you try to exaggerate the character of Little Red, to make the portrayal similar to that of M. Woolf?

1   LITTLE RED: Bon soir, tout le monde. I am Little Red
2   Riding Hood, preparing to visit the house of my dear
3   grandmother in the middle of the deep, dark, Bois de
4   Boulogne. My grandmother [a toss of the curls] is the
5   extraordinary person who gave me this little red
6   hood which I wear everywhere and by which I am
7   everywhere known. [another insupportable smile] You
8   will notice that I speak American quite perfectly. But
9   you must not feel badly about that. *I* have two
10   languages and *you* have only one. This is life. This is
11   also the result of the superior training all French
12   children receive in their little lycées — where it is
13   understood that Americans can speak no language
14   but their own. For language, as everyone knows, is an
15   ability limited to the happy few — most of whom
16   dwell in my country. The happy few...the happy few.
17   This is a phrase I once read and liked very much. The
18   "happy few." It makes me think of my dear grand-
19   mother as well as myself, for my grandmother is also
20   a very unusual person... [an insupportable smile]
21
22
23
24
25
26
27
28
29
30
31
32
33
34
35

SCENE 3: One Male and One Female (and the Reader)

Little Red, no age given

M. Woolf, no age given

The Reader, any age

After the two monologs, Little Red assures her mother that she has the basket for her grandmother. She then explains to the audience that Grandmére is a professional woman. She assures her mother that she'll stay on the path to her grand-mother's and says that she has indeed heard stories of "Big Bad M. Woolf," who then begins to howl.

M. Woolf addresses the audience and says that they are as much animal as he is. Like him, they growl. To prove this, all they have to do is listen to their stomachs when they're hungry.

Little Red tells the audience her mother has fainted because she believed the Big Bad Wolf brushed past Little Red. She says that she is now going through the woods where she sometimes sees the Woodsman. However, M. Woolf tells the audience that there will be no Woodsman in this story. Suddenly, he hears Little Red picking flowers.

Offstage she can be heard singing a song about picking flowers for her grandmére, as well as berries to crush in the sink. This is because her grandmother loves to see dying, and animals in pain.

This scene follows. You can perform it with just Little Red and M. Woolf, or with the Reader who can be either male or female.

1. Why do you think the author included the character of the Reader? What does this add to the play? How would you approach playing this role?

2. Of course, it is not logical that Little Red not see that "M. Woods" really is M. Woolf. How would you then try to play the role — with "wide-eyed" innocence, for example, or by attempting to include the audience in the "joke"? Of course, these are only two ways to approach the role. There can be many more.

3. How would you play the role of M. Woolf? As an evil person? As a character who is only true to his nature? Or another

way? Discuss this with the class. Of course, if you are playing this scene in front of an audience, you and the other actors have to agree on a particular approach, so that the acting appears unified.

4. Why do you suppose the author made both Little Red and M. Woolf (and later the Grandmother) such vicious characters? What do you think is the theme of the play? For what purpose was it written?

5. What do you think is the significance of the long shadow that falls across Little Red and M. Woolf?

1   LITTLE RED: Oh my, oh my. How very familiar you look,
2   monsieur. And yet you are not the Woodsman with
3   the remarkable axe. No, no, you are certainly *not* the
4   Woodsman I know. But perhaps you are *another*
5   Woodsman? A... [she looks closely] hairier, damper
6   Woodsman?
7   M. WOOLF makes a surreptitious attempt to
8   smooth his arm fur, then whisks his handker-
9   chief across his dripping lower jaw. He
10   summons a reliable smile.
11   And if you *are* another Woodsman, monsieur, you
12   will know the path to the house of my dear grand-
13   mother and you will direct me to it. [and here LITTLE
14   RED quavers just a bit] For I seem, good M.
15   Woodsman, to have...just a little...lost my way.
16 M. WOOLF: Lost, chére mlle? Lost? Oh, do not say it.
17   Though these woods are deep, dark, and threatened
18   with meaninglessness, you are surely not lost. For,
19   charming child [an assessing glance] in the eleven to
20   fifteen-year-old category, you have found *me*. Me!
21   Moi, M. Wooo [the WOLF grabs his snout and censors
22   himself just in time] Woods. Ready, willing and able
23   to shine ze bright light of my attentions on your
24   leetle probleme.
25   M. WOOLF broadens his smile and a little
26   string of saliva appears at the stage right corner
27   of his lower jaw. From the seventh row of the
28   audience comes a warning: "Dwarf, dwarf, ya
29   dumb dwarf. He's gonna eat you."
30 LITTLE RED: You are not, then, a woodsman, kind sir. You
31   are only M. Woods?
32 M. WOOLF: Ah, charming child. Your beautiful youth must
33   be ze excuse for your ignorance. Zere is no longer a
34   woodsman in your leetle story. Ze woodsman was a
35   crude protuberance, an ugly thorn in ze primrose

1   path of our leetle meet. Meeth. Myt. You know what
2   I mean. A fiction with résonnance. No, zere ees no
3   woodsman, charming child, zere ees only me, alone
4   in all zis wooded space to guide you.
5   The image of Gaston Bachelard appears with
6   a postal sack on its back. It removes a card from
7   the sack and reads in a whisper: "Space has
8   always reduced me to silence," then disappears.
9   LITTLE RED: But I *insist* upon a woodsman! I *depend* upon
10   a woodsman! *I must have a woodsman!*
11 M. WOOLF: Dear child — in an *exceptionally* succulent
12   stage of development—not only is ze woodsman
13   absent from zis recital but I shall personally see to it
14   [and here M. WOOLF smiles a smile of unimaginable
15   wickedness and moisture from his salivary glands
16   finally passes the point of control] zat we do not 'ave
17   even a sweet old grandmozzer to obstruct our
18   wonderful duet. Your grandmozzer will be replaced wiz
19   something *simpler* — something on ze order of zis
20   placard. [and M. WOOLF points to the dripping ZERO]
21 LITTLE RED: That is *ridiculous*, M. Woods! There is *no*
22   *question* of replacing my remarkable grandmére! Why
23   in her youth Grandmother dearest was a *serious*
24   *professional* — the only female butcher in the Bois
25   de Boulogne! [proudly] Most of the tiny mammals of
26   the Bois have ended their lives on chére Grandmére's
27   butcher block. And now, *now* that she is *retired* you
28   wish to *replace* her?! No, no, M. Woods, my dear
29   grandmother will *never* be replaced!
30 M. WOOLF: [a paw raised in placation] I positively take
31   your point, charming child. So, ze old relative 'as a
32   good eye and a steady 'and, zen?
33 LITTLE RED: Better than that, M. Woods. Dear
34   Grandmother has a remarkably hard heart. It's a
35   quality which replaces almost every other quality.

1   But, M. Woods, dear *Grandmother* will not be
2   replaced *so just get over it!*
3   M. WOOLF: I take your point again, charming child. And
4   by ze way, your command of the American vernacular
5   is superbe. [slyly] I understand zis ability missed your
6   poor mother entirely.
7   LITTLE RED: I *have* heard that, M. Woods. I *have* heard that
8   Maman lacks a certain...oh... [shrugs] ...you know...
9   M. WOOLF: [top of his form] Ah, my dear child. Zere are
10   things I could tell you about your poor mozzer, things
11   only a man of my generation could know — but non,
12   non I *must* not. I *will* not. I *shall* not.
13   The image of Pierre Louys appears in a Paul
14   Poiret evening gown. It drops a shoulder strap
15   and says: "I will reveal something but not more
16   than is permitted." — then shimmers away.
17   And now, charming child, let me encourage you to
18   collect a few more forbidden blooms for your noble
19   grandmozzer. For I see zat ze bouquet you 'ave
20   assembled for ze old paragon is a little scanty.
21 LITTLE RED: Scanty, monsieur? Is it possible?
22 M. WOOLF: It ees, darling dryad. As you say, everyone in
23   zis deep, dark, forest knows ze reputation of your
24   extraordinary grandmozzer and no one would
25   begrudge 'er a full bouquet. So take zis leetle corsage
26   from me, [and M. WOOLF hands her a blighted
27   blossom] pin it to your cape, and pick ze proscribed
28   posies. Go on, go on! Enjoy yourself! And when you
29   'ave finished, zat is ze way to grandmozzer's 'ouse.
30   [and M. WOOLF turns to the audience with a
31   villainous whisper] In ze meantime, I shall snatch zis
32   delectable morsel's leetle basket, arrive at
33   Grandmozzer's dwelling, and swallow ze old monster
34   toute entiére. Cap, spectacles, ze knitting and, if
35   necessary, argh, ze needles.

1   LITTLE RED: Well, M. Woods. There is justice in what
2   you say. I would not care to approach
3   Grandmother dearest with anything less than the
4   best. But I must begin now — for I see that the
5   shadows are getting longer.
6   [A large shadow suddenly extends itself across
7   both M. WOOLF and LITTLE RED RIDING HOOD
8   — and just as suddenly retreats.]
9   [to the audience] And while this strange man,
10   deluded by my clever story, imagines me picking
11   flowers in a field, I shall run as rapidly as dignity
12   permits to the house of my dear grandmother, using
13   a short cut known only to me. For in this M. Woods I
14   am smelling a rat. I do not like the way his mouth
15   consistently drips moisture — though, to be sure, I
16   am too polite to say so. [to M. WOOLF] Au revoir, M.
17   Woods. I am on my merry way. Au revoir. [and she
18   forgets her basket as she backs out between the
19   velvet curtains]
20 M. WOOLF: [wiping his mouth on his sleeve and surrepti-
21   tiously slurping up the overflow] Slurp slurp. Au
22   revoir, charming child. And 'ow do zey say in
23   American vacationlands, take your time, my leetle
24   one. Take your time. Ze forbidden flower's cry out for
25   your attentions. [M. WOOLF whirls 'round to the
26   audience, a different wolf now, every one of his teeth
27   available for viewing] Aooow aaow aooooww! Ze leetle
28   hors d'oeuvre 'as left 'er basket to assist me in my
29   impe'sonation! M. Woolf 'as prevailed! Ha! Ha!
30   Grandmozzers beware! Leetle girls BEWARE! M. Woolf
31   *(Aooooow!)* is on ze loose once again!
32
33
34
35

SCENE 4: Two Females (and the Reader)

Grandmother, no age given

Little Red, no age given

Again the shadow falls, and Part I ends. The curtains part and M. Woolf comes out to address the audience. He asks them to look at their programs and read the text of the story there; it really is to be included with the program. The gist of it is that the wolf kills the grandmother and then devours Little Red Riding Hood.

This leads directly into the following scene.

1. Why do you suppose Schenkar made both Little Red and her grandmother so unlikable? Why do you think she made Little Red dumb and the Grandmother forgetful?

2. What sort of relationship do Little Red and Grandmother have? Explain.

3. How is exaggeration used in this scene? How might you point it up here?

1   *(PART II. The curtains open wider than they ever have on*
2   *the same little stage. It is now GRANDMOTHER's house*
3   *and the decor is that of a retired butcher who might at any*
4   *time resume her career. We see chopping blocks, a full set*
5   *of Sabatiers, and various small mammals hanging by*
6   *their hindquarters in gruesome disarray. GRANDMOTHER*
7   *sits in a rocking chair with cap, spectacles, two outsize*
8   *needles [but no knitting], and a bottle of blackberry wine.*
9   *She rocks and sips and sings her Grandmother song.)*
10 **GRANDMOTHER:**
11   **They think that I'll knit by night**
12   **They hope I'll crochet by day**
13   **They want their socks mended**
14   **Their sad problems ended**
15   **Well it won't be by me**
16   **Hee hee**
17   **Hee hee**
18   **No it won't be by me**
19   **Not by me.**
20   **A loud knocking sound — KNOCK KNOCK —**
21   **interrupts GRANDMOTHER's big aria. From off-**
22   **stage we hear: "Grandmother, dearest**
23   **grandmother! Open the door. Oh please, please,**
24   **please, please, please open the door!"**
25   **It's Little Red Riding Hood. For godssake, Little**
26   **Red Riding Hood! Are you blind? [to the audience]**
27   **She must be blind. The door is open. Raise the latch.**
28   **[knocking continues] For godssake Little Red Riding**
29   **Hood. Are you deaf? [to the audience] She must be**
30   **deaf. The latch! RAISE THE LATCH!**
31 **LITTLE RED: [entering] I raised the latch, Grandmére...**
32 **GRANDMOTHER: Smart girl. [to the audience] She's**
33   **coming along.**
34 **LITTLE RED: ...and I ran all the way thru the Bois de**
35   **Boulogne** *(Pant pant)* **to advise you** *(Pant pant)* **of the**

1 arrival of a very suspicious gentlemen with moisture
2 around his mouth.
3 GRANDMOTHER: That will be the wolf, Little Red Riding
4 Hood. I know this story very well.
5 LITTLE RED: [marvelling] The moist man with fur on his
6 hands was M. *Woolf*. That was M. WOOLF!
7 GRANDMOTHER: Sometimes I fear the girl has inherited
8 more traits from her mother than from *me*.
9 LITTLE RED: Do not say it, Grandmother dearest! I
10 beg you.
11 GRANDMOTHER: Well sit down and drink with me, grand-
12 daughter, and we'll discuss why I forgot your visit
13 and what to do about the possible new monsieur.
14 LITTLE RED: I am too young to drink, Grandmère. Maman
15 says it is drink that has dissolved your memory.
16 GRANDMOTHER: Drink is the proper partner for meat,
17 Little Red Riding Hood, and it is meat that makes a
18 memory. Or so we butchers always say. (*Gulp gulp*)
19 Now describe the strange monsieur for me. I must see
20 him before I can deal with him.
21 LITTLE RED: [carefully] He was...hairy...damp...unctuous
22 ...and full of fine phrases.
23 GRANDMOTHER: It's the wolf, alright.
24 LITTLE RED: *Really*, Grandmother dearest. That was
25 *really* M. Woolf?!
26 GRANDMOTHER: Oh, for *godssake*, Little Red Riding Hood.
27 LITTLE RED: Well, then, Grandmère. M. Woolf is coming to
28 eat us both and with my little basket, too, which in
29 my haste, I abandoned.
30 GRANDMOTHER: *My* little basket, you mean. [avariciously]
31 What's in it? *Fresh meat*? Did you put *fresh* meat in
32 my basket?
33 LITTLE RED: Six bottles of blackberry wine, some wilting
34 flowers, and one deceased songbird at the bottom,
35 dear Grandmother.

1   GRANDMOTHER: Six bottles! Good for you, Granddaughter!
2   I detest cut flowers as you well know but the bird is
3   a *wonderful* touch. I'll pop him in a pâte brilé. If I
4   remember. Now in just a moment that *awful* wolf will
5   be at the door trying to imitate *you*, Little Red Riding
6   Hood.
7   LITTLE RED: Is he *that* stupid, Grandmother dearest? Or
8   does he think *you're* that stupid?
9   GRANDMOTHER: That is how the story goes, Little Red
10   Riding Hood. At least I *think* that is how the story
11   goes. My memory is as full of holes as a hairnet.
12   LITTLE RED: It's the wine, isn't it, Grandmére?
13   GRANDMOTHER: [taking a slurp] It's the *meat*, Little Red.
14   It's been days since I've had *fresh meat.* [looks at the
15   bottle] Of course, every pleasure has its penalties.
16   *(Glug glug glug)*
17   LITTLE RED: Well, but dearest Grandmére, what are we
18   to *do*?
19   GRANDMOTHER: [taking a slug] I'm thinking, Little Red.
20   LITTLE RED: You're *drinking*, Grandmére.
21   GRANDMOTHER: The one supports the other. *(Glug glug)* Or
22   so we butchers always say.
23   LITTLE RED: Thank heaven, chére Grandmére, that I do
24   not have your responsibilities.
25   GRANDMOTHER: Ha ha! I've *got* it. The *perfect solution!*
26   LITTLE RED: Oh, Grandmother. You are certainly the
27   cleverest old person in the Bois de Boulogne! Tell me
28   your solution!
29   GRANDMOTHER: [raises her head to speak, but memory
30   fails] Woops, it's gone! The idea has flown my mind
31   like a bird from a bough! [to herself] Must be a protein
32   deficiency. [to the audience] Old age is a *miracle* of
33   selective consciousness. A *miracle.*
34   LITTLE RED: We are lost! We are lost! Maman was right!
35   You have drunk your mind away!

1   GRANDMOTHER: Stop that gibbering you brainless child.
2   *No* one is lost. A *solution* is, that is all. And in one
3   minute, I will have another. [to the audience] Old age
4   is very resilient.
5
6
7
8
9
10
11
12
13
14
15
16
17
18
19
20
21
22
23
24
25
26
27
28
29
30
31
32
33
34
35

SCENE 5: One Male and Female (and the Reader)

M. Woolf, no age given

Grandmother, no age given

Reader, any age

Little Red allows her corsage to come into contact with Grandmother, who begins to sneeze. M. Woolf knocks on Grandmother's door and speaks in a falsetto voice, pretending to be Little Red. Grandmother tells Little Red to hide in the armoire where she'll find a "well-honed axe on your right-hand side!" She continues to sneeze but says this will save their lives.

Little Red makes it into the armoire just before M. Woolf, wearing a "cerise tablecloth and a cottonwool bib" enters. Grandmother pretends to think he's Little Red. This is where the scene picks up.

1. How might you point up the humor of M. Woolf's being affected by Grandmother's fake sobs? What are some other ways humor is used in this scene?

2. Do you like this play? Why? Would you enjoy seeing it performed? Or performing in it? Why?

1   M. WOOLF: Oooh, dear Grandmozzer. I was in such a hurry
2   to arrive zat I forgot to look in ze basket. [he flips
3   quickly through the top layer] But you weel immedi-
4   ately find plaisir in zees lovely flowers which I
5   labored to gather for you.
6   GRANDMOTHER: Have you dropped an oar in the water,
7   Little Red Riding Hood? You *know* I'm violently
8   allergic to *anything* that grows. ACHOO ACHOOO
9   ACHOO. Why, the moment I come into contact with
10   chlorophyll [and here she touches a leaf] I break out
11   in hideous pustules, boils filled with slime, wens,
12   warts, carbuncles, and large purple spots! Look!
13   Look! And anyone who touches me suffers the very
14   same affliction.
15   M. WOOLF: [pulling back in horror] Do you mean, dear
16   Grandmozzer, zat I cannot embrace you, encompass
17   you, put my, uh, mouse, moufe, mout, I *cannot* say
18   zis word but you know what I mean — ze area below
19   my nose — cannot kees your beautiful wizzered
20   cheek? Your neck full of exquisite veins running in
21   blood? [M. WOOLF's bib fills with saliva]
22   GRANDMOTHER: ACHOO, Little Red Riding Hood, ACHOO.
23   Do you remember what happened the last time you
24   approached me with a bouquet in hand?
25   M. WOOLF: Uh...I am a leetle vague on that subject, dear
26   Grandmozzer.
27   GRANDMOTHER: Why, we had to rush you right to the
28   hospital, Little Red Riding Hood. Your lips swelled up
29   like soccer balls, your eyes looked like fresh pample-
30   mousse, even your ears were affected. [peers] Why
31   Little Red Riding Hood, I believe your ears are *still*
32   affected. How very large they look.
33   M. WOOLF: The better to hear you with, ancient relative.
34   GRANDMOTHER: And your mouth. Surely you had some
35   serious dental work since your last visit? Your teeth

1   seem twice as large as they once were.

2 M. WOOLF: No, no, dear Grandmozzer. I assure you my

3   teeth are in a terrible condition. [touches them.]

4   Aooww.

5 GRANDMOTHER: And your nose, dear child. What

6   happened to your nose?

7 M. WOOLF: Eet is ze way of adolescence, Grandmozzer

8   dearest. You know how quickly one feature can

9   outstrip anozzer in ze process of growth. And now I

10   can smell you so much better. Sniff sniff. Sniff sniff.

11   I can smell you *and* something else. Are you certain

12   we are quite alone, dear Grandmozzer? Sniff sniff —

13 GRANDMOTHER: I was expecting no one but you,

14   Granddaughter, ACHOO ACHOO, and now you have

15   entirely forgotten my basket of presents which was

16   so terribly important to me, living alone as I do so

17   entirely and without consolation. SOB SOB.

18   GRANDMOTHER's loud, false sobs touch M.

19   WOOLF as real emotion never could.

20 M. WOOLF: [to the audience] Oh, my goodness, I deed not

21   calculate ze affects of my avidity on ze old woman.

22   Zis touches me very much, very much indeed.

23   [GRANDMOTHER sobs louder] I sink I must kill ze

24   poor thing quickly to put 'er out of 'er extreme

25   misery. [GRANDMOTHER instantly cries more softly]

26   But 'ow can I kill 'er if I cannot *touch* 'er?

27 GRANDMOTHER: Boo hoo hoo. Alone! Forsaken! Under-

28   nourished!

29 M. WOOLF: Eet ees clearly time to reveal myself and

30   accomplish ze classical deed, but all zis emotion is,

31   'ow you say in American business circles, keeling my

32   appetite for power.

33 GRANDMOTHER: Poor, poor, poor Grandmother with

34   nothing but a distant daughter, an ingrate grand-

35   child, and a dull collection of carving knives!

1   Boo! Hoo! Hoo!
2   M. WOOLF: Really, I cannot tolerate zis display of
3   emotion. Grandmozzer, dear Grandmozzer! Cease
4   your crying! Desist from your depression! See! See!
5   [he holds up the basket while rummaging through it]
6   I have brought you 1, 2, 3, 4, 5, 6, six bottles of, of
7   zis maroon liquid to drink. And beneath them ...Argh!
8   A dead hen of some sort.
9   GRANDMOTHER: I believe that's a songbird, Little Red
10   Riding Hood.
11   M. WOOLF: Whatever it is, dear Grandmozzer, I am certain
12   it will make someone a very good meal. [M. WOOLF
13   begins to drip a little] Now dry your dreadful tears
14   and think about cooking.
15   GRANDMOTHER: I'd rather think about drinking, darling
16   Granddaughter. Your foolish flowers have begun to
17   raise welts on my skin. See here and here.
18   M. WOOLF: Mon dieu! Could ze old dragon be correct? Her
19   forearm looks anyway like a bas-relief map of the
20   Pyrenees. [to GRANDMOTHER] Grandmozzer dearest.
21   Eet ees true, zen. You are poisonous to ze touch?
22   GRANDMOTHER: Lay a hand on me, Little Red, and that
23   hand will never again be the same.
24   M. WOOLF: Heureusement, my appetite is momentarily
25   suppressed by ze old lady's histrionics and, besides, I
26   'ave already confessed it, my serious preference is for
27   prepubescent cheeldren. SLURP DROOL. Mon dieu!
28   Mon bib! Uh, Grandmozzer. Whatever can I do to offer
29   you consolation for zis hideous condition?
30   GRANDMOTHER: Open a bottle for me, Little Red, and
31   allow me to drown my misery in fermented black-
32   berry juices.
33   M. WOOLF: Eet seems a small sing to ask, dear Grand-
34   mozzer, 'ere you are. [hands her a bottle]
35   GRANDMOTHER: Salut salope. *(Glug glug glug)* Ahhh. Much,

1   much better. But when thirst is satisfied, hunger
2   begins to speak. Or so we butchers always say.
3   [LITTLE RED sneezes in the armoire]
4   M. WOOLF: [freezes in a predatory attitude] *Aha*, Grand-
5   mozzer. Zere is someone in your armoire.
6   GRANDMOTHER: Is it possible?
7   M. WOOLF: Years of serious training 'ave allowed me to
8   identify ze smallest sound of prospective prey. Eef
9   only I could 'ear it again.
10   LITTLE RED: ACHOO ACHOO.
11   M. WOOLF: Merci.
12   GRANDMOTHER: [to the audience] The little fool is
13   allergic to mothballs.
14   LITTLE RED: ACHOO ACHOO ACHOO
15   M. WOOLF: Oh merci merci. Now zat, eef I am not
16   mistaken, is a female sneeze in ze eleven- to fifteen-
17   year-old category. It is a blonde sneeze, moreover,
18   and more zan likely ze sneeze 'as blue eyes. Am I
19   warm, dear Grandmozzer?
20   GRANDMOTHER: You're running a temperature, Little Red
21   Riding Hood.
22   M. WOOLF: I can only conclude, dear Grandmozzer, zat in
23   your armoire is concealed a dreadful, female 'oping
24   to supplant me in your abundant affections.
25   GRANDMOTHER: Could it be M. *Woolf*, Little Red? Could
26   it actually be the *big, bad, wolf* and could that *wolf*
27   be a *female*?!
28   M. WOOLF: Aoww. Aowwww. Even my name uttered by
29   anozzer person affects me 'orribly. Woooooolf!
30   Woooooolf! Aoooww! Aoooww! Pardon, dearest
31   Grandmozzer. I am overly excited. I sink we might 'ave
32   located ze terrible M. [whispers.] Woolf in your
33   armoire. I must enter and vanquish him. Or 'er, in zis
34   case.
35   GRANDMOTHER: Go right ahead, darling Granddaughter. I

1   will sit here with my bottle and my needles and my
2   knives at the ready.
3 M. WOOLF: At last! At last! My appetite will be satisfied!
4   At last! Justice for ze Wolf. Aaaaooowwww!
5
6
7
8
9
10
11
12
13
14
15
16
17
18
19
20
21
22
23
24
25
26
27
28
29
30
31
32
33
34
35

M. Woolf goes into the armoire; Little Red at first can't find the axe. Then there are sounds of battle. Little Red hacks M. Woolf "into small, steak-like pieces" but complains that the axe was dull. Now Grandmother decides she can't put up with Little Red's smile for another decade, or her voice for another year. So she sings her a lullaby. Once Little Red is asleep, Grandmother plunges her knitting needles again and again into Little Red's body.

Wine in the Wilderness

by Alice Childress

Born in Charleston, South Carolina, Alice Childress moved to Harlem when she was five and was raised by her grandmother, whom she credits with inspiring her to become a writer.

Childress opened the New York stage to black women playwrights because of the success of her play *Gold Through the Trees,* produced off-Broadway in 1952.

A novelist as well as a playwright, Childress was forced to quit high school when both her mother and grandmother died. She attempted to read two books a day afterwards in an effort to educate herself.

For years, she was an actress with the American Negro Theatre, which she helped to found. In 1955 her play *Trouble in the Mind* won an Obie Award for the best off-Broadway play. It tells the story of an experienced black actress's protest against playing a stereotypical "darkie" role in a Broadway-bound play. Two of her plays, produced in 1950 and 1952, were the first by a black woman to be professionally produced with Actors Equity Association, that is, union actors.

The action in *Wine in the Wilderness* occurs during a 1964 race riot in Harlem. The play opens with Bill Jameson, an artist and self-styled intellectual, rebuking Oldtimer for bringing back things he has picked up in the streets — suits, clothing and liquor.

Unable to convince Oldtimer to get rid of the stuff, Bill returns to his current project, a triptych containing two of the three final paintings. The first is an innocent child, the second a beautiful and regal black woman, who symbolizes "Wine in the Wilderness" or "Mother Africa."

The third will be a lost woman, defeated and with nothing of substance in her life. As he is beginning to tell Oldtimer about this third painting, two friends, a married couple named Cynthia (a social worker) and Sonny-man (a writer) call to say they have found a perfect model for the final panel.

They bring her to his studio. She says her name is Tommy and she begins to size up Bill as potential husband material. He agrees that she is a "messed up chick," a good choice as a model.

She says before she'll pose, she needs something to eat. Her apartment has been nearly destroyed in a fire resulting from the riot, and she isn't allowed back in.

While the men are gone, Tommy asks Cynthia how she can win Bill's interest and affection. Cynthia gently tries to tell her that maybe she's aiming too high.

Later when Bill wants to paint her in her wig and mismatched clothes, a result of not being allowed back into her apartment, she objects. Of course, not knowing what the painting is to be, she wants to look her best. For starters, this means taking off her wig.

Bill is very patronizing, telling her she's just like most black women, eager to create a matriarchal society which robs men of their masculinity. He plays the intellectual, quizzing her about black people and white sympathizers throughout recent history. In effect, he keeps implying that he's better than she is. He's an intellectual, she a common or grass-roots woman.

She sees a painting he did of a white woman, and tells him she is certain he treated her with respect.

While they exchange words, she upsets an orange drink on herself. He gives her an African wrap and tells her to change into it. When she's behind a screen, the phone rings. She hears Bill telling the caller about the magnificent woman in his painting, "the finest" in the world. Tommy, whose real name is Tomorrow Marie, thinks he's talking about her. As a result, she gains self-respect and actually transforms herself into a beautiful woman.

Bill asks her to put on the wig again. She doesn't want to, saying she doesn't really like wigs. As she is posing, he asks her to tell about herself, which she does. She also tells him some black history he doesn't know, things about which she is not the least bit pretentious.

Bill has become enchanted by her transformation but now can't recapture the image of her he wanted to paint. They are drawn to each other.

The next morning while Bill is showering, Oldtimer comes and explains to Tommy the idea behind the triptych. Tommy is furious, feeling she has been taken advantage of, or worse still, been treated as dirt. She lashes out at Bill and Cynthia and

Sonny-man. She tells Oldtimer he is a fool for letting middle-class people treat him like he's invisible. They hadn't even known his real name. She then turns back to the three others. She says when whites call Negroes nigger, "they mean educated you, uneducated me." "I called you a 'nigger' but I love you." She tells them that they think they are superior to the masses, but they are the masses and just don't know it.

Bill comes to realize that his vision was wrong and that his painting of "Mother Africa" does not actually represent the black women of America. He says he just dreamed this up out of the "junk room of my mind" and that Tommy really is the "Wine in the Wilderness" because she (or her family) has survived slavery and race riots and still holds her head high.

Because of this Bill decides he will do a new triptych of black womanhood.

SCENE 1: Two Males

Bill Jameson, 33

Oldtimer, in his 60s

The play takes place in the summer of 1964. The setting is "a one room apartment in a Harlem tenement." It was a three-room apartment, but Bill has broken down the walls so that the kitchen is part of the room, as is the bedroom. There is a screen at the foot of the bed. "The room is obviously black-dominated, pieces of sculpture, wall hangings, paintings." Drapery hides the canvas on an artist's easel. Two other canvases the same size are next to it, also covered. "The place is in a beautiful, rather artistic state of disorder." "There is a raised platform for model posing. On the platform is a backless chair."

As the curtain rises, "The tail end of a riot is going on out in the street..."

Bill sits on the floor, his back to the wall, drawing on a sketch pad. The phone rings; it's Sonny-man, who is in a bar, having been prevented from coming up the block. Sonny-man says he and Cynthia have found a model for him. Bill says he prefers to get his own models. There is yelling off-stage about the riots being over.

Then this scene begins.

315

1. What sort of person is Oldtimer? Is he a likeable man? What makes you think so? What do you think of his argument that it's okay to bring home the loot he found because he isn't the one who stole it?

2. What sort of person is Bill? What sort of relationship does he have with Oldtimer? How does he feel about him?

3. What does Oldtimer mean when he says Bill "oughta be fed up with your people sometimes"? Is this a valid comment? Why?

4. What are Oldtimer's views on life? How are they different from Bill's?

5. Disregarding what you read earlier about the plot of the play, what do you think of Bill's idea about the three paintings? Do you think it's a good one? Why? How do you feel about his trying to find a "messed up chick" to paint?

1   **BILL: What's this! Oh, no, no, no, Oldtimer, not here...**

2   *(Faint sound of a police whistle)*

3   **BILL: The police after you? What you bring that stuff in**

4   **here for?**

5   **OLDTIMER:** *(Runs past BILL to center as he looks for a place*

6   *to hide the loot.)* **No, no, they not really after me but...I**

7   **was in the basement so I could stash this stuff...but**

8   **a fella told me they pokin' 'round down there...in the**

9   **back yard pokin' 'round...the police doin' a lotta**

10   **pokin' 'round.**

11   **BILL: If the cops are searchin', why you wanna dump your**

12   **troubles on me?**

13   **OLDTIMER: I don't wanta go to jail. I'm too old to go to**

14   **jail. What we gonna do?**

15   **BILL: We can throw it the hell outta the window. Didn't**

16   **you think of just throwin' it away and not worry**

17   **'bout jail?**

18   **OLDTIMER: I can't do it. It's like...I'm Oldtimer but my**

19   **hands and arms is somebody else that I don' know-**

20   **a-tall.**

21   *(BILL pulls stuff out of OLDTIMER'S arms and places loot*

22   *on the kitchen table. OLDTIMER's arms fall to his sides.)*

23   **OLDTIMER: Thank you, son.**

24   **BILL: Stealin' ain't worth a bullet through your brain, is**

25   **it? You wanna get shot down and drown in your own**

26   **blood...for what? A suit, a bottle of whiskey? Gonna**

27   **throw your life away for a damn ham?**

28   **OLDTIMER: But I ain't really stole nothin', Bill, 'cause I**

29   **ain't no thief. Them others...they smash the**

30   **windows, they run in the stores and grab and all. Me,**

31   **I pick up what they left scattered in the street.**

32   **Things they drop...things they trample underfoot.**

33   **What's in the street ain't like stealin'. This is**

34   **leavin's. What I'm gon' do if the police come?**

35   **BILL:** *(Starts to gather the things in the tablecloth that is on the*

1   *table.)* **I'll throw it out the air-shaft window.**

2   **OLDTIMER:** *(Places himself squarely in front of the air-shaft*

3   *window.)* **I be damn. Uh-uh, can't let you do it, Billy-**

4   **Boy.** *(Grabs the liquor and holds on.)*

5   **BILL:** *(Wraps the suit, the ham and the salami in the tablecloth*

6   *and ties the ends together in a knot.)* **Just for now, then**

7   **you can go down and get it later.**

8   **OLDTIMER:** *(Getting belligerent)* **I say I ain't gon' let you do it.**

9   **BILL: Sonny-man calls this "The people's revolution." A**

10   **revolution should not be looting and stealing.**

11   **Revolutions are for liberation.**

12   *(OLDTIMER won't budge from before the window.)*

13   **BILL: Okay, man, you win. It's all yours.** *(Walks away from*

14   *OLDTIMER and prepares his easel for sketching.)*

15   **OLDTIMER: Don't be mad with me, Billy-Boy, I couldn't**

16   **help myself.**

17   **BILL:** *(At peace with the old man)* **No hard feelin's.**

18   **OLDTIMER:** *(As he uncorks bottle)* **I don't blame you for**

19   **bein' fed up with us...Fella like you oughta be fed up**

20   **with your people sometime. Hey, Billy, let's you and**

21   **me have a little taste together.**

22   **BILL: Yeah, why not.**

23   **OLDTIMER:** *(At the table pouring drinks)* **You mustn't be too**

24   **hard on me. You see, you talented, you got somethin'**

25   **on the ball, you gonna make it on past these white**

26   **folk...but not me, Billy-Boy, it's too late in the day for**

27   **that. Time, time, time...time done put me down.**

28   **Father Time is a bad white cat. Whatcha been paintin'**

29   **and drawin' lately? You can paint me again if you**

30   **wanta...no charge. Paint me, 'cause that might be the**

31   **only way I get to stay in the world after I'm dead and**

32   **gone. Somebody'll look up at your paintin' and**

33   **say..."Who's that?" And you say "That's Oldtimer."**

34   *(BILL joins OLDTIMER at table and takes one of the*

35   *drinks.)*

1   OLDTIMER: **Well, here's lookin' at you and goin' down me.**
2   *(Gulps down drink.)*
3   BILL: *(Raising his glass)* **Your health, Oldtimer.**
4   OLDTIMER: **My day we didn't have all this grants and**
5   **scholarship like now. Whatcha been doin'?**
6   BILL: **I'm working on the third part of a triptych.**
7   OLDTIMER: **A what tick?**
8   BILL: **A triptych.**
9   OLDTIMER: **Hot-damn, that call for another drink. Here's**
10   **to the trip-tick. Down the hatch. What is one-a-**
11   **those?**
12   BILL: **It's three paintings that make one work...three**
13   **paintings that make one subject.**
14   OLDTIMER: **Goes together like a new outfit...hat, shoes**
15   **and suit.**
16   BILL: **Right. The title of my triptych is..."Wine in the**
17   **Wilderness"...Three canvases on black womanhood...**
18   OLDTIMER: *(Eyes light up.)* **Are they naked pitchers?**
19   BILL: *(Crosses to paintings.)* **No, all fully clothed.**
20   OLDTIMER: *(Wishing it was a naked picture)* **Man, ain'**
21   **nothin' dirty 'bout naked pitchers. That's art. What**
22   **you call artistic.**
23   BILL: **Right, right, right, but these are with clothes. That**
24   **can be artistic too.** *(Uncovers one of the canvases and*
25   *reveals painting of a charming little girl in Sunday dress*
26   *and hair ribbon.)* **I call her..."Black Girlhood."**
27   OLDTIMER: **Awwwww, that's innocence! Don't know what**
28   **it's all about. Ain't that the little child that live right**
29   **down the street? Yeah. That call for another drink.**
30   BILL: **Slow down, Oldtimer, wait till you see this.** *(He covers*
31   *the painting of the little girl, then uncovers another canvas*
32   *and reveals a beautiful woman, deep mahogany*
33   *complexion; she is cold but utter perfection, draped in star-*
34   *tling colors of African material, very "Vogue" looking. She*
35   *wears a golden headdress sparkling with brilliants and*

1   *sequins applied over the paint.)* **There she is…"Wine in**
2   **the Wilderness"…Mother Africa, regal, black woman-**
3   **hood in her noblest form.**
4   **OLDTIMER: Hot damn. I'd die for her, no stuff…Oh, man.**
5   **"Wine in the Wilderness."**
6   **BILL: Once, a long time ago, a poet named Omar told us**
7   **what a paradise life could be if a man had a loaf of**
8   **bread, a jug of wine and…a woman singing to him in**
9   **the wilderness. She is the woman; she is the bread;**
10   **she is the wine; she is the singing. This Abyssinian**
11   **maiden is paradise…perfect black womanhood.**
12   **OLDTIMER:** *(Pours for BILL and himself.)* **To our Abyssinian**
13   **maiden.**
14   **BILL: She's the Sudan, the Congo River, the Egyptian**
15   **Pyramids …Her thighs are African mahogany…she**
16   **and speaks and her words pour forth sparkling clear**
17   **as the waters…Victoria Falls.**
18   **OLDTIMER: Ow! Victoria Falls! She got a pretty name.**
19   **BILL:** *(Covers her up again.)* **Victoria Falls is a waterfall, not**
20   **her name. Now, here's the one that calls for a drink.**
21   *(Snatches cover from the empty canvas.)*
22   **OLDTIMER:** *(Stunned by the empty canvas)* **Your…your**
23   **pitcher is gone.**
24   **BILL: Not gone…she's not painted yet. This will be the third**
25   **part of the triptych. This is the unfinished third of**
26   **"Wine in the Wilderness." She's gonna be the kinda**
27   **chick that is grass roots…no, not grass roots…I mean**
28   **she's underneath the grass roots. The lost**
29   **woman…what the society has made out of our women.**
30   **She's as far from my African queen as a woman can get**
31   **and still be female; she's as close to the bottom as you**
32   **can get without crackin' up…She's ignorant, unfemi-**
33   **nine, coarse, rude…vulgar…a poor, dumb chick that's**
34   **had her behind kicked until it's numb…and the sad**
35   **part is…she ain't together, you know,…there's no**

1   hope for her.
2   OLDTIMER: Oh, man, you talkin' 'bout my first wife.
3   BILL: A chick that ain't fit for nothin' but to...to...just
4   pass her by.
5   OLDTIMER: Yeah, later for her. When you see her, cross
6   over to the other side of the street.
7   BILL: If you had to sum her up in one word it would be
8   nothin'!
9   OLDTIMER: *(Roars with laughter.)* That call for a double!
10   BILL: *(Beginning to slightly feel the drinks. He covers the
11   canvas again.)* Yeah, that's a double! The kinda
12   woman that grates on your damn nerves. And Sonny-
13   man just called to say he found her runnin' 'round in
14   the middle-a this riot; Sonny-man say she's the real
15   thing from underneath them grass roots. A back-
16   country chick right outta the wilds of
17   Mississippi...but she ain't never been near there.
18   Born in Harlem, raised right here in Harlem...but
19   back country. Got the picture?
20   OLDTIMER: *(Full of laughter)* When...when...when she get
21   here let's us stomp her to death.
22   BILL: Not till after I paint her. Gonna put her right here on
23   this canvas. *(Pats the canvas, walks in a strut around
24   the table.)* When she gets put down on canvas...then
25   triptych will be finished.
26   OLDTIMER: *(Joins him in the strut.)* Trip-tick will be
27   finish...trip-tick will be finish.
28   BILL: Then "Wine in the Wilderness" will go up against the
29   wall to improve the view of some post office...or
30   some library ...or maybe a bank...and I'll win a
31   prize...and the queen, my black queen will look down
32   from the wall so the messed up chicks in the neigh-
33   borhood can see what a woman oughta be...and the
34   innocent child on the side of her and the messed up
35   chick on the other side of her...MY STATEMENT.

SCENE 2: Two Females

Tommy, 30

Cynthia, 25

Sonny-man and Cynthia bring Tommy to Bill's apartment. Tommy is surprised to learn that nobody knows Oldtimer's name. He says it's Edmond Lorenzo Matthews. Tommy says she cut her own name to Tommy or sometimes Tommy-Marie. In reference to Tommy, Sonny-man says, "Did I tell you!" She refers to blacks as "niggers," and Bill tells her they don't use that word. They use Afro-Americans, instead. She says it was the "Afro-Americans" who burned down her house and everything is gone. All she has is her mismatched clothes.

When Bill says he wants to paint her, she wonders why he doesn't do "pretty girls" instead. When he insists that she's the one he wants to paint, she asks that he wait till she gets some clothes out of the cleaners. He says he wants to paint her right away.

She says she's hungry and would like Chinese food. The men leave to get the food. This is where the following scene picks up.

1. In what way has Tommy misinterpreted what Cynthia has done? Explain.

2. What type of person is Tommy? List as many of her character traits as you can. Point to specific lines that illustrate these traits.

3. What type of person is Cynthia? Use lines in this scene to illustrate what you say?

4. Why do you think Cynthia tells Tommy if she wants to, she can just leave? What trait of Tommy's does it illustrate when she refuses? Explain.

5. In what way is Cynthia not treating Tommy as an individual here? In what way is she?

6. Why does Tommy say white people are the dullest people in the world? From her point of view, do you think this is justified? Why?

7. Why does Cynthia make the statement that she thinks Tommy is too good for Bill? Is this an honest statement? Why?

8. Do you think all the advice Cynthia gives Tommy is good? Explain.

1   **TOMMY: Turn that off.** *(CYNTHIA turns off record player.)*
2   How could I forget your name, good as you been to
3   me this day. Thank you, Cynthia, thank you. I like
4   him. Oh, I like him. But I don't wanta push him too
5   fast. Oh, I got to play these cards right.
6   **CYNTHIA:** *(A bit uncomfortable)* **Oh, honey...Tommy, you**
7   don't want a poor artist.
8   **TOMMY: Tommy's not lookin' for a meal ticket. I been**
9   doin' for myself all my life. It takes two to make it in
10   this high-priced world. A black man see a hard way to
11   go. The both of you gotta pull together. That way you
12   accomplish.
13   **CYNTHIA: I'm a social worker...and I see so many broken**
14   homes. Some of these men! Tommy, don't be in a
15   rush about the marriage thing.
16   **TOMMY: Keep it to yourself...but I was thirty my last**
17   birthday and haven't ever been married. I coulda
18   been. Oh, yes, indeed, coulda been. But I don't want
19   any and everybody. What I want with a no-good
20   piece-a nothin'? I'll never forget what the Reverend
21   Martin Luther King said..."I have a dream." I liked
22   him sayin' it 'cause truer words have never been
23   spoke. *(Straightening the room)* **I have a dream, too.**
24   **Mine is to find a man who'll treat me just half-way**
25   **decent...just to meet me half-way is all I ask, to**
26   **smile, be kind to me. Somebody in my corner. Not to**
27   **wake up by myself in the mornin' and face this world**
28   **all alone.**
29   **CYNTHIA: About Bill, it's best not to ever count on**
30   anything, anything at all, Tommy.
31   **TOMMY:** *(This remark bothers her for a split second but she*
32   *shakes it off.)* **Of course, Cynthia, that's one of the**
33   **foremost rules of life. Don't count on nothin'!**
34   **CYNTHIA: Right, don't be too quick to put your trust in**
35   these men.

1   TOMMY: You put your trust in one and got yourself a
2   husband.
3   CYNTHIA: Well, yes, but what I mean is...Oh, you know. A
4   man is a man and Bill is also an artist and his work
5   comes before all else and there are other factors...
6   TOMMY: *(Sits facing CYNTHIA.)* **What's wrong with me?**
7   CYNTHIA: I don't know what you mean.
8   TOMMY: Yes you do. You tryin' to tell me I'm aimin' too
9   high by lookin' at Bill.
10   CYNTHIA: Oh, no, my dear.
11   TOMMY: Out there in the street, in the bar, you and your
12   husband were so sure that he'd like me and want to
13   paint my picture.
14   CYNTHIA: But he does want to paint you; he's very
15   eager to...
16   TOMMY: But why? Somethin' don't fit right.
17   CYNTHIA: *(Feeling sorry for TOMMY)* **If you don't want to do
18   it, just leave and that'll be that.**
19   TOMMY: Walk out while he's buyin' me what I ask for,
20   spendin' his money on me? That'd be too dirty. *(She
21   looks at books and takes one from shelf.)* **Books, books,
22   books everywhere. "Afro-American History." I like
23   that. What's wrong with me, Cynthia? Tell me, I
24   won't get mad with you, I swear. If there's somethin'
25   wrong that I can change, I'm ready to do it. Eighth
26   grade, that's all I had of school. You a social worker;
27   I know that means college. I come from poor people.**
28   *(Examining the book in her hand)* **Talkin' 'bout poverty
29   this and poverty that and studyin' it. When you in it
30   you don' be studyin' 'bout it. Cynthia, I remember
31   my mother tyin' up her stockin's with strips-a rag
32   'cause she didn't have no garters. When I get home
33   from school she'd say...Nothin' much here to eat."
34   Nothin' much might be grits, or bread and coffee. I
35   got sick-a all that, got me a job. Later for school.**

1   CYNTHIA: The Matriarchal Society.

2   TOMMY: What's that?

3   CYNTHIA: A matriarchal society is one in which the
4   women rule ...the women have the power...the
5   women head the house.

6   TOMMY: We didn't have nothin' to rule over, not a pot nor
7   a window. And my papa picked hisself up and ran off
8   with some finger-poppin' woman and we never hear
9   another word til ten, twelve years later when a under-
10   taker call up and ask if Mama wanta claim his body.
11   And don'cha know, Mama went on over and claimed
12   it. A woman need a man to claim, even if it's a dead
13   one. What's wrong with me? Be honest.

14   CYNTHIA: You're a fine person ...

15   TOMMY: Go on, I can take it.

16   CYNTHIA: You're too brash. You're too used to looking out
17   for yourself. It makes us lose our femininity...it
18   makes us hard...it makes us seem very hard. We do
19   for ourselves too much.

20   TOMMY: If I don't, who's gonna do for me?

21   CYNTHIA: You have to let the black man have his
22   manhood again. You have to give it back, Tommy.

23   TOMMY: I didn't take it from him, how I'm gonna give it
24   back? What else is the matter with me? You had
25   school, I didn't. I respect that.

26   CYNTHIA: Yes, I've had it, the degrees and the whole bit.
27   For a time I thought I was about to move into
28   another world, the so-called "integrated" world, a
29   place where knowledge and know-how could set you
30   free and open all the doors, but that's a lie. I turned
31   away from that idea. The first thing I did was give up
32   dating white fellas.

33   TOMMY: I never had none to give up. I'm not soundin' on
34   you. White folks, nothin' happens when I look at 'em.
35   I don't hate 'em, don't love 'em...just nothin' shakes

1   a-tall. The dullest people in the world. The way they
2   talk..."Oh, hooty, hooty, hoo"...Break it down for me
3   to A, B, Cs. That Bill...I like him, with his black,
4   uppity, high-handed ways. What do you do to get a
5   man you want? A social worker oughta tell you
6   things like that.
7   CYNTHIA: Don't chase him...at least don't let it look that
8   way. Let him pursue you.
9   TOMMY: What if he won't? Men don't chase me much, not
10   the kind I like.
11   CYNTHIA: *(Rattles off instructions glibly.)* Let him do the
12   talking. Learn to listen. Stay in the background a
13   little. Ask his opinion..."What do *you* think, Bill?"
14   TOMMY: Mmmm, "Oh, hooty, hooty, hoo."
15   CYNTHIA: But why count on him? There are lots of other
16   nice guys.
17   TOMMY: You don't think he'd go for me, do you?
18   CYNTHIA: *(Trying to be diplomatic)* Perhaps you're not really
19   his type.
20   TOMMY: Maybe not, but he's mine. I'm so lonesome...I'm
21   lonesome...I want somebody to love. Somebody to
22   say..."That's all right," when the world treats me mean.
23   CYNTHIA: Tommy, I think you're too good for Bill.
24   TOMMY: I don't wanta hear that. The last man that told
25   me I was too good for him...was tryin' to get away.
26   He's good enough for me. *(Straightening room)*
27   CYNTHIA: Leave the room alone. What we need is a little
28   more sex appeal and a little less washing, cooking
29   and ironing.
30   *(TOMMY puts down the room straightening.)*
31   CYNTHIA: One more thing...do you have to wear that wig?
32   TOMMY: *(A little sensitive)* I like how your hair looks. But
33   some of the naturals I don't like. Can see all the lint
34   caught up in the hair like it hasn't been combed
35   since know not when. You a Muslim?

1   CYNTHIA: No.
2   TOMMY: I'm just sick-a hair, hair, hair. Do it this way,
3   don't do it, leave it natural, straighten it, process, no
4   process. I get sick-a hair and talkin' 'bout it and
5   foolin' with it. That's why I wear the wig.
6   CYNTHIA: I'm sure your own must be just as nice or nicer
7   than that.
8   TOMMY: It oughta be. I only paid nineteen ninety-five
9   for this.
10 CYNTHIA: You ought to go back to using your own.
11 TOMMY: *(Tensely)* I'll be givin' that some thought.
12 CYNTHIA: You're pretty nice people just as you are. Soften
13   up, Tommy. You might surprise yourself.
14 TOMMY: I'm listenin'.
15 CYNTHIA: Expect more. Learn to let men open doors for
16   you...
17 TOMMY: What if I'm standin' there and they don't open it?
18 CYNTHIA: *(Trying to level with her)* You're a fine person. He
19   wants to paint you, that's all. He's doing a kind of
20   mural thing and we thought he would enjoy painting
21   you. I'd hate to see you expecting more out of the
22   situation than what's there.
23 TOMMY: Forget it, sweetie-pie, don' nothin' happen that's
24   not suppose to.
25
26
27
28
29
30
31
32
33
34
35

SCENE 3: One Male and One Female

Tommy, 30

Bill, 33

The next scene occurs a few minutes after Cynthia and Tommy have their conversation. The three men return, and then everyone leaves except Tommy and Bill.

1. Why do you think Tommy reacts so strongly to getting a frankfurter instead of Chinese food? What is Bill's attitude about this? Are both attitudes justified? Why?

2. Do you agree with what Bill says about the black revolution in the line that begins, "Let's face it, our folks are not together?" Why?

3. How do you interpret Tommy's response that "what everybody need is somebody like you?" What tone is she taking with him here? Explain. How about when she says, "You're a very correctable person, aren't you?"

4. If you were Tommy, how would you react to being quizzed about John Brown, Harriet Tubman and so on? What does this show about Bill's attitude to her? Explain.

5. How many instances can you find of Bill's patronizing or even putting down Tommy's way of life? Why do you think he feels he has to do this? How do you feel about this?

6. Why do you think Tommy continues to be interested romantically in Bill in spite of the way he insults her?

7. Bill accuses Tommy of being a stereotypical black female. In what ways is he, too, a stereotype? Explain.

8. Bill accuses Tommy of not being beautiful and yet objects to her wanting to take off her wig and to wear different clothes to pose for him. Why do you think there is this contradiction?

1   (*TOMMY notices nothing that looks like Chinese food. BILL*
2   *is carrying a small bag and a container.*)
3   **TOMMY: Where's the Foo-Yong?**
4   **BILL: They blew the restaurant, baby. All I could get was a**
5   **couple-a franks and a orange drink from the stand.**
6   **TOMMY:** (*Tersely*) **You brought me a frank-footer? That's**
7   **what you think-a me, a frank-footer?**
8   **BILL: Nothin' to do with what I think. Place is closed.**
9   **TOMMY:** (*Quietly surly*) **This is the damn city-a New York,**
10   **any hour on the clock they sellin' the chicken in the**
11   **basket, barbecue ribs, pizza pie, hot pastrami**
12   **samitches; and you brought me a frank-footer?**
13   **BILL: Baby, don't break bad over somethin' to eat. The**
14   **smart set, the jet set, the beautiful people, kings and**
15   **queens eat frankfurters.**
16   **TOMMY: If a queen sent you out to buy her a bucket-a Foo-**
17   **Yong, you wouldn't come back with no lonely-ass**
18   **frank-footer.**
19   **BILL: Kill me 'bout it, baby! Go 'head and shoot me six**
20   **times. That's the trouble with our women, y'all**
21   **always got your mind on food.**
22   **TOMMY: Is that our trouble?** (*Laughs.*) **Maybe you right.**
23   **Only two things to do. Either eat the frank-footer or**
24   **walk outta here. You got any mustard?**
25   **BILL:** (*Gets mustard from the refrigerator.*) **Let's face it, our**
26   **folks are not together. The brothers and sisters have**
27   **busted up Harlem...no plan, no nothin'. There's your**
28   **black revolution, heads whipped, hospital full and we**
29   **still in the same old bag.**
30   **TOMMY:** (*Seated at the kitchen table*) **Maybe what everybody**
31   **need is somebody like you, who know how things**
32   **oughta go, to get on out there and start some action.**
33   **BILL: You still mad about the frankfurter?**
34   **TOMMY: No. I keep seein' pitchers of what was in my room**
35   **and how it all must be spoiled now.** (*Sips the orange*

1   *drink)* **A orange never been near this. Well, it's cold.**
2   *(Looking at an incense burner)* **What's that?**
3   BILL: **An incense burner, was given to me by the Chinese**
4   **guy, Richard Lee. I'm sorry they blew his restaurant.**
5   TOMMY: **Does it help you to catch the number?**
6   BILL: **No, baby, I just burn incense sometime.**
7   TOMMY: **For what?**
8   BILL: **Just 'cause I feel like it. Baby, ain't you used to**
9   **nothin'?**
10   TOMMY: **Ain't used to burnin' incent for nothin'.**
11   BILL: *(Laughs.)* **Burnin' what?**
12   TOMMY: **That stuff.**
13   BILL: **What did you call it?**
14   TOMMY: **Incent.**
15   BILL: **It's not incent, baby. It's incense.**
16   TOMMY: **Like the sense you got in your head. In-sense.**
17   **Thank you. You're a very correctable person, ain't you?**
18   BILL: **Let's put you on canvas.**
19   TOMMY: *(Stubbornly)* **I have to eat first.**
20   BILL: **That's another thing 'bout black women, they wanta**
21   **eat 'fore they do anything else. Tommy...Tommy...I**
22   **bet your name is Thomasina. You look like a**
23   **Thomasina.**
24   TOMMY: **You could sit there and guess till your eyes pop**
25   **out and you never would guess my first name. You**
26   **might could guess the middle name but not the first**
27   **one.**
28   BILL: **Tell it to me.**
29   TOMMY: **My name is Tomorrow.**
30   BILL: **How's that?**
31   TOMMY: **Tomorrow...like yesterday and** *tomorrow,* **and the**
32   **middle name is just plain Marie. That's what my**
33   **father name me. Tomorrow Marie. My mother say he**
34   **thought it had a pretty sound.**
35   BILL: **Crazy! I never met a girl named Tomorrow.**

1   **TOMMY: They got to callin' me Tommy for short, so I stick**
2   **with that. Tomorrow Marie...Sound like a promise**
3   **that can never happen.**
4   **BILL:** *(Straightens chair on stand. He is very eager to start*
5   *painting.)* **That's what Shakespeare said...Tomorrow**
6   **and tomorrow and tomorrow." Tomorrow, you will be**
7   **on this canvas.**
8   **TOMMY:** *(Still uneasy about being painted)* **What's the hurry?**
9   **Rome wasn't built in a day...that's another saying.**
10   **BILL: If I finish in time, I'll enter you in an exhibition.**
11   **TOMMY:** *(Loses interest in the food. She examines the room,*
12   *and looks at portrait on the wall.)* **He looks like some-**
13   **body I know or maybe saw before.**
14   **BILL: That's Frederick Douglass. A man who used to be a**
15   **slave. He escaped and spent his life trying to make us**
16   **all free. He was a great man.**
17   **TOMMY: Thank you, Mr. Douglass. Who's the light-colored**
18   **man?** *(Indicates a frame next to the Douglass.)*
19   **BILL: He's white. That's John Brown. They killed him for**
20   **tryin' to shoot the country outta the slavery bag. He**
21   **dug us, you know. Old John said, "Hell no, slavery**
22   **must go."**
23   **TOMMY: I heard all about him. Some folks say he was**
24   **crazy.**
25   **BILL: If he had been shootin' at *us* they wouldn't have**
26   **called him a nut.**
27   **TOMMY: School wasn't a great part-a my life.**
28   **BILL: If it was you wouldn't-a found out too much 'bout**
29   **black history cause the books full-a nothin' but**
30   **whitey...all except the white ones who dug us...they**
31   **not there either. Tell me...who was Elijah Lovejoy?**
32   **TOMMY: Elijah Lovejoy...Mmmm. I don't know. Have to do**
33   **with the Bible?**
34   **BILL: No, that's another white fella...Elijah had a printin'**
35   **press and the main thing he printed was "Slavery got**

1	to go." Well, the man moved in on him, smashed his
2	press time after time...but he kept puttin' it back
3	together and doin' his thing. So, one final day, they
4	came in a mob and burned him to death.
5	TOMMY: *(Blows her nose with sympathy as she fights tears.)*
6	That's dirty.
7	BILL: *(As TOMMY glances at titles in book case)* **Who was**
8	**Monroe Trotter?**
9	TOMMY: Was he white?
10	BILL: No, soul brother. Spent his years tryin' to make it all
11	right. Who was Harriet Tubman?
12	TOMMY: I heard-a her. But don't put me through no test,
13	Billy. *(Moving around studying pictures and books)* **This**
14	**room is full-a things I don' know nothin' about.**
15	**How'll I get to know.**
16	BILL: Read, go to the library, bookstores, ask somebody.
17	TOMMY: Okay, I'm askin'. Teach me things.
18	BILL: Aw, baby, why torment yourself? Trouble with our
19	women...they all wanta be great brains. Leave some-
20	thin' for a man to do.
21	TOMMY: *(Eager to impress him)* **What you think-a Martin**
22	**Luther King?**
23	BILL: A great guy. But it's too late in the day for the
24	singin' and prayin' now.
25	TOMMY: What about Malcolm X?
26	BILL: Great cat...but there again...Where's the program?
27	TOMMY: What about Adam Powell? I voted for him. That's
28	one thing 'bout me. I vote. Maybe if everybody vote
29	for the right people...
30	BILL: The ballot box. It would take me all my life to
31	straighten you on that hype.
32	TOMMY: I got time.
33	BILL: You gonna wind up with a king-size headache. The
34	matriarchy gotta go. Y'all throw them suppers
35	together, keep your husband happy, raise the kids.

1   TOMMY: I don't have a husband. Course, that could be
2   **fixed.** *(Leaving the unspoken proposal hanging in the air)*
3   BILL: You know the greatest thing you could do for your
4   people? Sit up there and let me put you down on
5   canvas.
6   TOMMY: Bein' married and havin' family might be good for
7   your people as a race, but I was thinkin' 'bout myself
8   a little.
9   BILL: Forget yourself sometime, sugar. On that canvas
10   you'll be givin' and givin' and givin'...That's where
11   you do your thing best. What you stallin' for?
12   TOMMY: *(Returns to table and sits in chair.)* I...I don't want to
13   pose in this outfit.
14   BILL: *(Patience wearing thin)* Why, baby, why?
15   TOMMY: I don't feel proud-a myself in this.
16   BILL: Art, baby, we talkin' art. Whatcha want...Ribbons?
17   Lace? False eyelashes?
18   TOMMY: No, just my white dress with the orlon sweater
19   ...or anything but this what I'm wearin'. You oughta
20   see me in that dress with my pink linen shoes. Oh,
21   hell, the shoes are gone. I forgot 'bout the fire...
22   BILL: Oh, stop fightin' me! Another thing...our women
23   don't know a damn thing 'bout bein' feminine. *Give*
24   *in* sometime. It won't kill you. You tellin' me how to
25   paint? Maybe you oughta hang out your shingle and
26   give art lessons! You too damn opinionated. You
27   gonna pose or you not gonna pose? Say somethin'.
28   TOMMY: You makin' me nervous! Hollerin' at me. My
29   mama never holler at me. Hollerin'.
30   BILL: I'll soon be too tired to pick up the brush, baby.
31   **TOMMY:** *(Eye catches picture of white woman on the wall.)*
32   That's a white woman! Bet you never hollered at her
33   and I bet she's your girlfriend...too, and when she
34   posed for her pitcher I bet y'all was laughin'...and you
35   didn't buy her no frank-footer!

1   BILL: *(Feels a bit smug about his male prowess.)* **Awww, come**
2   **on, cut that out, baby. That's a little blonde, blue-**
3   **eyed chick who used to pose for me. That ain't where**
4   **it's at. This is a new day, the deal is goin' down**
5   **different. This is the black moment, doll. Black, black,**
6   **black is bee-yoo-tee-full. Got it?** *Black is beautiful.*
7   TOMMY: **Then how come it is that I don't** *feel* **beautiful**
8   **when you talk to me?!**
9   BILL: **That's your hang-up, not mine. You supposed to**
10   **stretch forth your wings like Ethiopia, shake off**
11   **them chains that been holdin' you down. Langston**
12   **Hughes said let 'em see how beautiful you are. But**
13   **you determined not to ever be beautiful. Okay, that's**
14   **what makes you Tommy.**
15   TOMMY: **Do you** *have* **a girlfriend? And who is she?**
16   BILL: *(Now enjoying himself to the utmost)* **Naw, naw, naw, doll.**
17   **I know people, but none-a this "tie-you-up-and-I-own-**
18   **you" jive. I ain't mistreatin' nobody and there's**
19   **enough-a me to go around. That's another thing with**
20   **our women...they wanta** *latch* **on. Learn to play it by**
21   **ear, roll with the punches, cut down on some-a this**
22   **"got-you-to-the-grave" kinda relationship. Was today**
23   **all right? Good, be glad...take what's at hand because**
24   **tomorrow never comes, it's always today.**
25   *(TOMMY begins to cry.)*
26   BILL: **Awwww, I didn't mean it that way...I forgot your**
27   **name.** *(He brushes her tears.)* **You act like I belong to**
28   **you. You're jealous of a picture?**
29   TOMMY: **That's how women are, always studyin' each**
30   **other and wonderin' how they look up 'gainst the**
31   **next person.**
32   BILL: *(A bit smug)* **That's human nature. Whatcha call**
33   **healthy competition.**
34   TOMMY: **You think she's pretty?**
35   BILL: **She was, perhaps still is. Long, silky hair. She could**

1   sit on her hair.

2   **TOMMY:** *(With bitter arrogance)* **Doesn't everybody?**

3   **BILL:** You got a head like a rock and gonna have the last

4   word if it kills you. Baby, I bet you could knock out

5   Muhammad Ali in the first round, then rare back and

6   scream like Tarzan..."Now, I am the greatest!"

7

8

9

10

11

12

13

14

15

16

17

18

19

20

21

22

23

24

25

26

27

28

29

30

31

32

33

34

35

SCENE 4: Female Monolog

Tommy, 30

Tommy wants to take off her wig; Bill says it's a part of her; she has a reason for wearing it. She grabs her orange drink and accidentally spills it in her lap. The phone rings, and he tosses her an African wrap and answers it. She goes behind the screen. The call is about his exhibition. He tells the caller: "You oughta see her. The finest black woman in the world...This gorgeous satin chick is...is...black velvet moonlight...an ebony queen of the universe."

Tommy is astounded, thinking he's talking about her. As he continues talking, she "is suddenly awakened to the feeling of being loved and admired." She dons the wrap, takes off her wig, and studies herself in the mirror. She is "taller, more relaxed and sure of herself."

She does not wear the wig when she poses. Trying to remember the earlier image of her, Bill has trouble painting anything. He asks Tommy to tell him about herself. This is what she says.

1. The monolog sounds like stream of consciousness at first. Why do you suppose she does this? Why doesn't she say anything more substantial at first?

2. Then she starts talking about the Elks and goes on with it. Why do you think she does that?

1   **TOMMY:** *(Now on sure ground)* **I was born in Baltimore,**
2   **Maryland and raised here in Harlem. My favorite**
3   **flower is "Four o'clocks," that's a bush flower. My**
4   **wearin' flower, corsage flower, is pink roses. My**
5   **mama raised me, mostly by herself, God rest the**
6   **dead. Mama belonged to "The Eastern Star." Her**
7   **father was a "Mason." If a man in the family is a**
8   **"Mason" any woman related to him can be an**
9   **"Eastern Star." My grandfather was a member of "The**
10   **Prince Hall Lodge." I had an uncle who was an "Elk"...**
11   **a member of the "The *Improved* Benevolent Protective**
12   **Order of Elks of *the World*": "The Henry Lincoln**
13   **Johnson Lodge." You know, the white "Elks" are called**
14   **"The Benevolent Protective Order of Elks" but black**
15   **"Elks" are called "The Improved Benevolent**
16   **Protective Order of Elks of the World." That's because**
17   **the black "Elks" got copyright first but the white**
18   **"Elks" took us to court about it to keep us from usin'**
19   **the name. Over fifteen hundred black folk went to jail**
20   **for wearin' the "Elk" emblem on their coat lapel.**
21   **Years ago...that's what you call history.**
22
23
24
25
26
27
28
29
30
31
32
33
34
35

SCENE 5: Three Males and Two Females

Oldtimer, 60s

Tommy, 30

Bill, 33

Sonny-man, 27

Cynthia, 25

Tommy tells Bill about the history of the Elks, the A.M.E. church, and that her ancestors were slaves in what is now a part of Norfolk.

Bill tells her about his family — post office workers. He says they all bought aluminum doors with ducks on them and bought houses in Jamaica, Long Island. He tells her of a dream where people are looking at his work in a gallery and everything is laughed away. Finally, he tells her, "Let's save each other, let's be kind and good to each other while it rains and the angels roll those hoops and bicycle wheels." (She'd earlier told him that thunder was caused by this.)

The scene shifts to the following day, Tommy and Bill happy with each other, probably beginning to fall in love. Oldtimer comes to the door and doesn't recognize Tommy at first. She tells him to come in. "She wears another throw [African design] draped around her."

They talk as Bill is taking a shower. This is what happens; it takes us to the end of the play.

1. Why do you suppose Oldtimer slips up and mentions the unfinished painting and what it is to represent?

2. How do you suppose Cynthia and Sonny-man feel when they find out what Oldtimer has said? What about Oldtimer? What is he feeling? What do you think are the various emotions Tommy is feeling?

3. What are Bill's feelings when he enters the room?

4. Who do you think has the more realistic view of life, Tommy or Bill? Explain.

5. Do you think there is any validity to Tommy's saying that Bill and his friends "dig" black people in history books but not living people? Explain.

6. What is the most important single emotion you would want to convey to an audience throughout this scene? What other important emotions would you want to convey? Explain.

7. This is an extremely powerful scene. What do you think makes it so?

8. What do you think makes Bill change his mind about "Wine in the Wilderness"?

9. The Greek philosopher Aristotle said that all drama should make the audience undergo a catharsis, which means a cleansing of the soul, a release. Do you think *Wine in the Wilderness* accomplishes this? Explain.

1   OLDTIMER: Everything I put my hand and mind to do, it

2   turn out wrong...Nothin' but mistakes...When you

3   don' know, you don' know. I don' know nothin'. I'm

4   ignorant.

5   TOMMY: Hush that talk...You know lotsa things, every-

6   body does. (*Helps him remove wet coat.*)

7   OLDTIMER: Thanks. How's the trip-tick?

8   TOMMY: The what?

9   OLDTIMER: *Trip-tick.* That's a paintin'.

10   TOMMY: See there, you know more about art than I do.

11   What's a trip-tick? Have some coffee and explain me

12   a trip-tick.

13   OLDTIMER: (*Proud of his knowledge*) Well, I tell you...a trip-

14   tick is a paintin' that's in three parts...but they all

15   belong together to be looked at all at once. Now...

16   this is the first one...a little innocent girl...

17   Unveils picture.)

18   TOMMY: She's sweet.

19   OLDTIMER: And this is "Wine in the Wilderness"...The

20   Queen of the Universe...the finest chick in the world.

21   TOMMY: (*She is thoughtful as he unveils the second picture.*)

22   That' not me.

23   OLDTIMER: No, you gonna be this here last one. The worst

24   gal in town. A messed-up chick that — that — (*He*

25   *unveils the third canvas and is face to face with the*

26   *almost blank canvas, then realizes what he has said. He*

27   *turns to see the stricken look on TOMMY's face.*)

28   TOMMY: The messed-up chick, *that's* why they brought

29   me here, ain't it? That's why he wanted to paint me!

30   Say it!

31   OLDTIMER: No, I'm lyin', I didn't mean it. It's the society

32   that messed her up. Awwwwww, Tommy, don't look

33   that-a-way. It's art...it's only art...He couldn't mean

34   you...it's art...

35   (*The door opens. CYNTHIA and SONNY-MAN enter.*)

1   SONNY-MAN: Anybody want a ride down...down...
2   down...downtown? What's wrong? Excuse me...
3   *(Starts back out.)*
4   TOMMY: *(Blocking the exit to CYNTHIA and SONNY-MAN)* No,
5   come on in. Stay with it..."Brother"..."Sister." Tell
6   'em what a trip-tick is, Oldtimer.
7   CYNTHIA: *(Very ashamed)* Oh, no.
8   TOMMY: You don't have to tell 'em. They already know.
9   The messed-up chick! How come you didn't pose for
10   that, my sister? The messed-up chick lost her home
11   last night...burnt out with no place to go. You and
12   Sonny-man gave me comfort, you cheered me up and
13   took me in...*took me in!*
14   CYNTHIA: Tommy, we didn't know you, we didn't mean...
15   TOMMY: It's all right! I was lost but now I'm found! Yeah,
16   the blind can see! *(She dashes behind the screen and*
17   *puts on her clothing, sweater, skirt, etc.)*
18   OLDTIMER: *(Goes to bathroom.)* Billy, come out!
19   SONNY-MAN: Billy, step out here, please!
20   *(BILL enters shirtless, wearing dungarees.)*
21   SONNY-MAN: Oldtimer let it out 'bout the triptych.
22   BILL: The rest of you move on.
23   TOMMY: *(Looking out from behind the screen)* No, don't go a
24   step. You brought me here, see me out!
25   BILL: Tommy, let me explain it to you.
26   TOMMY: *(Coming out from behind screen)* I gotta check out
27   my apartment, and my clothes and money.
28   Cynthia...I can't wait for anybody to open the door or
29   look out for me and all that kinda crap you talk. A
30   bunch-a liars!
31   BILL: Oldtimer, why you...
32   TOMMY: Leave him the hell alone. He ain't said nothin'
33   that ain' so!
34   SONNY-MAN: Explain to the sister that some mistakes
35   have been made.

1   BILL: Mistakes have been made, baby. The mistakes were
2   yesterday, this is today...
3   TOMMY: Yeah, and I'm Tomorrow, remember? Trouble is I
4   was Tommy to all of you..."Oh, maybe they gon' like
5   me."...I was your fool, thinkin' writers and painters
6   know moren' me, that maybe a little bit of you would
7   rub off on me.
8   CYNTHIA: We are wrong. I knew it yesterday. Tommy, I
9   told you not to expect anything out of this...this
10   arrangement.
11   BILL: This is a relationship, not an arrangement.
12   SONNY-MAN: Cynthia, I tell you all the time, keep outta
13   other people's business. What the hell you got to do
14   with who's gonna get what outta what? You and
15   Oldtimer, yakkin' and hakkin'. *(To OLDTIMER)* Man,
16   your mouth gonna kill you.
17   BILL: It's me and Tommy. Clear the room.
18   TOMMY: Better not. I'll kill him! The "black people" this
19   and the "Afro-American"...that...You ain't got no use
20   for none-a us. Oldtimer, you their fool too. 'Til I got
21   here they didn't even know your damn name. There's
22   something inside-a me that says I ain' suppose to let
23   *nobody* play me cheap. Don't care how much they
24   know! *(She sweeps some of the books to the floor.)*
25   BILL: Don't you have any forgiveness in you? Would I be
26   beggin' you if I didn't care? Can't you be generous
27   enough...
28   TOMMY: Nigger, I been too damn generous with you
29   already. All-a these people know I wasn't down here
30   all night posin' for no pitcher, nigger!
31   BILL: Cut that out, Tommy, and you not going anywhere!
32   TOMMY: You wanna bet? Nigger!
33   BILL: Okay, you called it, baby. I did act like a low,
34   degraded person...
35   TOMMY: *(Combing out her wig with her fingers while holding it)*

1	Didn't call you no low, degraded person. Nigger! *(To*
2	*CYNTHIA who is handing her a comb)* "Do you have to
3	wear a wig?" Yes! To soften the blow when y'all go up
4	side-a my head with a baseball bat. *(Going back to*
5	*taunting BILL and ignoring CYNTHIA's comb)* Nigger!
6	BILL: That's enough-a that. You right and you're wrong too.
7	TOMMY: Ain't a-one-a us you like that's alive and walkin'
8	by you on the street. You don't like flesh and blood
9	niggers.
10	BILL: Call me that, baby, but don't call yourself. That what
11	you think of yourself?
12	TOMMY: If a black somebody is in a history book, or
13	printed on a pitcher, or drawed on a paintin'...or if
14	they're a statue...dead, and outta the way, and can't
15	talk back, then you dig 'em and full-a so much-a
16	damn admiration and talk 'bout "our" history. But
17	when you run into us livin' and breathin' ones, with
18	the life's blood still pumpin' through us...then you
19	comin' on 'bout we ain' never together. You hate us,
20	that's what! *You hate black me!*
21	BILL: *(Stung to the heart, confused and saddened by the half*
22	*truth which applies to himself.)* I never hated you, I
23	never will, no matter what you or any of the rest of
24	you do to *make* me hate you. I won't! Hell, woman,
25	why do you say that! Why would I hate you?
26	TOMMY: Maybe I look too much like the mother that give
27	birth to you. Like the Ma and Pa that worked in the
28	post office to buy you a house and a screen door with
29	a damn duck on it. And you so ungrateful you didn't
30	even like it.
31	BILL: No, I didn't, baby. I don't like screen doors with
32	ducks on 'em.
33	TOMMY: You didn't like who was livin' behind them screen
34	doors. Phoney nigger!
35	BILL: That's all! Dammit! Don't go there no more!

1   **TOMMY: Hit me, so I can tear this place down and scream**
2   **bloody murder.**
3   **BILL:** *(Somewhere between laughter and tears)* **Looka here,**
4   **baby, I'm willin' to say I'm wrong, even in fronta the**
5   **room fulla people...**
6   **TOMMY:** *(Through clenched teeth)* **Nigger.**
7   **SONNY-MAN: The sister is upset.**
8   **TOMMY: And you stop callin' me "the" sister...if you**
9   **feelin' so brotherly why don't you say *"my"* sister?**
10   **Ain't no we-ness in your talk. "The" Afro-American,**
11   **"the" black man, there's no we-ness in you. Who you**
12   **think *you* are?**
13   **SONNY-MAN: I was talkin' in general er...my sister, 'bout**
14   **the masses.**
15   **TOMMY: There he go again. "The" masses. Tryin' to make**
16   **out like we pitiful and you got it made. You the**
17   **masses your damn self and don't even know it.**
18   *(Another angry look at BILL)* **Nigger.**
19   **BILL:** *(Pulls dictionary from shelf.)* **Let's get this ignorant**
20   **"nigger" talk squared away. You can stand some**
21   **education.**
22   **TOMMY: You treat me like a nigger, that's what. I'd rather**
23   **be called one than treated that way.**
24   **BILL:** *(Questions TOMMY.)* **What is a nigger?** *(Talks as he is*
25   *trying to find word.)* **A nigger is a low, degraded person,**
26   *any low* **degraded person. I learned that from my**
27   **teacher in the fifth grade.**
28   **TOMMY: Fifth grade is a liar! Don't pull that dictionary**
29   **crap on me.**
30   **BILL:** *(Pointing to the book)* ***Webster's New World Dictionary***
31   ***of the American Language, College Edition.***
32   **TOMMY: I don't need to find out what no college white**
33   **folks say nigger is.**
34   **BILL: I'm tellin' you it's a low, degraded person. Listen.**
35   *(Reads from the book.)* **Nigger, n-i-g-g-e-r...A Negro...A**

1   **member of any dark-skinned people...Damn.** *(Amazed*
2   *by dictionary description)*
3   **SONNY-MAN: Brother Malcolm** *said* **that's what they**
4   **meant... nigger is a Negro, Negro is a nigger.**
5   **BILL:** *(Slowly finishing his reading)* **A vulgar, offensive term**
6   **of hostility and contempt. Well, so much for the fifth**
7   **grade teacher.**
8   **SONNY-MAN: No, they do not call low, degraded white**
9   **folks niggers. Come to think of it, did you ever hear**
10   **whitey call Hitler a nigger? Now if some whitey digs**
11   **us...the others might call him a nigger-***lover***, but they**
12   **don't call him no nigger.**
13   **OLDTIMER: No, they don't.**
14   **TOMMY:** *(Near tears)* **When they say "nigger,"just dry-long-**
15   **so, they mean educated you and uneducated me.**
16   **They hate you and call you "nigger," I called you**
17   **"nigger" but I love you.** *(There is dead silence in the*
18   *room for a split second.)*
19   **SONNY-MAN:** *(Trying to establish peace)* **There you go. There**
20   **you go.**
21   **CYNTHIA:** *(Cautioning SONNY-MAN)* **Now is not the time to**
22   **talk, darlin'.**
23   **BILL: You love me? Tommy, that's the greatest compli-**
24   **ment you could...**
25   **TOMMY:** *(Sorry she said it)* **You must be runnin' a fever,**
26   **nigger, I ain' said nothin' 'bout lovin' you.**
27   **BILL:** *(In a great mood)* **You did, yes, you did.**
28   **TOMMY: Well, you didn't say it to me.**
29   **BILL: Oh, Tommy...**
30   **TOMMY:** *(Cuts him off abruptly.)* **And don't you dare say it**
31   **now. I'm tellin' you...it ain't to be said now.** *(Checks*
32   *through her paper bag to see if she has everything. She*
33   *starts to put on the wig, changes her mind, holds it to end*
34   *of scene, turns to the others in the room.)* **Oldtimer...my**
35   **brothers and my sister.**

1   OLDTIMER: I wish I was a thousand miles away; I'm so
2   sorry. *(He sits at the foot of the model stand.)*
3   TOMMY: I don't stay mad; it's here today and gone
4   tomorrow. I'm sorry your feelin's got hurt...but when
5   I'm hurt I turn and hurt back. Somewhere, in the
6   middle of last night, I thought the old me was gone
7   ...lost forever, and gladly. But today was flippin' time,
8   so back I flipped. Now it's "turn the other cheek"
9   time. If I can go through life other-cheekin' the white
10   folk...guess y'all can be other-cheeked too. But I'm
11   going back to the nitty-gritty crowd, where the talk
12   is we-ness and us-ness. I hate to do it but I have to
13   thank you cause I'm walkin' out with much more
14   than I brought in. *(Goes over and looks at the queen in*
15   *the "Wine in the Wilderness" painting.)* Tomorrow Marie
16   had such a lovely yesterday.
17   *(BILL takes her hand; she gently removes it from his*
18   *grasp.)*
19 TOMMY: Bill, I don't have to wait for anybody's by-your-
20   leave to be a "Wine in the Wilderness" woman. I can
21   be it if I wanta...and I *am*. I am. I am. I'm not the one
22   you made up and painted, the very pretty lady who
23   can't talk back...but I'm "Wine in the Wilderness"...
24   alive and kickin', me...Tomorrow Marie, cussin' and
25   fightin' and lookin' out for my damn self 'cause ain'
26   nobody else 'round to do it, dontcha know. And,
27   Cynthia, if my hair is straight, or if it's natural, or if
28   I wear a wig, or take it off, that's all right; because
29   wigs...shoes...hats...bags and even this *(She picks up*
30   *the African throw she wore a few moments before*
31   *...fingers it.)* They're just what...what you call...
32   access... *(Fishing for the word)* ...like what you wear
33   with your Easter outfit.
34 CYNTHIA: Accessories.
35 TOMMY: Thank you, my sister. Accessories. Somethin' you

1   **add on or take off. The real thing is takin' place on**
2   **the inside...that's where the action is. That's "Wine**
3   **in the Wilderness"...a woman that's a real one and a**
4   **good one. And y'all just better believe I'm it.** *(She*
5   *proceeds to the door.)*
6   **BILL: Tommy.**
7   *(TOMMY turns. He takes the beautiful queen, "Wine in the*
8   *Wilderness" from the easel.)*
9   **BILL: She's not it at all, Tommy. This chick on the canvas,**
10   **...nothin' but accessories, a dream I drummed up**
11   **outta the junk room of my mind.** *(Places the "queen" to*
12   *one side.)* **You are and...** *(Points to OLDTIMER)*...**Edmund**
13   **Lorenzo Matthews...the real beautiful people...**
14   **Cynthia.**
15   **CYNTHIA:** *(Bewildered and unbelieving)* **Who? Me?**
16   **BILL: Yeah, honey, you and Sonny-man, don't know how**
17   **beautiful you are.** *(Indicates the other side of model*
18   *stand.)* **Sit there.**
19   **SONNY-MAN:** *(Places cushions on the floor at the foot of the*
20   *model stand.)* **Just sit here and be my beautiful self.**
21   *(To CYNTHIA)* **Turn on, baby, we gonna get our picture**
22   **took.** *(CYNTHIA smiles.)*
23   **BILL: Now there's Oldtimer, the guy who was here before**
24   **there were scholarships and grants and stuff like that,**
25   **the guy they kept outta the schools, the man the facto-**
26   **ries wouldn't hire, the union wouldn't let him join.**
27   **SONNY-MAN: Yeah, yeah, rap to me. Where you goin' with**
28   **it, man? Rap on.**
29   **BILL: I'm makin' a triptych.**
30   **SONNY-MAN: Make it, man.**
31   **BILL:** *(Indicating CYNTHIA and SONNY-MAN)* **On the other**
32   **side, Young Man and Woman, workin' together to do**
33   **our thing.**
34   **TOMMY:** *(Quietly)* **I'm goin' now.**
35   **BILL: But you belong up there in the center, "Wine in the**

1 **Wilderness"...that's who you are.** *(Moves the canvas of*
2 *"the little girl" and places a sketch pad on the easel.)* **The**
3 **nightmare, about all that I've done disappearing**
4 **before my eyes. It was a good nightmare. I was**
5 **painting in the dark, all head and no heart. I couldn't**
6 **see until you came, baby.** *(To CYNTHIA, SONNY-MAN*
7 *and OLDTIMER)* **Look at Tomorrow. She came through**
8 **the biggest riot of all...somethin' called "Slavery,"**
9 **and she's even comin' through the "now" scene...**
10 **folks laughin' at her, even her own folks laughin' at**
11 **her. And look** *how...***with her head high like she's**
12 **poppin' her fingers at the world.** *(Takes up charcoal*
13 *pencil and tears old page off sketch pad so he can make a*
14 *fresh drawing.)* **Aw, let me put it down, Tommy. "Wine**
15 **in the Wilderness," you gotta let me put it down so all**
16 **the little boys and girls can look up and see you on the**
17 **wall. And you know what they're gonna say? "Hey,**
18 **don't she look like somebody we know?"**
19 *(TOMMY slowly returns and takes her seat on the stand.*
20 *TOMMY is holding the wig in her lap. Her hands are very*
21 *graceful looking against the texture of the wig.)*
22 BILL: **And they'll be right, you're somebody they know...**
23 *(He is sketching hastily. There is a sound of thunder and*
24 *the patter of rain.)* **Yeah, roll them hoops and bicycle**
25 **wheels.**
26 *(Music in low; music up higher as BILL continues to*
27 *sketch.)*
28
29
30
31
32
33
34
35

Acknowledgments

FAMILY SCENES by Ivette M. Ramirez. Copyright © 1989 by Ivette M. Ramirez. Excerpts from "Family Scenes" edited by John Antush are reprinted with permission from the publisher of *Recent Puerto Rican Theatre: Five Plays From New York* (Houston: Arte Publico Press — University of Houston, 1991).

LETTERS TO A STUDENT REVOLUTIONARY by Elizabeth Wong. Copyright © 1989, Elizabeth Wong. All inquiries for performing rights should be addressed to: Writers and Artists, 19 West 44th St., Suite 1000, New York, NY 10036.

MIGHTIER THAN THE SWORD by Nirmala Moorthy. Copyright © 1987 by Nirmala Moorthy. Reprinted by permission of the author.

PAINTING CHURCHES by Tina Howe. Copyright © 1982 by Tina Howe. All rights reserved. Used by permission of Flora Roberts, Inc.

THE UNIVERSAL WOLF by Joan M. Schenkar. Copyright © 1990, 1991, 1992 by Joan M. Schenkar. All rights, including professional, amateur, motion picture, television, public reading, broadcasting in any form, reproduction in any form, and rights of translation are strictly reserved. All inquiries should be addressed to Joan M. Schenkar, P.O. Box 814, North Bennington, VT 05257.

WINE IN THE WILDERNESS by Alice Childress. Copyright © 1969 by Alice Childress. All rights reserved. Used by permission of Flora Roberts, Inc.

ABOUT THE AUTHOR/EDITOR

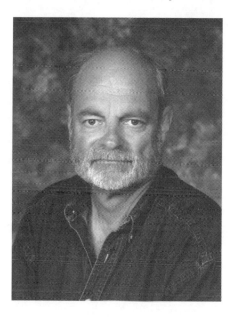

Marsh Cassady has written more than forty books including novels, short story and drama collections, haiku, biography, and books on theatre and storytelling. His audio and stage plays have been widely performed (including off-Broadway), and he has written and recorded a three-set audio tape on storytelling.

A former actor/director and university professor with a Ph.D. degree in theatre, Cassady has worked with more than a hundred productions. Currently fiction/drama editor of *Crazyquilt Quarterly*, he also co-edits a commercial magazine. Since 1981, he has conducted an all-genre writing workshop in San Diego and has taught various creative writing classes at UCSD and elsewhere. While teaching at Montclair State in the 1970s, he started a program of workshops, classes and special projects in playwriting. His own writing has won numerous regional and national awards.

ALSO BY MARSH CASSADY

Characters in Action

The Theatre and You

Acting Games — Improvisations and Exercises

The Art of Storytelling

ORDER FORM

MERIWETHER PUBLISHING LTD.
P.O. BOX 7710
COLORADO SPRINGS, CO 80933
TELEPHONE: (719) 594-4422

Please send me the following books:

_____ **Great Scenes From Women Playwrights**
#TT-B119   **$14.95**
by Marsh Cassady
Classic and contemporary scenes for actors

_____ **Characters in Action #TT-B106**   **$14.95**
by Marsh Cassady
Playwriting the easy way

_____ **The Theatre and You #TT-B115**   **$14.95**
by Marsh Cassady
An introductory text on all aspects of theatre

_____ **Acting Games — Improvisations and**
Exercises #TT-B168   **$12.95**
by Marsh Cassady
A textbook of theatre games and improvisations

_____ **The Art of Storytelling #TT-B139**   **$12.95**
by Marsh Cassady
Creative ideas for preparation and performance

_____ **Truth in Comedy #TT-B164**   **$12.95**
by Charna Halpern, Del Close and Kim "Howard" Johnson
The manual of improvisation

_____ **The Scenebook for Actors #TT-B177**   **$14.95**
by Norman A. Bert, Ph.D
Great monologs and dialogs for auditions

These and other fine Meriwether Publishing books are available at your local bookstore or direct from the publisher. Use the handy order form on this page.

NAME: _____

ORGANIZATION NAME: _____

ADDRESS: _____

CITY:_____ STATE: _____ ZIP: _____

PHONE: _____
  ❑ **Check Enclosed**
  ❑ **Visa or MasterCard #** _____

Signature: _____ *Expiration Date:* _____

(required for Visa/MasterCard orders)

COLORADO RESIDENTS: Please add 3% sales tax.
SHIPPING: Include $2.75 for the first book and 50¢ for each additional book ordered.

❑ *Please send me a copy of your complete catalog of books and plays.*

ORDER FORM

MERIWETHER PUBLISHING LTD.
P.O. BOX 7710
COLORADO SPRINGS, CO 80933
TELEPHONE: (719) 594-4422

Please send me the following books:

_____ **Great Scenes From Women Playwrights**
#TT-B119 $14.95
by Marsh Cassady
Classic and contemporary scenes for actors

_____ **Characters in Action #TT-B106** $14.95
by Marsh Cassady
Playwriting the easy way

_____ **The Theatre and You #TT-B115** $14.95
by Marsh Cassady
An introductory text on all aspects of theatre

_____ **Acting Games — Improvisations and**
Exercises #TT-B168 $12.95
by Marsh Cassady
A textbook of theatre games and improvisations

_____ **The Art of Storytelling #TT-B139** $12.95
by Marsh Cassady
Creative ideas for preparation and performance

_____ **Truth in Comedy #TT-B164** $12.95
by Charna Halpern, Del Close and Kim "Howard" Johnson
The manual of improvisation

_____ **The Scenebook for Actors #TT-B177** $14.95
by Norman A. Bert, Ph.D
Great monologs and dialogs for auditions

These and other fine Meriwether Publishing books are available at your local bookstore or direct from the publisher. Use the handy order form on this page.

NAME: _____

ORGANIZATION NAME: _____

ADDRESS: _____

CITY:_____ STATE: _____ ZIP: _____

PHONE: _____
   ❏ **Check Enclosed**
   ❏ **Visa or MasterCard #** _____

   Expiration
Signature: _____ Date: _____
      (required for Visa/MasterCard orders)

COLORADO RESIDENTS: Please add 3% sales tax.
SHIPPING: Include $2.75 for the first book and 50¢ for each additional book ordered.

   ❏ *Please send me a copy of your complete catalog of books and plays.*